S0-AYA-375

Western Public Lands
and Environmental Politics

WESTERN PUBLIC LANDS AND ENVIRONMENTAL POLITICS

edited by

CHARLES DAVIS

COLORADO STATE UNIVERSITY

WestviewPress

A Division of HarperCollins*Publishers*

All rights reserved. Printed in the United States of America. No part of this publication may be re-produced or transmitted in any form or by any means, electronic or mechanical, including photocopy, recording, or any information storage and retrieval system, without permission in writing from the publisher.

Copyright © 1997 by Westview Press, A Division of HarperCollins Publishers, Inc.

Published in 1997 in the United States of America by Westview Press, 5500 Central Avenue, Boulder, Colorado 80301-2877, and in the United Kingdom by Westview Press, 12 Hid's Copse Road, Cumnor Hill, Oxford OX2 9JJ

Library of Congress Cataloging-in-Publication Data
Western public lands and environmental politics / edited by Charles Davis.
    p. cm.
Includes bibliographical references and index.
ISBN 0-8133-8947-X (hc) — ISBN 0-8133-2970-1 (pbk.)
    1. Environmental policy—West (U.S.) 2. Public lands—Government policy—West (U.S.) 3. Land use—Government policy—West (U.S.)
I. Davis, Charles E. , 1947–   .
GE185.U6W47   1997
333.73′15′0978—dc21   96-48499
                                                                            CIP

The paper used in this publication meets the requirements of the American National Standard for Permanence of Paper for Printed Library Materials Z39.48-1984.

10   9   8   7   6   5   4   3   2   1

Contents

Preface   vii

List of Acronyms   ix

1   Introduction: The Context of Public Lands Policy Change,
    Charles Davis   1

PART ONE
PARTICIPANTS, PROCESSES, AND
THE POLICY FRAMEWORK

2   Fighting over Public Lands: Interest Groups, States, and the
    Federal Government, *Sandra K. Davis*   11

3   A Critique of the Multiple Use Framework in Public Lands
    Decisionmaking, *R. McGreggor Cawley and John Freemuth*   32

PART TWO
PROGRAMS

4   From Localism to Legalism: The Transformation of Federal
    Forest Policy, *George Hoberg*   47

5   Politics and Public Rangeland Policy,
    Charles Davis   74

6   Reform at a Geological Pace: Mining Policy on the Federal
    Lands, 1964–1994, *Christopher McGrory Klyza*   95

7   Energy on Federal Lands, *David Howard Davis*   122

8   National Parks Policy, *William R. Lowry*   150

9   Wilderness Policy, *Craig W. Allin*   172

PART THREE
POLICY CHANGE

10   Conclusion: Public Lands and Policy Change,
     Charles Davis   193

About the Book   203
About the Editor and Contributors   204
Index   206

Preface

Few policy issues evoke the degree of passion and concern among contending parties as does the controversy over who manages western federal lands and for what purpose. A key question is whether U.S. land management agencies such as the Forest Service, the Bureau of Land Management, and the National Park Service should pay more attention to ecological values and make decisions that tread more lightly on the land or whether they should defer to the policy priorities of traditional user groups wishing to continue extractive land use activities such as mining, logging, and livestock grazing.

Public officials representing the interests of industry and environmentalists alike have turned up the volume in advocating policy positions that have historically held little interest for people residing east of the Mississippi River. On May 16, 1994, Interior Secretary Bruce Babbitt referred to the giveaway of mineral-rich federal lands to companies holding patents as "the biggest gold heist since the days of Butch Cassidy."[1] Conversely, Representative Craig Thomas (R-WY), a proponent of existing mining laws, testified at a 1993 committee hearing that the "entire debate on the 1872 law is simply another follow-up on the Babbitt-Clinton assault on the West."[2]

Rhetorical one-upmanship effectively symbolizes the growing importance of the public lands policy arena in recent years. Since the 1960s, policy debates have become increasingly strident as Congress has responded to the growing political strength of environmental groups by passing legislation requiring federal land managers to place greater emphasis on ecological values in making use allocation decisions. Land use restrictions to preserve scenic areas or wildlife habitat have become more common, resulting in a greater number of conflicts pitting group against group and, occasionally, states against the federal government.

The origins of this project can be traced to my efforts to find up-to-date materials for a public lands policy seminar that I developed in the fall semester of 1993. It was a time of considerable interest in increasingly controversial policy issues such as protecting spotted owl habitat within the timber-rich old-growth forests of the Pacific Northwest under provisions of the Endangered Species Act. Efforts were under way as well to reform policies dealing with livestock grazing on public rangelands and hardrock mining practices. Much of the writing on public lands policymaking was overly descriptive, was focused on single issues, or was out-of-date.

Nevertheless, it was relatively easy to identify political scientists who had written about specific public land policies. The idea for this book developed as an outgrowth of the seminar, and in summer 1994, a number of individuals were contacted and asked to contribute chapters on particular policy areas, focusing on changes that had occurred over time. Two questions were used to guide each author's discussion: What changes have taken place in your program since the advent of the environmental era in 1960? Are changes in policy attributable to a new demographic landscape such as the urbanization of the West, presidential policy priorities, economic conditions, or value shifts? In the concluding chapter here, I have attempted to assess the results of the preceding chapters to determine whether the same factors tend to account for changes found across policy issue areas. I hope that the book offers a greater degree of thematic consistency as a result.

My thanks go out to the chapter contributors, whose efforts not only provided the primary body of information for this project but also made the editing task relatively painless. Comments offered by manuscript reviewers helped to sharpen the focus of the book and were very much appreciated. I would also like to acknowledge the assistance and encouragement of Westview editors, particularly Julia Joun and Rebecca Ritke, for keeping things moving at a reasonable pace. I have personally benefited from an association with like-minded colleagues and graduate students in a department committed to environmental education. Finally, I would like to thank Sandy and Kevin for their love and support on the home front.

NOTES

1. Cited in Catalina Camia, "House Names Negotiators on Mining Law Overhaul," *CQ Weekly Report* 52 (May 21, 1994):1294.
2. Cited in Bob Benenson, "House Easily Passes Overhaul of 1872 Mining Law," *CQ Weekly Report* 51 (November 20, 1993):3191.

Acronyms

AMC	American Mining Congress
AMPs	allotment management plans
ANILCA	Alaska National Interest Lands Conservation Act
APC	Alaska Pulp Corporation
AUM	animal unit month
BLM	Bureau of Land Management
BP	British Petroleum
CCC	California Coastal Commission
CIA	Central Intelligence Agency
CMU	Classification and Multiple Use Act
CRS	Congressional Research Service
DOE	Department of Energy
DOI	Department of the Interior
EIS	environmental impact statement
EPA	Environmental Protection Agency
FCLAA	Federal Coal Leasing Amendments Act
FEMA	Federal Emergency Management Agency
FERC	Federal Energy Regulatory Commission
FLPMA	Federal Land Policy and Management Act
FWS	Fish and Wildlife Service
GAO	General Accounting Office
GMP	General Management Plan
GSA	General Services Administration
LASER	League for the Advancement of States' Equal Rights
LWCF	Land and Water Conservation Fund
MUSY	Multiple Use and Sustained Yield Act

NEPA	National Environmental Policy Act
NFMA	National Forest Management Act
NIMBY	not in my back yard
NPCA	National Parks and Conservation Association
NPS	National Park Service
NRDC	Natural Resources Defense Council
NSC	National Security Council
OMB	Office of Management and Budget
OPEC	Organization of Petroleum Exporting Countries
OSM	Office of Surface Mining
PAC	political action committee
PILT	Payment in Lieu of Taxes Act
PLLRC	Public Land Law Review Commission
PRIA	Public Range Improvement Act
RARE I	Roadless Area Review and Evaluation I
RARE II	Roadless Area Review and Evaluation II
RCRA	Resource Conservation and Recovery Act
SCLDF	Sierra Club Legal Defense Fund
SMCRA	Surface Mining Control and Reclamation Act
TTRA	Tongass Timber Reform Act
USDA	U.S. Department of Agriculture
USDA/DI	U.S. Departments of Agriculture and the Interior
USFS	U.S. Forest Service
USGS	U.S. Geological Survey

1

Introduction: The Context of Public Lands Policy Change

CHARLES DAVIS

A look at U.S. public lands policy from the latter part of the nineteenth century until the mid-1960s reveals a clear pattern of resource development priorities from Congress and federal land use management agencies. National forests and rangelands were managed for commodity production purposes, activities that were undertaken in accord with existing policy mandates. Under its Organic Act of 1897, the U.S. Forest Service (USFS) was authorized to administer public forests for timber and watershed protection, and the primary objective of the Taylor Grazing Act of 1934 was to create a rancher-friendly policy for the management of rangelands under the jurisdiction of the U.S. Department of the Interior. This perspective toward land use was compatible with national policy goals such as the settlement of the West and the provision of economic development opportunities for incoming residents (Dana and Fairfax, 1980; Hays, 1959).

Even land management agencies with a more preservationist bent leaned more heavily toward resource use than resource conservation. The U.S. National Park Service (NPS) consistently placed emphasis on attracting more visitors to the parks despite mounting evidence that tourist services were maintained or increased at the expense of other values such as the preservation of wildlife habitat (Foresta, 1984). In like fashion, the U.S. Fish and Wildlife Service sought to balance conservation policy objectives with program activities aimed at cultivating political support from hunting and fishing organizations (Tobin, 1990).

The most visible examples of political accommodation to more extractive land use decisionmaking could be observed in the development of policy subsystems, or the "iron triangle" form of governance. A policy subsystem consists of a tripartite alliance between congressional committees, executive departments or bureaus, and interest groups with a common interest in a particular area of policy (Maas, 1949; Freeman, 1965; Cater, 1964). Policymaking within this arena is relatively

1

closed, is less visible, and tends to be stable over a long period of time (Ripley and Franklin, 1984). Programs developed within policy subsystems have historically distributed benefits (e.g., subsidized resource use) to a relatively small number of individuals or firms, while spreading the cost among all U.S. taxpayers.

Subsystems aptly characterize a variety of natural resource policy concerns, including public land programs. Beneficiaries include miners, loggers, ranchers, and energy firms. Contributing to the enactment of favorable programs and the preservation of program benefits are trade associations (e.g., the National Cattlemen's Association and the American Mining Congress, among others), the disproportionate representation of western legislators on the House and Senate interior committees (since renamed the House Resources Committee and the Senate Energy and Natural Resources Committee), and administrators working for the U.S. Forest Service (headquartered in the U.S. Department of Agriculture) and the Department of the Interior.

Noticeably absent from the policy debates for much of the twentieth century was a viable environmental constituency to present an ecological perspective on land use options. By midcentury, public consciousness about the need to preserve western federal lands was beginning to grow, thanks to the writings of Bernard DeVoto, Edward Abbey, and Wallace Stegner. In addition, activists such as David Brower waged well-publicized political campaigns to save wild places. A notable example was his successful effort to persuade political authorities to refrain from constructing a dam near Dinosaur National Monument (Udall, 1988).

However, things began to change in the 1960s with the emergence of both environmental and economic concerns. Growing public support for environmental causes was accompanied by the development of political organizations to advance ecologically friendly goals within the federal lands policy arena. This new wave of group leaders, along with like-minded supporters in Congress and in the executive branch, provided the political and organizational apparatus for change (Caulfield, 1989; Bosso, 1994). A smaller subset of legislators and staffers within the U.S. Bureau of the Budget (later renamed the Office of Management and Budget [OMB]) began to question the economic rationale for the continuation of federal subsidies to traditional land use constituencies in the mid-1960s and recommended that the government charge "fair market value" for the use or development of natural resources within federal lands.

Post-1960 Public Land Policies

Numerous changes in public land policy have occurred since 1960 (see Table 1.1). Some of the newer statutes have been designed to accommodate a wider range of uses, whereas others have dealt with procedural shifts. The Multiple Use and Sustained Yield Act of 1960 provided the Forest Service with a statutory mandate to broaden its mission beyond timber production and watershed management to include recreation and wildlife preservation as well. The Bureau of Land

TABLE 1.1   Major Public Land Laws, 1960 to 1996

Multiple Use and Sustained Yield Act of 1960
Classification and Multiple Use Act of 1964
Wilderness Act of 1964
Land and Water Conservation Fund Act of 1964
National Environmental Policy Act of 1969
Endangered Species Act of 1973
Federal Land Policy and Management Act of 1976
Surface Mining Control and Reclamation Act of 1976
National Forest Management Act of 1976
Public Rangelands Improvement Act of 1978
Alaska National Interest Lands Conservation Act of 1980
Energy Act of 1992

Management (BLM) was given a similar multiple use mandate in 1976 with the enactment of the Federal Land Policy and Management Act (FLPMA).

However, the stage for important changes in both substance and procedure was set in 1964 with the passage of the Wilderness Act. This law allowed lands under the jurisdiction of the Forest Service, National Park Service, and the Fish and Wildlife Service to be designated as wilderness if the areas under consideration possessed outstanding scenic and recreational qualities, were largely unaffected by previous developmental activities, and were of sufficient size (at least 5,000 acres) to justify their withdrawal from most extractive land uses. But Congress also added opportunities for public comment within the wilderness designation process.

Lawmakers sympathetic to the conservationist policy agenda subsequently expanded the range of permissable participatory activities to include litigation as well as written or oral comments. Consequently, environmentalists were able to expand their influence over land management decisions through procedural requirements contained within later policies such as the National Environmental Policy Act (NEPA), the Wild and Scenic Rivers Act, the Federal Land Policy and Management Act, and the National Forest Management Act, among others. As Paul Culhane (1981) and others have indicated, the net result of these changes was to enlarge not only the constituency base of public land management agencies but also the number of institutional venues, such as the courts, where policy battles could be waged.

It is also important to direct attention to the crossover impact of both public land and general environmental policies. For environmentalists, the NEPA-based requirement that federal agencies prepare an environmental impact statement (EIS) prior to undertaking any new project or activity with potentially harmful effects on environmental quality provided a key weapon in their efforts to delay or halt developmental activities such as logging or grazing on federal land. Agencies such as the BLM or the Forest Service were routinely sued by such organizations as the Sierra Club Legal Defense Fund or the Natural Resources Defense Council for failing to complete an EIS that incorporated the amount of information necessary to prevent or mitigate environmental damage (Wenner, 1993).

Other "wedge policies" that have proven to be strategically useful to environmentalists include the Endangered Species Act and the National Forest Management Act, which place restrictions on logging and related developmental activities that can occur within critical habitat areas set aside for threatened or endangered species. The Clean Water Act has provided a legal vehicle for Environmental Protection Agency (EPA) or land management agencies to address problems of ecological damage stemming from careless hardrock mining practices or from overgrazing by livestock in riparian areas. Likewise, provisions of the Clean Air Act gave the EPA the authority to protect scenic vistas in national parks that were threatened by nearby industrial activity such as pollution from smelters or power plants.

Explaining Public Lands Policymaking

How can we account for shifts in public land use policies, given the political clout of ranchers, miners, loggers, and energy firms? The magnitude and direction of change has been influenced by a variety of contextual factors, for example, by the geographical distribution of population growth, land use patterns, the number of policy participants operating within and outside of the traditional subsystem, value shifts, and election results.

One factor receiving increasing attention within the policy literature and the press is the changing demographics of the American West. Most western states have become more urbanized, a trend that is associated with higher levels of income and education, increasing environmental group membership, and stronger public support for recreational uses on the public lands (Hays, 1991; Alm and Witt, 1995). Consequently, urban-rural differences over public land policy are likely to be especially contentious since they go beyond abstract notions of user preference to include the availability of employment opportunities for longstanding rural residents in extractive natural resource industries (Kamieniecki, Kahn, and Goss, 1991). However, the assumption that the "urban west" is inexorably linked to a rise in the number of pro-environmental legislators and to a more conservation-oriented federal land use policy is largely unexamined and may offer fertile ground for policy research in the near future.

A second factor deals with shifts in public land use patterns over time. If we compare the two primary commodity development activities—logging and livestock grazing—on BLM lands and the national forests with recreation, the results are noteworthy. The number of permits issued to ranchers for livestock grazing by land management agencies has declined slightly over the years. The amount of timber harvested within the national forests (including the BLM's holdings in western Oregon) increased steadily from the 1960s and 1970s and peaked in the 1980s with a yearly average of 11 billion board feet (Wilkinson, 1992). Since the onset of restrictions on logging in the Pacific Northwest to preserve old-growth habitat for the northern spotted owl, the volume of timber actually harvested has been reduced by approximately 50 percent (Farnham and Mohai, 1995).

In contrast, recreation on lands administered by federal agencies (measured in terms of visitor days) has risen steadily from 1977 through 1993. The magnitude of this increase was relatively modest within national wildlife refuges but was quite pronounced within the national parks, BLM lands, and the national forests (Council on Environmental Quality, 1993).

The participants in the public lands policymaking process comprise the third source of influence. The number of stakeholders in public lands policy has increased considerably, particularly within the environmental community (see Chapter 2). Organizations representing the interests of commodity producers have mushroomed as well, including umbrella groups covering a wide array of developmental interests and groups more narrowly focused on specific issues such as property rights. In addition, both industry and environmentalists have sought to broaden their respective political coalitions to include university experts and public officials at all levels of government.

Participants also include public officials operating both within and outside of government. One relevant indicator of their influence is the proportion of western legislators serving on committees with jurisdiction over public land programs. Another is the ability of committee and executive agency leaders to maintain exclusive control over a particular area of policy. Both are structural sources of influence that favor entrenched program interests by containing issues at a state or regional level rather than allowing these issues to be expanded to the national policy agenda. And all participants seek to maximize their influence over policy by controlling the way an issue is defined and perceived by the public (Baumgartner and Jones, 1992).

Fourth, shifts in political values may eventually contribute to policy change through the election of legislators and chief executives with a distinct orientation toward federal land use policies. Although a candidate's views on environmental protection rarely dictate voter choice per se, partisan differences on policy issues with distinct trade-offs between the environment and other concerns have become increasingly common. These differences are reinforced when elected officials representing different parties are in control of Congress and the White House. Sharply divergent views on the direction of public lands policy were clearly visible in interbranch disputes spanning the Reagan, Bush, and Clinton administrations.

With the notable exception of the timber summit convened in Portland, Oregon, in 1993 by Bill Clinton, presidents are rarely involved in the details of public land policy. Instead, policy influence occurs through the appointment of individuals to head key agencies such as the Department of the Interior, the Forest

Service, and the Environmental Protection Agency and through budgetary recommendations, the promotion of legislation developed by agency program spe-
cialists, and administrative actions such as reorganization or executive orders.
Congressional policy preferences are demonstrated through traditional activities
such as program development, Senate confirmation of presidential appointments, and the budgetary process. In recent years, members of Congress have increasingly conducted oversight hearings on agency operations and have relied
upon policy riders to appropriations bills in an effort to shape policy decisions.

The Rest of the Book

This book offers an analysis of public lands policy and change from 1960 to 1996.
The contributors to Part One examine the involvement of interest groups and political institutions in policy debates, the intergovernmental context of programmatic disputes, and the decisional frameworks that shape federal land management choices. Thus, land use policy controversies are viewed from both the
external political environment and the differing organizational contexts of decisionmaking.

   In Chapter 2, Sandra Davis analyzes the development of interest groups and
strategies affecting policy disputes as well as the ongoing battles between the federal government and the states over the fundamental question of who decides—
that is, she addresses whether the primary authority for making land use decisions should lie in the hands of federal or state officials. In Chapter 3, Gregg
Cawley and John Freemuth offer their assessment of how disagreement over land
use allocation decisions is exacerbated by the differing decisionmaking frameworks used by the National Park Service, the Forest Service, the Bureau of Land
Management, and the Fish and Wildlife Service.

   Although a general discussion of both interest groups and intergovernmental
relations adds much to our understanding of public lands policy, it is conceivable
that the relative explanatory importance of organizational involvement, intergovernmental conflict, and other factors mentioned earlier may vary according
to the issue under consideration. Part Two addresses both developmental and
preservation-oriented programs. Commodity-based programs that attempt to
reconcile the development and conservation of natural resources within a multiple-use management framework include timber harvesting within national
forests (George Hoberg, Chapter 4), livestock grazing on public rangelands
(Charles Davis, Chapter 5), hardrock mining (Christopher Klyza, Chapter 6), and
energy (David Davis, Chapter 7).

   Much of the controversy affecting these programs can be attributed to efforts
to superimpose regulatory decisions pertaining to environmental protection onto
distributive policies that were designed to encourage resource development. The
politics of national parks (William Lowry, Chapter 8) and wilderness preservation (Craig Allin, Chapter 9) begins with a premise that federal lands possessing

scenic or other ecological values merit protection. However, the political price tag often includes a willingness on the part of park or wilderness proponents to accept a higher number of visitors, water restrictions, or historic uses (such as mining or livestock grazing) than they would prefer.

My primary objective in Part Three is to integrate and evaluate information gleaned from the preceding chapters. In Chapter 10, I review the findings pertaining to both public land policies and participants to determine whether the factors discussed earlier advance our understanding of how change is likely to occur. Are most policy issues explained by electoral shifts, demographic trends, interest group pressures, or changing land use preferences? Or do alterations in policy tend to be more idiosyncratic?

REFERENCES

Alm, Lesley, and Stephanie Witt. 1995. "Environmental Policy in the Intermountain West: The Rural-Urban Linkage." *State and Local Government Review* 27 (Spring):127–136.

Baumgartner, Frank, and Bryan D. Jones. 1992. *Agendas and Instability in American Politics.* Chicago: University of Chicago Press.

Bosso, Christopher. 1994. "After the Movement: Environmental Activism in the 1990s." In Norman Vig and Michael Kraft, eds., *Environmental Policy in the 1990s*. Washington, DC: CQ Press.

Cater, Douglass. 1964. *Power in Washington.* New York: Random House.

Caulfield, Henry. 1989. "The Conservation and Environmental Movements: An Historical Analysis." In James P. Lester, ed., *Environmental Politics and Policy: Theories and Evidence.* Durham, NC: Duke University Press.

Council on Environmental Quality. 1993. *Environmental Quality: The 1993 Annual Report of the Council on Environmental Quality.* Washington, DC: Government Printing Office.

Culhane, Paul. 1981. *Public Lands Politics.* Washington, DC: Resources for the Future.

Dana, Samuel T., and Sally Fairfax. 1980. *Forest and Range Policy.* 2d ed. New York: McGraw-Hill.

Farnham, Timothy J., and Paul Mohai. 1995. "National Forest Timber Management over the Past Decade: A Change in Emphasis for the Forest Service?" *Policy Studies Journal* 23 (Summer):268–280.

Foresta, Ronald. 1984. *America's National Parks and Their Keepers.* Washington, DC: Resources for the Future.

Freeman, J. Lieper. 1965. *The Political Process.* 2d ed. New York: Random House.

Hays, Samuel P. 1959. *Conservation and the Gospel of Efficiency.* Cambridge: Harvard University Press.

_____. 1991. "The New Environmental West." *Journal of Policy History* 3 (3):223–248.

Kamieniecki, Sheldon, Matthew Kahn, and Eugene Goss. 1991. "Western Governments and Environmental Policy." In Clive Thomas, ed., *Politics and Public Policy in the Contemporary American West.* Albuquerque: University of New Mexico Press.

Maas, Arthur. 1949. *Muddy Waters.* Cambridge: Harvard University Press.

Ripley, Randall, and Grace Franklin. 1984. *Congress, the Bureaucracy, and Public Policy.* Homewood, IL: Dorsey Press.

Tobin, Richard. 1990. *The Expendable Future.* Durham, NC: Duke University Press.

Udall, Stewart. 1988. *The Quiet Crisis.* 2d ed. Salt Lake City: Peregrine Smith Books.

Wenner, Lettie McSpadden. 1993. "The Courts in Environmental Politics: The Case of the Spotted Owl." In Zachary Smith, ed., *Environmental Politics and Policy in the West.* Dubuque, IA: Kendall/Hunt.

Wilkinson, Charles. 1992. *Crossing the Next Meridian: Land, Water, and the American West.* Washington, DC: Island Press.

PART ONE

PARTICIPANTS, PROCESSES, AND THE POLICY FRAMEWORK

2

Fighting over Public Lands: Interest Groups, States, and the Federal Government

SANDRA K. DAVIS

For over two hundred years there have been conflicts and agreements between the national and state governments over public lands. Too often the role of the state and local government has been minimized because a simple model of federal-state conflict is inappropriate. Yet, as Gregg Cawley and Sally Fairfax have argued, states are central actors (Fairfax and Cawley, 1991, 435; Cawley and Fairfax, 1991, 423). To better understand recent public lands decisions, I use an intergovernmental relations framework in this chapter.

I suggest here that policy is made through a matrix of power relations among government entities at different levels that pursue their own policy concerns and variously respond to the demands of private interests (Krane, 1993, 187). Policymaking occurs within a policy context that includes historical agreements about public land, competing philosophies on the use of natural resources, demographic changes, and political events such as elections and presidential executive orders. I use this meld of intergovernmental relations, policy analysis, and coalitional politics to examine changes in public lands policy that have occurred since the 1960s. I first discuss the issues that divide state and federal officials and the historical context of public lands decisionmaking.

Public Land Issues: States as Managers of Their Own Land

Beginning with the General Land Ordinance of 1785, the national government granted land to new states to produce revenue to support state programs for education, roads, and other ventures (Cawley, 1993, 105). States made different choices about these lands. Nevada sold most of its lands, whereas Arizona retained large portions of its holdings. Critics complain that states often disposed of their land, but they also point out that when they kept it, they expended so few resources per acre that it could not be properly managed (Graf, 1990, 229). State supporters argue that states greatly expanded their capacity to manage natural resources and work with federal agencies (Fairfax and Cawley, 1991, 443).

States have a number of grievances about the question of public land ownership. First, many states have asserted claims to a sizable amount of acreage that was promised but never received when they joined the Union (Fairfax, 1984, 84). In 1980, many states still had not received the acreage they were owed. In Arizona, for example, another 190,000 acres remain to be transferred to state control by the BLM (Graf, 1990, 9). The BLM has been slow to act upon state requests that such land be conveyed, and its wilderness programs have withdrawn land that states can no longer choose, diminishing the choices left to the states. Second, more direct conflict that has arisen concerns the states' attempts to manage the lands earmarked to support education and other programs. These holdings are often isolated sections that are sometimes surrounded by federal land. States sometimes wish to develop the resources on these sections in a way that conflicts with BLM management plans for the surrounding areas. Although it is possible to negotiate federal-state land swaps to minimize state problems in managing their lands, such swaps are time consuming and difficult to achieve (Fairfax, 1984, 85).

State or Federal Supremacy?

Although there are few court cases in which the issue of the supremacy of state versus federal authority arises, there are a few examples, and they generally work against the states. These disputes often occur between a third party and a government rather than being a direct dispute between state and federal governments. The third party is usually a regulated interest that is trying to avoid more stringent regulation by one government by arguing that another government with less restrictive regulation has authority to make a public land decision (Fairfax and Cawley, 1991, 446). Nonetheless, these decisions have important implications for the states' ability to manage their own resources and to form management partnerships with federal entities.

In several decisions, federal authority has been expanded through the preemption of state or local authority. In one such case, the U.S. Supreme Court extended federal authority to protect wild horses and burros and undermined established state authority over wildlife (Fairfax, 1984, 84).[1] In another case, the Federal Power Act preempted an Iowa law requiring that hydroelectric facilities obtain a state water permit before beginning construction.[2] Consequently, in California, Ventura County's attempt to stop oil exploration in a national forest contained within a county-designated open space was overruled.[3]

When the issue of federal preemption was tested again, the states did receive two rulings in their favor. This occurred in the late 1970s and early 1980s when

Texas and midwestern utilities challenged Montana's 30 percent severance tax on coal. The utilities argued that this tax violated the supremacy and commerce clauses of the U.S. Constitution. This time, third parties argued against states' rights to spare themselves the unwanted burden of the severance tax. Nevertheless, the Supreme Court ruled in favor of Montana's tax (Cawley, 1993, 79–81). In a more recent decision, the Supreme Court narrowly upheld the California Coastal Commission's (CCC) requirement that industry officials wanting to locate a mine in a national forest within the state's coastal zone obtain a CCC permit.[4]

States and Receipt Sharing Programs

Contrary to the threats posed by some preemption cases, states have greatly benefited from receipt-sharing programs funded by the federal government. Federal revenues from the sale or leasing of land and minerals were initially used to induce state officials to relinquish claims on federal lands, to refrain from taxing federal property, and to wait five years before taxing newly settled land in the hands of private owners (Fairfax and Cawley, 1991, 438). Later on, federal receipts were used by members of Congress to pacify state officials with the argument that land would be permanently held in reserve for the benefit of all states. In 1908, Congress established the states' share of receipts from forest reserves at 25 percent and specified that the money was to be used to support the costs of building and maintaining roads and schools.

The Mineral Leasing Act of 1920 gave 37.5 percent of mineral leasing revenues to states to do with as they wished, with 52.5 percent of the funds allocated to the Reclamation Fund to pay for water projects. State officials argued that mineral leasing would promote economic activity and population growth, requiring public services that should be financed from federal receipts since local and state taxes would not be forthcoming from federal lands. Western states got the best of both worlds. The leasing programs stimulated economic development, which the states very much wanted, and at the same time, the states were paid to undergo the "burden" of development (Fairfax and Cawley, 1991, 439–440).

There have been some changes in receipt sharing since 1960. On the one hand, states continue to be rewarded for their developmental "burdens." For example, western states took advantage of the energy crisis and the push to mine more low-sulfur coal by asking for extra protection. While officials from other regions loudly objected, western producers acquired additional federal funds when the Surface Mining Control and Reclamation Act (SMCRA) was passed in 1977.

On the other hand, change did occur. The Payment in Lieu of Taxes (PILT) Act of 1976 awarded funds to both western and eastern states; in fact, it extended one-third of its revenues to eastern states as "compensation" for national parks (Cawley, 1993, 79). The PILT Act is a pork barrel program in which states from all regions benefit. Unlike the funds granted in earlier decisions, these payments were not prompted by a change in federal land authority that was traded for federal revenue (Fairfax and Cawley, 1991, 441–442). So far, this changing rationale for PILT payments has not significantly affected public land policy.

States are important participants in public lands policy in ways that transcend direct federal-state conflict. They are involved as managers of their own resources, as recipients of federal revenues, as landowners affected by federal wilderness and other environmental regulations, and as political organizations that pursue greater control of federal lands.

Public Land Policy Before 1960

The General Land Ordinances of 1785 and 1787 settled claims that states made on western territories and provided Congress with the authority to regulate this territory. Despite this authority, no real effort was made to manage these lands. From the 1790s to the 1880s, Congress chose to dispose of the land to establish and settle new states (Fairfax and Cawley, 1991, 438; Francis and Ganzel, 1984, 15–17), to provide revenue for the federal treasury, to reward veterans, support internal improvements such as schools, roads, and railroads, and to promote the growth of a class of small landholders (Cawley and Fairfax, 1991, 421; Francis and Ganzel, 1984, 15).

The numerous disagreements over these decisions were typically settled as states bargained and negotiated within Congress to convey the land to state and private owners (Cawley and Fairfax, 1991, 420–421). Even during these earliest years, there were receipt-sharing programs in which federal revenues from the land were transferred to the states (Fairfax and Cawley, 1991, 436).

Later in the nineteenth century, as western states began to enter the Union, they, too, sought to have unappropriated land transferred to themselves or to private owners. But existing states objected, arguing that they struggled for the public domain, which should be held in federal reserves to benefit all. Unable to acquire the unappropriated land, western states agreed to federal land preserves in return for getting federal grants, speedy land surveys, and other concessions (Cawley and Fairfax, 1991, 421).

Increasingly, debates in Congress arose about the use of specific resources within public lands. These were marked by three sagebrush rebellions in which unhappy westerners sought to exert more control over natural resources. In the late 1880s, westerners reacted against a federal law to withhold land from public sale that might be developed for irrigation until a survey of likely water project sites could be compiled. Fearing this could slow efforts to spur economic growth, opponents staged the first Sagebrush Rebellion to release land for unrestricted development (Graf, 1990, 16–17).

In 1890, the sagebrush rebels introduced a bill to cede all unappropriated lakes and rivers to state or territorial control. The proposal was defeated, but their demand to give states control over federal resources was to reappear in subsequent rebellions. Reformers did pass the General Revision Act of 1891 to reduce corruption and begin shifting federal policy from disposal to federal reservation and management of public lands. This event served to mark both the end of the first rebellion over irrigation lands and the beginning of the second rebellion over forest lands (Graf, 1990).

By 1893, mining companies, ranchers, and timber companies realized that reservation of large tracts of land threatened the economic activities they wished to pursue. After complaining about limited access to resources on federal lands, rebels began to push for states' rights. This time they met stiff opposition from President Theodore Roosevelt and Gifford Pinchot, head of the Division of Forestry within the Department of the Interior. The sagebrush rebels failed to acquire the same unified support they had enjoyed earlier from western interests, and the rebellion faded. Federal policy began evolving from allowing private exploitation of public resources to supporting federally managed resource use (Graf, 1990).

The third Sagebrush Rebellion, from the 1920s to the late 1940s, focused on grazing fees and set off two major efforts to convey public lands to the states and private individuals. The sagebrush rebels received important support from President Herbert Hoover, who recommended that Congress transfer public lands (without mineral rights) to western states. This stimulated opposition from professional land managers who wished to apply scientific management principles, from authors such as Bernard DeVoto and others who depicted transfer proposals as a raid of national resources, and from some congressional representatives and governors who did not wish to undertake management of lands that would produce limited revenues. Consequently, the proposal was rejected, prompting ranching interests and western legislators to push for the enactment of the Taylor Grazing Act, which provided for substantial local control over grazing land (Graf, 1990, 147–184).

During the latter part of the third rebellion, ranchers attacked federal efforts to manage livestock grazing as well as proposals to increase grazing fees. After spirited attempts to sell lands into private ownership and disband federal land management agencies met with an equally vehement defense of federal land ownership, the rebellion ended, with public lands now falling under the management of the newly created BLM and other federal agencies (Graf, 1990, 163–170).

Politics and Participants in the Pre-1960s Era

There was a recurring pattern of participants and politics in the three rebellions. After decades of private sector use and resource development, federal agencies were created and began applying scientific management principles to determine resource use. Scientists—geologists, geographers, foresters, and soil scientists—conducted research and played an important role in justifying public land decisions. Scientific input, however, did nothing to stem the sagebrush rebels' anger at agency restriction on land use, and this hostility was vented within Congress as western legislators (and especially senators) championed commodity interests (Graf, 1990, 261).

Agency management practices were often criticized by western legislators, and attempts were made to transfer land to private or state ownership (Cawley, 1993, 72–74). Even as westerners complained that snobbish easterners (i.e., agency managers) were in control of western resources, they failed to get federal land transferred to states. Instead, they had to content themselves with federal land use concessions wrung from Congress or federal agencies (Fairfax, 1984, 80).

Commodity use supporters often argued their case in terms of states' rights, but in some crucial negotiations, state officials were minimally involved. First, many of the battles occurred in Congress as federal legislators advocated issue positions on behalf of state interests. This followed the well-established pattern of negotiation among states, a pattern that had been established as far back as 1785 (Cawley and Fairfax, 1991, 419–421).

Second, the conservation movement at the turn of the twentieth century operated during the Progressive Era, with its reliance upon policy control from the national government and its distrust of state and local governments. The Progressives' attack on state and local government and their policy reforms limited states' ability to develop a natural resource policy on their own (Francis and Ganzel, 1984, 16–17). Third, even when President Hoover offered states the opportunity to acquire federal land (without mineral rights) prior to the depression, state officials refused because of political opposition and concerns about their ability to shoulder land management costs (Graf, 1990, 147).

States, however, were involved as recipients of various receipt-sharing programs that were initiated by the U.S. government to prompt states to accept changes in federal land policy. Federal officials encouraged incoming states not to tax or lay claim to unappropriated federal land in return for land grants and a percentage of land sales. By the end of the nineteenth century, new western states, unable to secure state ownership, agreed to federal land preserves in return for a share of money raised through land and mineral sales and leases (Graf, 1990).

Western critics did not achieve the transfer of public lands to either states or private individuals during any of the early sagebrush rebellions for several reasons. One factor was the opposition of nonwestern states that blocked western states' efforts to secure title over these lands. Legislators from northeastern and midwestern states offered enough inducements to persuade western public officials to accept federal payments and management concessions once these officials recognized the difficulty of wresting away federal control of public land (Cawley and Fairfax, 1991, 419–423; Francis and Ganzel, 1984, 18). By the 1940s, the rebels' strength had eroded even more, as a split between small and larger ranchers had deprived the movement of unified support (Graf, 1990, 169). Finally, federal agencies and their desire to implement professional management principles thwarted the sagebrush rebels' complete domination of policy. Even the BLM, which was criticized as a captured agency during this period, struggled with and then usually gave way to commodity interests; although bloodied, the agency did resist (Fairfax, 1984, 81). With this history of serial conflict over public land management, it is not surprising that disputes have continued into the 1990s.

Changes in Public Lands Policy Since the 1960s

The Fourth Sagebrush Rebellion

Disgruntlement with public land policy began in the late 1970s during the Carter administration, when westerners complained about Carter's hit list of water projects and public lands decisions. For example, Secretary of the Interior Cecil Andrus used FLPMA authority to temporarily withdraw 110 million acres of Alaskan public land from development in 1978 (Cawley, 1993, 85). In 1980, the Carter administration produced several grazing environmental impact statements, calling for a reduction of grazing rights by one-third in some areas of New Mexico. Quickly reacting to the EISs, western cattlemen battled the proposal in the courts and Congress, winning a court injunction against the grazing reduction and the passage of the McClure Amendment within the Public Rangelands Improvement Act of 1978, which limited grazing reductions in the West to 10 percent per grazing permit (Durant, 1992).

By 1980, the BLM had begun making concessions to commodity users, but it was too late. The sagebrush rebels began considering state laws to transfer federal lands to state control (Durant, 1992, 103–107). They were quite effective from 1980 through 1982 in promoting their policies with Congress and the national media. However, by the end of the first Reagan term, they had failed because the expected support from the Reagan administration, their own movement, and their home states was not forthcoming.

A variety of changes had occurred in the western states by the 1960s that worked to the detriment of the rebels. First, a wave of new residents who did not share rural or commodity development interests had moved into urban areas in western states. They made it increasingly difficult for the rebels to build unified support within their own states. Second, to compound this problem, rural interests within state legislatures were weakened as a result of court-ordered reapportionment. Third, the economy of many western cities diversified and boomed at the same time that rural economies were often in decline (Graf, 1990, 248–252). Thus, the political context that had supported commodity users was changing (Cawley, 1993, 76), and this, in turn, gave rise to a modified set of participants.

Coalition Participants

Environmentalists. A new group of participants—environmentalists—became active in public land policy and launched an aggressive campaign to redefine conservation in the 1960s. The more traditional definition of conservation, developed in the nineteenth century, emphasized human control of the earth and the development of resources to provide "the greatest good for the greatest number in the long run" (Cawley, 1993, 17–20). This interpretation lent legitimacy to the claims of commodity users to develop resources (Cawley, 1993, 32). To Pinchot and others, a failure to develop and use resources could be as serious a problem as the depletion of resources (Cawley, 1993, 24). The environmentalists, in contrast, emphasized preservation of resources to provide for aesthetics, animals, plants, and wilderness experience.

With their preservation mandate, environmental groups such as the Sierra Club, the National Wildlife Federation, the Wilderness Society, the Friends of the Earth, and the Natural Resources Defense Council have led the opposition to the more recent sagebrush rebellions (Cawley, 1993, 33). The Sierra Club, founded by John Muir, has been one of the most involved. The National Wildlife Federation, which began as an organization for hunters and fishermen, has pursued the protection of wildlife habitat. The Wilderness Society has focused solely on public land issues, and its members have brought great expertise to the society's efforts (Gifford, 1990, 77). The Friends of the Earth, one of the smaller and "purer" organizations, was created when leader David Brower came to believe that the Sierra Club had become too moderate in its views (Bosso, 1994, 37). The Natural Resources Defense Council has been an aggressive legal advocate, actively using the court system to produce desired policy.

These and other organizations have lobbied Congress and agencies for legislation and rules that would provide greater protection for larger areas of land. They have engaged in confirmation battles over nominees for the offices of EPA administrator and secretary of the interior, lending support or criticism as they have seen fit. They also became active in electoral politics for the first time during the Reagan years. In 1982, a coalition of environmental groups endorsed congressional candidates. Two years later, the environmentalists' frustration with the Reagan administration's policy became apparent when the Sierra Club, the Friends of the Earth, and several prominent environmental leaders formally endorsed Walter Mondale for president (Cawley, 1993, 145–150).

Federal Land Agencies. Land agencies such as the Forest Service and BLM have remained players, but in important respects they have become changed agencies because of the multiple use doctrine. The Forest Service officially received its mandate in 1960 (from the Multiple Use and Sustained Yield Act) to legitimize the management philosophy it espoused throughout the twentieth century. Despite the agency's professed support for multiple use, its application was seen by environmentalists as allowing one use to dominate while allowing secondary uses that did not interfere (Cawley, 1993, 19–20). As a result, environmentalists have used the Wilderness Act of 1964 and other means to pressure the Forest Service to manage resources for purposes other than timber production.

For the BLM, it was not until 1976 that the Federal Land Policy Management Act was passed, officially making it a multiple use agency. The livestock industry and other commodity interests viewed the BLM's new mandate as an attempt by the agency to dominate land policy while relegating grazing to an inferior position (Cawley, 1993, 23). Although this intention was denied by the BLM, it was evident the agency was a stronger participant in land policy than it had previously been (Cawley, 1993, 76).

Lack of Participation by Scientists. Few scientists participated in the fourth rebellion, as they had in earlier sagebrush rebellions. The result was that the debate centered more on moral and philosophical grounds, and the public was left to make as much sense of the rhetoric as it could with little environmental research to rely upon (Graf, 1990, 244).

State Legislatures. One atypical feature of the fourth Sagebrush Rebellion was that state legislatures declared ownership of the public lands. Between 1979 and 1981, eleven state legislatures considered bills to transfer control of BLM (and sometimes Forest Service) lands to the states. Nevada was the leader, passing the first bill, which protected established lease agreements and allowed the sale of land to private owners. Recognizing that such a transfer would raise legal questions, the bill authorized the state's attorney general to undertake the legal steps necessary to implement the transfer (Graf, 1990, 226). Of the other ten states, four successfully enacted bills, one passed a bill that was voided by a citizen referendum, two passed bills that were vetoed by the governor, and three failed to get the legislation passed (Francis, 1984, 37).[5]

Sagebrush Rebellion Organizations. New organizations advanced the cause of the sagebrush rebels. The League for the Advancement of States' Equal Rights (LASER), Sagebrush Rebellion, Inc., and the Public Lands Council worked to secure the transfer of federal land to state ownership (Graf, 1990, 225–226). In late 1980, LASER held a conference in Salt Lake City attended by six hundred people at which it successfully publicized a number of policy demands. There were presentations by well-known rebels and by federal legislators, and there was even a formal hearing of the U.S. House Subcommittee on Mines and Mining. The event received substantial media coverage, making it the height of the rebellion success (Graf, 1990, 230).

How did the various policy actors proceed? In the agenda-setting phase, activists publicized the problem to convince others to make policy decisions. This happened when western commodity interests were again angered at being unable to develop natural resources as they saw fit. They complained that BLM policy had been captured by environmentalists and that the rebellion was, at least partially, a protest against the influence of environmentalists, with their emphasis on preservation (Cawley, 1993, 89; Graf, 1990, 216–221).

Although the issue of states' rights was the activists' clarion call, this rhetoric was partially (Cawley, 1993, 95; Cawley and Fairfax, 1991, 427–428) or wholly

(Williams, 1995, 133; Graf, 1990, 228; McCurdy, 1986, 90–93) a smoke screen for an attack on environmentalists and an attempt to regain unfettered access to natural resources. Implementation of multiple use principles, wilderness planning, new environmental regulations, and Carter's hit list for water projects (Cawley, 1993, 82) prompted western anger to boil over into the fourth rebellion. The LASER conference stimulated media coverage, bringing the issue to the attention of a larger public.

In the policy formulation phase, the rebels made strategic decisions to promote their policy goals in several institutional venues. At the national level, western legislators in Congress introduced the Western Lands Act to convey lands and mineral rights to the states. At the state level, states passed legislation to claim federal lands as their own. State officials hoped to accomplish two things. First, they emphasized states' rights to minimize the dispute over preservation and development of resources. Second, they made a public statement of the states' wish to control federal land rather than a bona fide attempt to seize immediate control.

The rebels tried to buy time to build support before they went into court to convince judges that federal land ownership violated states' equal footing in the Union.[6] Since the legal precedents for winning this argument were not promising, the rebels wanted to achieve as many political successes as they could before moving into the courts to do battle. Even if the rebels lost in the courts, they might capitalize upon political victories within the states to win a consolation prize, that is, policy concessions from federal land agencies (Cawley, 1993, 95).

With the election of Ronald Reagan, who was an avowed Sagebrush Rebellion supporter, the future looked bright for the rebels. Many of Reagan's appointees favored deregulation and states' rights, suggesting that the rebels had a better chance of winning their policy goals through the efforts of agencies headed by Reagan loyalists or via the initiatives of western legislators. Yet with all this promise, the rebels were not able to achieve their policy goals; in fact, the rebellion and its policy goals went into a period of latency or incubation.

The inability of the rebels to win or even sustain their movement is explained by a number of factors. First, the rebellion failed because the political, social, and economic factors that were transforming the western states meant that the rebels were unable to build the necessary political support (Graf, 1990, 248–255). Second, Sagebrush Rebellion, Inc. led a strident but poorly organized campaign (Lewis, 1995, 15). And finally, Reagan appointees were not all states' rights proponents. Secretary of the Interior James Watt was a puzzle to the rebels. On the one hand, they liked his confrontational style and his rejection of the new definition of conservation, with its emphasis on preservation. On the other hand, he opposed conveyance of land to the states. Watt argued that if the federal government managed lands wisely, development of resources would be compatible with environmental protection. He proposed that the federal agencies would be such good neighbors that the rebellion could die out because of increased support for federal management (Cawley, 1993, 114–117).

Others within the Reagan administration brought their libertarian principles to bear and advocated privatization of natural resources. This flew in the face of the rebels' commitment to transfer the land to state management. Thus, the failure of the Reagan administration to support the transfer of public land to state management deflated the momentum of the Sagebrush Rebellion (Cawley, 1993, 124–135).

In sum, the fourth Sagebrush Rebellion resembled earlier rebellions in that agency restrictions on land had prompted the protest. As earlier, there were attempts by western legislators in Congress to protect commodity interests and there was an incumbent president who took a public position on public land issues.

There were differences this time, however. First, the opposition included well-organized groups that were insiders in national politics. In earlier rebellions, the opposition had come primarily from eastern states and conservation leaders who worked within agencies. Second, although the Reagan administration professed its support for the rebels, its top appointees championed other plans for the disposition of land. This created an obstacle with a double whammy. The rebels were lulled by the prospect of administration support and were quite unprepared to counter the conflict between those Reagan appointees who fought to maintain control of public lands and those who sought to privatize them. Third, the venues in which conflict was fought expanded. It was no longer just the congressional arena in which issues were debated and decided. More decisions than ever before were made by agencies with a multiple use mandate. The rebels planned (although they did not systematically follow through on the plan) to use the courts to produce favorable policy decisions. Finally, the state became a staging ground for the rebels, who passed bills within state legislatures calling for the conveyance of lands to the states.

How can we evaluate the impact of the fourth Sagebrush Rebellion? The rebels' attempt to increase their power over the use of resources and to dilute the influence of environmentalists, who they believed dominated federal land policy, may have been the below-board agenda, whereas the rebels' arguments for states' rights and state management of these resources (the aboveboard agenda) was just a stalking horse (Graf, 1990, 262; McCurdy, 1986, 90–93).

Historically, western states and protesters chose the pragmatic response of taking the concessions they could get once it was clear they were unable to win control of the land (Cawley and Fairfax, 1991, 424). Thus, the rebels' commitment to states' rights as the driving force for their protest is open to question; but it is a question that is difficult to answer without ascertaining the motivations of individual participants who were only loosely organized in protests that spanned over one hundred years.

National Public Lands Decisions in the 1980s

After the fourth Sagebrush Rebellion and the stalemate on public lands issues, the Reagan and Bush administrations sometimes resorted to administrative strategies to accomplish what they could not manage through legislative reform. For example, recommended funding cuts for the BLM (see Chapter 4) and Executive Order No. 12630, which required federal agencies to assess the impact of regulations on private property values (i.e., takings impact assessment), were administrative actions taken to blunt the effect of environmental regulations (Dennis, 1995, 158).

In the legislative arena, developers were as unable to open the Arctic National Wildlife Refuge to oil drilling as environmentalists were to pass grazing reform or hardrock mining reform. Many bills did not pass when opponents put up a spirited fight, indicating the contentious and competitive nature of the legislative arena for natural resource and public lands issues.

This situation remained the same after the 1992 election of Bill Clinton as president and his appointment of Bruce Babbitt as secretary of the interior. After several failed attempts to pass legislation that would increase grazing fees, Babbitt initiated an administrative strategy to promote consensus on grazing reforms. Borrowing from defeated bills, he administratively increased grazing fees and created multiple use advisory boards to replace the rancher-dominated grazing advisory boards (see Chapter 5). Despite legislative stalemate, implementation of environmental laws proceeded, arousing state and local anger at federal management. The rise of new participants and their interaction in the public lands policy arena are now addressed.

The 1990s: Wise Use, Property Rights, and the Counties Movements

As regulations pertaining to endangered species, wetlands, and logging were enforced, a revival of some of the concerns of earlier sagebrush rebels (Lewis, 1995, 15) arose in the form of the Wise Use Movement. This movement consolidated after two hundred organizations attended a 1988 conference and published the proceedings as *The Wise Use Agenda* (Echeverria and Eby, 1995, 11).

Two of this movement's three primary goals are consistent with the goals of recent sagebrush rebellions. The first is protection of jobs and economic development from federal regulatory decisions. Second, Wise Use members believe that environmentalists have so dominated federal management of public lands that a preservation doctrine has been implemented to lock up use of valuable resources. They advocate a shift in policy toward their view of genuine multiple use principles.

Like the sagebrush rebels, Wise Use activists initially focused on western conflicts. They chose their name from and emphasized ties to the traditional conservation philosophy of Gifford Pinchot, who defined conservation as the "wise use of resources" (Lewis 1995, 14–16). Wise Use members are committed to resource extraction and development, and their group originated in the Pacific Northwest while battles raged over logging and the protection of endangered species (Kriz, 1995, 31–32).

Wise Use's third theme, however, was not emphasized by previous sagebrush rebels. The idea of protection of property rights was borrowed from the property rights movement, which originated in eastern states, and derived its basic concept from libertarian philosophy. It has been nurtured by intellectual leaders such as Richard Epstein, a law professor at the University of Chicago, and Roger Pilon of the Cato Institute. The Wise Use Movement's adoption of the property rights issue has facilitated its appeals for political support and its likelihood of succeeding in legal cases (Echeverria, 1995, 147).

In addition, the Wise Use Movement has been joined by the county movement, whose principles parallel those of the fourth Sagebrush Rebellion in its emphasis on resource development, enmity toward environmentalists, and a desire to confront federal land managers for control over public lands. Centered in the western states, the county movement also bases its legal defense on property rights (Williams, 1995, 130). Both the property rights and county movements are closely allied to the Wise Use Movement; in fact, the three movements' goals seem to have melded together.

Although their ideas complement each other, the movements are still fairly autonomous. However, the Wise Use and property rights movements do work with each other to lobby in the nation's capital (Kriz, 1995, 31–32). Together, the three movements are composed of participants who choose diverse tactics and venues within which to work.

What is the membership base of the Wise Use and property rights movements? First, there are hundreds of local organizations that are funded by local citizens motivated by the fear that environmental regulations are destroying local jobs (Kriz, 1995, 28). Second, there are national and regional think tanks and advocacy organizations such as the Center for the Defense of Free Enterprise, the National Inholders Association, the Wilderness Impact Research Foundation (Lewis, 1995, 15–16), the Defenders of Property Rights, and the Pacific Legal Foundation (Echeverria, 1995, 147). Other participants include prodevelopment groups such as the National Association of Home Builders, International Council of Shopping Centers, and the National Farm Bureau (Echeverria, 1995, 147). There are also industry fronts with environmental names, groups that represent the lobbying and public relations arm of industry. For example, the Marine Preservation Association has fifteen oil company members, and its charter defines marine preservation as the promotion of petroleum and energy company interests (Lewis, 1995, 19–20). Finally, county commissioners seeking greater control over development decisions have been drawn to the movement since its inception (Ramos, 1995, 84).

Although critics assail the groups that are industry fronts and the willingness of some Wise Use groups to accept corporate money, this does not explain Wise

Use members' defense of private property, which is a dominant American political value (Roush, 1995, 5). As with the sagebrush rebels, it is the effects of members' actions and the implications of these actions for intergovernmental relations in public lands that are most important.

Let us examine the most recent political battles more closely. The Wise Use and county movements, whose activities constitute the fifth Sagebrush Rebellion, are a reaction to the implementation of environmental regulations (Williams, 1995, 130). Angry at their inability to use natural resources, western commodity interests have joined forces with the property rights groups that protest limitations on their ability to develop private property. Like the sagebrush rebels, the people in these movements want a definition of multiple use that provides for resource development and extraction as an economic base for the western economy. However, this time, the prodevelopment rebels have a key advantage in their struggle. Their emphasis on protection of property rights is a deeply held value that helps them attract support and members (Roush, 1995).

A legal defense based on property rights offers the likelihood of greater success in court suits (Echeverria, 1995, 147). In addition, these organizations are better financed and organized (Lewis, 1995, 15) to sustain a complex series of political assaults on environmental regulation in a variety of political arenas.

Realizing the folly of relying upon state legislation as a means of achieving policy goals, Wise Use groups turned to the courts in the late 1980s. They had some success within the U.S. Court of Federal Claims, which settles regulatory takings and other contractual claims against the national government involving more than $10,000 (Dennis, 1995, 161). With Reagan's appointee, Chief Judge Loren Smith, sitting on the court, it has ruled in favor of some individuals and companies that were prevented from developing their property by environmental rules (Lewis, 1995, 18).[7] Even so, other judges on the court have been less kindly disposed to takings claims (Dennis, 1995, 162).

Not content with these victories, Wise Use activists have sought a U.S. Supreme Court ruling to establish the principle that regulatory takings must be compensated. The search for compensation from regulatory losses is not a new legal challenge. Over one hundred years ago, a Kansas brewer sought compensation when prohibition laws put him out of business, but the Supreme Court ruled against him. In 1907 and again in 1978, the Supreme Court ruled against private property owners who sought relief from regulation.[8]

More recently, Supreme Court decisions have favored private property owners by finding that regulations were unjustified and required compensation.[9] At the same time, however, Wise Use groups face procedural obstacles in getting their cases heard before the high tribunal since all procedures must be exhausted within the state courts before appeal to the U.S. Supreme Court is possible. Even the most active groups lack the resources to actively litigate in state courts (Farole, 1995, 9–21).[10]

Wise Use groups have also been actively working for legislation on the state level (Farole, 1995, 16). By 1993, Utah, Arizona, and Delaware had passed mild bills requiring agencies to assess whether proposed regulations risk diminishing the value of private property (i.e., taking impact assessment). Similar bills were introduced in another twenty-three state legislatures, often when members of the Reagan administration became advisers on property rights legislation (Lavelle, 1995, 35–38).

Even before many states began to introduce property rights legislation, a movement was underway in counties across the West to protect the use and extraction of resources on federal land that was deemed vital to local economies. The movement was sparked by a Forest Service decision in New Mexico to reduce timber sales to protect the Mexican spotted owl. A local rancher persuaded commissioners in Catron County, New Mexico, to pass an emergency ordinance that required federal agencies to get local approval for all activities undertaken within the county or risk being arrested for actions that reduced the value of private property.

Catron County passed its ordinance in 1990, and by late 1992, dozens of counties in Montana, Idaho, Wyoming, New Mexico, Utah, Nebraska, and California had passed similar ordinances (Williams, 1995, 130–132). One such ordinance failed a state court test, and others may also.[11] Nevertheless, commissioners and local residents may still benefit if federal managers decide that consultation and concessions are a wise choice. In Catron County, one forest ranger notes that he now goes to county commission meetings, is more aware of sentiments within the county, and has not eliminated any grazing permits (Williams, 1995, 134).

In summary, the Wise Use, property rights, and county movements have picked up the disputes over federal lands where the most recent sagebrush rebels have left off. The movement supporters are a more diverse group with potentially stronger legal arguments, and they are pursuing policy decisions in multiple branches and levels of government. As of 1996, these movements have not faded away; rather, the 1994 elections have provided them with a rejuvenated forum for public land issues—Congress.

The 1994 Congressional Elections

The 1994 election returns drastically changed the composition of Congress, giving Republicans control of both the Senate and the House. House candidates, under the leadership of Representative Newt Gingrich (R-GA), ran on the Contract with America promises to balance the budget and ease the regulatory burden on Americans. The Republican victory has produced a new set of committee and subcommittee chairmen who often have little sympathy for environmental protection. They have unleashed a spate of bills that align the Republicans with disgruntled commodity users and developers who want greater access to resources found on public lands. Their proposals include

- Allowing oil drilling in Alaska's Arctic National Wildlife Refuge and greatly increased logging in the 17-million-acre Tongass National Forest.
- Allowing states to decide if they want to acquire all the BLM land within their borders and, if they accept, to determine whether to (1) keep the newly acquired land open to the public, (2) provide state management but close off public access to the land, or (3) sell the land to private owners.
- Forcing the U.S. Forest Service to sell forty-two ski areas on public land to operators without a prohibition against the development of private homes or businesses on the land. Although this proposal passed the House Resources Committee, it met with strenuous opposition by angry western constituents, who persuaded its sponsor, Senator Frank Murkowski (R-AK), to remove it from consideration (Bettelheim, 1995c; Obmascik, 1995b).
- Creating a commission to recommend that some less well-known national parks and monuments be closed. This proposal has been rejected twice. Supporters have argued it would reduce the cost of operating the National Park Service, but critics have said it would result in the privatization of parks and monuments. After being initially defeated in the House, it was included in a House and Senate budget bill until the Republican leadership withdrew the proposal (Bettelheim, 1995b; Biers, 1995).
- Adding environmental provisions to the House appropriation bills, including a repeal of a court settlement that limits logging in Idaho's Clearwater National Forest, a $1.00 limit on the funds to manage the Mojave National Park in California, a prohibition on any Fish and Wildlife Service review of a wetlands permit for a Texas golf course, and a 1.2 percent cut in rent paid by resorts that operate on Forest Service lands (Obmascik, 1995a).

Republican supporters vehemently argue that people in the states can do a better job managing public resources. Many proposals would also reduce the federal budget and limit environmental regulations. Opponents, in contrast, are fearful of state control for various reasons. First, using current environmental standards, only two states (Wyoming and New Mexico) could make a profit. Although this might mean that some states would reject taking control of the land,[12] others might accept the land and then sell it to private owners.[13] Second, since it would cost states more to manage these lands than they would receive in revenue, states acquiring the land would face the same fiscal constraints in the management of these new lands that they currently have with their own state lands.[14] Third, states would lose $99 million in PILT funds and the royalties that the federal government currently returns to them from oil, gas, and coal extraction. Finally, states would assume still other costs for such responsibilities as the cleanup of abandoned mines (Miller, 1995), fire fighting, and improvements on rangelands (Bettelheim, 1995a).

None of these proposals has been passed in the 104th Congress. What is clear, however, is that the 1994 elections have again made the U.S. Congress a prominent forum for the public lands debate, temporarily obscuring state and local efforts to influence environmental regulation.

Conclusions

Public land disputes have periodically been a source of contention since the founding of the United States. Over time, many of the discontents have remained the same, but institutional access has become greater than ever before and the number of participants across the branches of government and across different levels of governments has increased. The presidency can participate via executive orders, review of proposed regulations, and judicial and executive appointments. Congress continues its historical role of providing a venue in which legislators address public land issues. Federal courts, depending on the legal philosophies of their judges, may reject or accept the legal rationale made by western interests and environmentalists.

Public lands policymaking, however, is not confined to national institutions. Since the end of the eighteenth century, states have been active participants in settling disputes fought in Congress and have benefited from federal receipt-sharing programs. Furthermore, states have long-standing land claims and problems related to the management of their own public lands that are affected by federal wilderness and regulatory decisions. More recently, during the fourth Sagebrush Rebellion and the rise of the Wise Use Movement, state officials have passed state laws claiming ownership of federal lands or requiring that takings impact assessments be conducted.

Local and regional governments have also become more active in the Wise Use era. With government entities such as coastal control commissions requiring that developers acquire permission to undertake activities on federal land, developers and environmentalists will sue any party that rules against their interests. In the past, critics have argued that using the concept of states' rights was simply a rhetorical strategy geared toward promoting the self-interest of commodity groups. It now appears that self-interest may be promoted through local autonomy, states' rights, federal supremacy, or other federalism doctrines. Such rhetoric will continue to play a role in intergovernmental relations, and different levels of government will have to operate in a political setting in which private sector organizations argue for their own interests, wrapping themselves in the cloak of the most convenient federalism theory.

State and local officials, however, are not relegated to passively watching third parties operate to influence policy. State officials in the fourth Sagebrush Rebellion and the Wise Use Movement have chosen to openly enter the fray, defying federal supremacy over public lands. Some are spokespersons for development interests, but other officials push for their own concerns and interests.

Public lands policy is more complex than ever before. Just as more interest groups and branches of government have become increasingly active in this policy area, more government entities at more levels of government are forging meaningful roles for themselves. The result is a web of power relations across the federal, state, and local levels of government that is shaped by the coalitional demands of private interests (Krane, 1993, 187). For too long, the roles of state and local governments have been deemphasized. They are central to understanding this web and the public land decisions produced within it.

NOTES

1. The decision to extend federal authority over wildlife and preempt state authority was made in *Kleppe v. New Mexico* (1976).

2. *First Iowa Hydro-Electric Cooperative v. Federal Power Commission* (1946) (Fairfax and Cawley, 1991, 444–445).

3. *Ventura County v. Gulf Oil Corp* (1976) (Fairfax and Cawley, 1991, 445).

4. In *California Coastal Commission v. Granite Rock Co.* (1987) the Supreme Court's 5–4 decision cautioned that the state's permit was upheld in this case because CCC had not yet set the permit conditions. Thus, no actual conflict existed between federal and state that might justify federal preemption of state regulations (Fairfax and Cawley, 1991, 444–447).

5. The following states passed bills transferring land to state ownership: Nevada (1979), Wyoming (1980), Utah (1980), New Mexico (1980), and Arizona (1980). Washington state passed a bill in 1980, but it was voided by a citizen referendum. Colorado (1981) and California (1981) passed bills that were vetoed by the governor. Finally, Idaho (1981), Montana (1981), and Oregon (1981) failed to pass bills (although Oregon did establish "a commission to consider the reduction of federal land holdings") (Francis, 1984, 37).

6. When states entered the Union, they had to sign a disclaimer clause in which they agreed not to tax federal property or interfere with the disposal of this unappropriated property. In *Stearns v. Minnesota* (1900), Minnesota argued that having federal lands within its borders meant the state did not have equal footing with other states. The Supreme Court ruled against the state, saying that equal footing did not guarantee either social or economic equality, only political equality; furthermore, the presence of federal land in the state did not create a political hardship. Although Nevada planned to differentiate its legal position from Minnesota's, the Nevada legal claim was weak (Cawley, 1993, 96–100).

7. In *Loveladies Harbor Inc. v. United States* (1990), the U.S. Claims Court ruled that a New Jersey developer prevented from building on 12.5 acres of wetlands (out of 250 acres that cost $300,000) was awarded damages of $2.68 million. The court, focusing only on the 12.5 acres rather than on the parcel as a whole, concluded that the value of the land had been almost totally destroyed. Although precedent required that the parcel-as-a-whole doctrine be followed, the decision was affirmed by the Federal Circuit Court of Appeal. In a more recent case, however, the Claims Court criticized the Loveladies decision because it failed to apply the parcel-as-a-whole doctrine that had been applied in the *Tabb Lakes v. United States* case (1993) when the court rejected the company's takings claim. The Federal Circuit Court affirmed the rejection of the takings claim and emphasized that a

takings must be determined in relation to the property as a whole (Dennis, 1995, 163–165; Lewis, 1995, 18).

8. In 1907, the Supreme Court said that states may regulate to protect the environment despite the effect on property owners in *Hudson Water Company v. McCarter* (1907). Seventy-one years later, in *Penn Central v. New York* (1978), the court rejected the claim that a taking may be established only by showing that owners were unable to profit from their property (Lewis, 1995, 18).

9. In *First English v. Los Angeles* (1987), *Nollan v. California Coastal Commission* (1987), *Dolan v. Rigard* (1994), and, to a lesser degree, in *Lucas v. South Carolina Coastal Council* (1991), the U.S. Supreme Court favored property rights claims.

10. In five states, the groups most active in property rights cases in Congress, state legislatures, and the Supreme Court are Pacific Legal Foundation, Mountain States Legal Foundation, National Association of Home Builders, American Farm Bureau Federation, Sierra Club, National Wildlife Federation, and American Planning Association. They seldom enter state courts with takings cases because they lack the resources to pursue cases in multiple states. Many of these organizations have state affiliates, but they, too, are unable to sustain state litigation; in fact, they believe litigation is the responsibility of their national organization (Farole, 1995, 15–18). Pacific Legal Foundation and Mountain States Legal Foundation, with their mission to litigate cases, are best prepared and actually do take some cases into state court. Even these organizations prefer using the federal courts, where they believe they have a better chance of winning. They go into state courts only because they must do so before appealing a decision to the Supreme Court (Farole, 1995, 18–21).

11. Boundary County, Idaho, passed an ordinance to make it illegal for a federal agency's action to reduce the value of private property. The ordinance was challenged by environmental groups and citizens claiming that it violated the federal supremacy clause giving federal agencies the authority to manage public lands. In January 1994, a state court ruled that the ordinance was unconstitutional (Williams, 1995, 135).

12. Governor Romer of Colorado has stated that he doesn't want to manage BLM lands (Carrier, 1995). Utah Natural Resources Director Ted Stewart has said that Utah cannot afford the financial obligations that would come with BLM land (Bettelheim, 1995).

13. States have sold large tracts of land granted to them by the federal government before. Nevada sold 1,997,000 acres of land it received when it became a state and kept 3,000 acres to provide funds for schools. Colorado sold 25 percent of its initial grant of 4 million acres of school lands (Carrier, 1995).

14. In New Mexico, BLM currently has 800 employees to manage 13 million acres, and the state also manages 13 million of its own acres with a staff of 140 employees (Carrier, 1995).

REFERENCES

Barone, Michael, and Grant Ujifusa, with Richard E. Cohen. 1995. *The Almanac of American Politics, 1996.* Washington, DC: National Journal.

Bettelheim, Adriel. 1995a. "States May Get Federal Land." *Denver Post,* September 10:1A.

_____. 1995b. "House Rejects Hefley's Park-Closure Proposal." *Denver Post,* September 20:3A.

_____. 1995c. "Plan to Sell U.S.-Owned Ski Areas Dies." *Denver Post,* September 22:20A.

Biers, John M. 1995. "GOP Drops 'For Sale' Plan for Parks." *Denver Post,* October 15:16A.

Bosso, Christopher J. 1994. "After the Movement: Environmental Activism in the 1990s." In Norman J. Vig and Michael E. Kraft, eds., *Environmental Policy in the 1990s.* 2d ed. Washington, DC: CQ Press.

Carrier, Jim. 1995. "Vision of Zane Grey West or Moonscape?" *Denver Post,* September 22:1A.

Cawley, R. McGreggor. 1993. *Federal Land, Western Anger: The Sagebrush Rebellion and Environmental Politics.* Lawrence: University Press of Kansas.

Cawley, R. McGreggor, and Sally K. Fairfax. 1991. "Land and Natural Resource Policy, I: Development and Current Status." In Clive S. Thomas, ed., *Politics and Public Policy in the Contemporary American West.* Albuquerque: University of New Mexico Press.

Dennis, Sharon. 1995. "The Takings Debate and Federal Regulatory Programs." In John Echeverria and Raymond Booth Eby, eds., *Let the People Judge: Wise Use and the Private Property Rights Movement.* Washington, DC: Island Press.

Durant, Robert F. 1992. *The Administrative Presidency Revisited.* Albany: State University of New York Press.

Echeverria, John, and Raymond Booth Eby, eds. 1995. *Let the People Judge: Wise Use and the Private Property Rights Movement.* Washington, DC: Island Press.

Echeverria, John D. 1995. "The Takings Issue." In John Echeverria and Raymond Booth Eby, eds., *Let the People Judge: Wise Use and the Private Property Rights Movement.* Washington, DC: Island Press.

Fairfax, Sally K. 1984. "Beyond the Sagebrush Rebellion: The BLM as Neighbor and Manager in the Western States." In John G. Francis and Richard Ganzel, eds., *Western Public Lands: The Management of Natural Resources in a Time of Declining Federalism.* Totowa, NJ: Rowman and Allanheld.

Fairfax, Sally K., and R. McGreggor Cawley. 1991. "Land and Natural Resource Policy, II: Key Contemporary Issues." In Clive Thomas, ed., *Politics and Public Policy in the Contemporary American West.* Albuquerque: University of New Mexico Press.

Farole, Donald J., Jr., 1995. "Interest Groups and Takings Legislation in State and Federal Courts." Paper presented at the 1995 Annual Meeting of the Southern Political Science Association, Tampa, Florida.

Francis, John. 1984. "Environmental Values, Intergovernmental Politics, and the Sagebrush Rebellion." In John Francis and Richard Ganzel, eds., *Western Public Lands.* Totowa, NJ: Rowman and Allanheld.

Francis, John G., and Richard Ganzel, eds. 1984. *Western Public Lands: The Management of Natural Resources in a Time of Declining Federalism.* Totowa, NJ: Rowman and Allanheld.

Gifford, Bill, and the Editors. 1990. "Inside the Environmental Groups." *Outside* (September):69–78.

Graf, William L. 1990. *Wilderness Preservation and the Sagebrush Rebellions.* Savage, MD: Rowman and Littlefield.

Krane, Dale. 1993. "American Federalism, State Governments and Public Policy: Weaving Together Loose Theoretical Threads." *PS: Political Science and Politics* 26 (June):186–190.

Kriz, Margaret. 1995. "Land Mine." In John Echeverria and Raymond Booth Eby, eds., *Let the People Judge: Wise Use and the Private Property Rights Movement.* Washington, DC: Island Press.

Lavelle, Marianne. 1995. "The Property Rights Revolt." In John Echeverria and Raymond Eby, eds., *Let the People Judge: Wise Use and the Private Property Rights Movement.* Washington, DC: Island Press.

Lewis, Thomas A. 1995. "Cloaked in Wise Disguise." In John Echeverria and Raymond Booth Eby, eds., *Let the People Judge: Wise Use and the Private Property Rights Movement.* Washington, DC: Island Press.

McCurdy, Howard. 1986. "Environmental Protection and the New Federalism: The Sagebrush Rebellion and Beyond." In Sheldon Kamieniecki, Robert O'Brien, and Michael Clarke, eds., *Controversies in Environmental Policy.* Albany: State University of New York Press.

Miller, Ken. 1995. "Western Faction Pushing for Sale of BLM Lands." *Denver Post,* October 7:6A.

Obmascik, Mark. 1995a. "In Bills in Congress, the Devil Is in the Details." *Denver Post,* October 17:1B.

_____. 1995b. "Ski Area Sale Plan Gets OK." *Denver Post,* September 20:1A.

Ramos, Tarso. 1995. "Wise Use in the West." In John Echeverria and Raymond Booth Eby, eds., *Let the People Judge: Wise Use and the Private Property Rights Movement.* Washington, DC: Island Press.

Roush, Jon. 1995. "Freedom and Responsibility: What We Can Learn from the Wise Use Movement." In John Echeverria and Raymond Booth Eby, eds., *Let the People Judge: Wise Use and the Private Property Rights Movement.* Washington, DC: Island Press.

Williams, Florence. 1995. "Sagebrush Rebellion II." In John Echeverria and Raymond Booth Eby, eds., *Let the People Judge: Wise Use and the Private Property Rights Movement.* Washington, DC: Island Press.

3

A Critique of the Multiple Use Framework in Public Lands Decisionmaking

R. MCGREGGOR CAWLEY

& JOHN FREEMUTH

In a refrain expressing the confusion and frustration of antiwar protests during the 1960s, Buffalo Springfield sang: "Something's happening here/What it is ain't exactly clear." Much the same might be said of events in the federal land policy arena over the past thirty years. The 1960s and 1970s were a period in which the traditional emphasis on commodity resource production (timber, grazing, and mining) receded as Congress enacted a large body of legislation that demanded greater attention to the preservation or restoration of the federal estate's environmental quality (Culhane, 1981). By the end of the 1970s, then, "few observers expected major changes in the environmental agenda" (Vig and Kraft, 1984, 20). Nevertheless, change was underway.

In 1979, the Nevada Legislature adopted a bill that asserted a moral and legal claim to lands within the state's boundaries that are administered by the Bureau of Land Management. This action marked the beginning of a protest movement among commodity interests in the western United States, dubbed the "Sagebrush Rebellion." One year later, Ronald Reagan was elected president, and his subsequent appointment of James Watt to the post of secretary of the interior confirmed that the Reagan administration intended to make fundamental changes in the environmental agenda (Cawley, 1993).

Over the next eight years, environmentalists struggled to develop an appropriate strategy in dealing with the Reagan administration. Although they were successful in blocking most of the more radical administration initiatives, the environmental community was unable to reclaim the momentum it had enjoyed in the 1970s. Thus, by the mid-1980s, it was clear that federal land policy dialogue had become mired in gridlock (Hays, 1987).

With the end of the Reagan administration came new, albeit guarded, hopes for reestablishing the environmental era. Although neither Republican presidential candidate George Bush nor his Democratic opponent Michael Dukakis had much of an environmental record, both candidates seem to signal an end to the open hostility of the Reagan years. Indeed, during a campaign visit to the Boston harbor, Bush announced his intention to be an "environmental president" if elected. As it turned out, Bush's election and subsequent choice of Manuel Lujan for interior secretary simply guaranteed that gridlock would continue to define the character of federal land policy discussions.

Set against this background, it is not difficult to understand why Bill Clinton's election in 1992 set off a flurry of speculations. Clinton's environmental record was somewhat sparse, but he had indicated that his views were consistent with those of Vice President Al Gore. Gore, in turn, provided a detailed chronicle of personal commitment to the environmental cause in his 1992 book *Earth in the Balance: Ecology and the Human Spirit.* Moreover, Clinton's choices for key posts within the administration seemed to affirm that environmental issues would be pursued by knowledgeable and dedicated personnel. Especially important in this regard was his choice of Bruce Babbitt for the interior secretary position. Babbitt had long been a champion of environmentally responsible land management and as governor of Arizona had been an outspoken critic of the Sagebrush Rebellion. In short, there was ample reason for the environmental community to believe that a return to the pre-Reagan era of federal land policy might be at hand.

The environmental community's optimism was balanced by the pessimism of its opponents. Shortly after Clinton's election and just before her own death, Dixy Lee Ray (1993, 188), a former governor (R-WA) asserted that the new administration's efforts would likely produce a "severe case of very expensive environmental overkill," an assessment gaining some currency among those looking for less costly ways to protect the environment. Other opponents pointed to Gore's book and Clinton's appointments as evidence that the administration was populated with "environmental extremists." And throughout the western United States, warnings were issued that the Clinton administration marked the beginning of a "new war on the West."

At this writing (1995), it is clear that neither the optimism of the environmental community nor the pessimism of its opponents has been realized. The only major environmental federal lands victory during the 103rd Congress was the California Desert Protection Act, and none of the administration's initiatives, including major reforms of range management and mining, were implemented.

In this chapter, we present a somewhat unorthodox interpretation of the curious turn of events in federal land policy. Rather than focusing on the competing interests in the federal lands policy arena, we contend that the key problem is the structure of the decision process. More specifically, we argue that the current gridlock and acrimony in the federal lands arena results from an event that occurred on June 12, 1960. On that date, President Dwight D. Eisenhower signed the Multiple Use and Sustained Yield Act (MUSY) into law. We argue that the management regime envisioned by MUSY, which was intended to provide the Forest Service, and subsequently the Bureau of Land Management, with a mechanism to deal with growing controversies over federal land use decisions, has simultaneously exacerbated federal land policy arguments and reduced the ability of land managers to resolve them.

We begin with a brief overview of the management regime defined by MUSY and consider some of the contemporary criticism of multiple use management. Building on this criticism, we identify what we see as the flaw in the logic of multiple use management. Finally, we offer some general suggestions about changes that might move federal land policy in more productive directions.

On Being in the Middle

The pluralist component has badly served liberalism by propagating the faith that a system built primarily upon groups and bargaining is self-corrective.
—Theodore Lowi, 1979

In 1953, then USFS Chief Richard McArdle noted that the growing diversity of demands for the use of national forests frequently put forest managers in the middle of conflict. Yet, McArdle also noted, "Being in the middle is exactly where we ought to be. I believe that our inability to satisfy completely each and every group of national-forest users is a definite sign of success in doing the job assigned to us. When each group is somewhat dissatisfied, it is a sign that no one group is getting more than its fair share" (1953, 325). Seven years later, Congress provided a statutory basis for McArdle's view when it enacted MUSY.

One of the more succinct federal land statutes at merely one page long, MUSY directed that national forests should be "administered for outdoor recreation, range, timber, watershed, and wildlife and fish purposes." A subsequent passage identified the "establishment and maintenance of areas of wilderness" as being consistent with the purposes of the act.[1] MUSY also contained a rather complicated definition of multiple use management.

The basic mandate called for utilization of the various forest resources in a "combination that will best meet the needs of the American people." The act also recognized that meeting this mandate would require "periodic adjustments in use to conform to changing needs and conditions." Finally, the act directed land managers to base their decisions on the "relative values of the various resources, and not necessarily the combination of uses that will give the greatest dollar return or the greatest unit output."

In 1964, Congress provided limited authorization for multiple use management on BLM-administered lands. This limited authorization became a formal mandate for the BLM with the enactment of the Federal Land Policy and Management Act of 1976. Thus, roughly 580 million acres of federal land, about 80 percent of the total federal estate, is now managed following the basic principles outlined in MUSY. And as we have already noted, federal land policy since the 1960s has been animated by ongoing dissatisfaction among virtually all federal land users. If we use the criteria suggested by McArdle, then it would appear that multiple use management has been successful. Participants at a recent workshop sponsored by the Congressional Research Service (CRS) arrived at a different assessment, however.

In a description nearly identical to the one offered by McArdle forty years earlier, the CRS staff note: "Over the years, increasing demands and pressures for resources and services from these Federal lands [USFS and BLM], plus heightened public interest in how these lands are used, have caused management and administration to become more complex and contentious." This situation has produced a "growing sense of dissatisfaction . . . not only over individual uses of Federal lands and resources, but also over the fundamental operating principles of multiple use and sustained yield" (CRS, 1992, vii).

Although certainly not unanimous in their assessment, the participants at this workshop generally agreed on two important points. First, the original goal of multiple use management was to provide land managers with a mechanism for resolving the political disputes among competing user groups. Second, after thirty years of experience, it seemed clear that multiple use management had not only failed to fulfill its original goal but may also have exacerbated the disputes over federal land use policy.

For instance, a Northern Arizona University forestry professor, Richard Behan, characterized the practice of multiple use management as an example of "predatory pluralism," in which "coalitions of single-resource users and single-resource professional managers transform multiple use into an adversarial game of adjacent, single-resource, land use allocations" (CRS, 1992, 98). James Magagna, president of the American Sheep Association, offered a similar assessment. While believing that multiple use management is theoretically sound, Magagna argues its implementation has been marred by user groups who approach land use decisions with an attitude "expressed as 'I must restrict or eliminate your use to protect my use.'" And land managers "often find it expedient to restrict or eliminate the use of the least politically powerful constituency rather than seek to achieve the delicate balance called for by the multiple use philosophy" (CRS, 1992, 92).

What begins to take shape here is the possibility that the roots of the gridlock now affecting federal land policy can be traced, at least in part, to multiple use management. Stated differently, if multiple use management transformed the federal lands policy arena into a zero-sum game and the field upon which the game is played has been leveled, then it is not at all surprising that politics of federal lands has been more attentive to confrontation and contention than compromise. Indeed, the logic of a zero-sum game encourages the various participants to concentrate their energies on the task of blocking the moves of their opponents rather than on seeking to establish a common ground upon which compromises could be constructed. Moreover, a predictable outcome of a zero-sum game in which the players are relatively equal is stalemate.

In an attempt to extricate themselves from the legacy of multiple use management, federal land management agencies have moved to adopt a new approach called "ecosystem management." Although still largely embryonic (GAO, 1994), one formal venture to implement this new approach has been launched. In 1990, the USFS and NPS announced plans to resolve long-standing management problems of the greater Yellowstone area by adopting an ecosystem management regime. However, this endeavor produced an episode of open conflict, replete with charge and countercharge of political conspiracy, that eventually forced the agencies to abandon their original plan. Today, the ecosystem management battleground has moved to the Pacific Northwest, as the USFS and BLM attempt to bring about ecosystem management through the Eastside and Upper Columbia River Basin projects.

Although some observers view ecosystem management as a way to overcome the gridlock in federal lands policy, experiences to date suggest that it has not lived up to its promise. Indeed, both the character of the argument over Yellowstone and broader discussions of ecosystem management contain obvious parallels to the criticism of multiple use management (Cawley and Freemuth, 1993; Freemuth and Cawley, 1993). These parallels, in turn, help expose the need to view current and future federal land policy disputes as *political problems* requiring *political solutions*.

The Logic of Multiple Use

To define an issue is to make an assertion about what is at stake and who is affected,
and therefore, to define interests and the constitution of alliances.
—Deborah Stone, 1988

This much seems clear: Multiple use management was intended as a response to three interrelated issues. First, the post–World War II era witnessed a significant increase in the numbers of organized groups seeking to influence national forest land use decisions. Second, the demands raised by these various groups represented reasonable expressions of the public purposes that the national forests might serve. Third, attempts by the USFS to respond to these various demands succeeded primarily in making the agency a target of criticism from all sides (Hirt, 1994).

These issues became particularly troublesome because they created a profound challenge to the traditional management philosophy of the USFS. Since the days of the early conservation movement, the USFS had approached its job from the perspective that forest management was largely a technical matter best carried out by trained professionals (Hays, 1975; Kaufman, 1960). Although this philosophy never went unchallenged, it generally assigned forest managers the task of determining the public interest to be served by the national forests. And although forest management had always embraced a diverse array of activities, including the management of wilderness areas, any use of forest areas other than to provide a long-term source of timber for the nation's needs was treated as secondary (McCloskey, 1961).

The challenge, then, was twofold. First, the proliferation of organized interests in the policy arena made clear that timber production was no longer the dominant public use of the national forests. Second, the growing criticism of the USFS also made clear that regardless of past philosophies, future forest management could not be viewed as simply a technical matter. To be sure, technical considerations would still be an important part of forest management. But as McArdle's comment above acknowledged, resolving disputes among competing forest users turned more on issues of equity and fairness than on technical determinations.

Viewed in this light, we can begin to understand why the underlying logic of MUSY set federal land policy on the path that has led to the current state of gridlock. On the one hand, MUSY can be interpreted as a congressional statement affirming the equity among various potential uses of the national forest resources. On the other hand, MUSY grants the USFS authority to develop management plans that treat these various uses unequally, as in these directives: "making the most judicious use of the land for *some* or all of these resources"; "some land will be used for *less* than all of the resources" (emphasis added). Nor does MUSY offer any other guiding principles on how to allocate those uses.

As should be obvious, this logic is custom-made for the kind of zero-sum game that has developed in federal land policy. For example, all forest users might agree with the concept that implementation of multiple use management will result in some land being used for less than all resources. However, it does not necessarily follow that forest users will therefore view a decision to limit or exclude their access in a specific area as fair or equitable. Indeed, as Behan and Magagna suggest, another possible outcome is that forest users will agree with the need to restrict some access, as long as their own access is not prohibited. And of course, if all user groups adopt this attitude, then the decision process becomes gridlocked.

Although our comments up to this point have focused on the USFS, they also apply to the BLM. From the 1930s, when the Taylor Grazing Act placed the remnants of the public domain under federal management, to the 1960s, the BLM lands were managed primarily for domestic livestock grazing. In 1964, Congress adopted the Multiple Use Classification Act, which directed the BLM to adopt a management approach modeled after MUSY, pending the completion of a thorough review of federal land policy by the Public Land Law Review Commission (PLLRC). In 1970, the PLLRC recommended a continuation of the multiple use approach for BLM, and in 1976, BLM received formal statutory authority for multiple use management in the Federal Land Policy and Management Act.

If, as we are arguing here, the logic of multiple use explains the pattern of increasing controversy over federal land policy during the past thirty years, then it is appropriate to ask whether there are ways to move beyond the current gridlock. It is to that task that we now turn.

Dealing with Gridlock

Extend the sphere and you take in a greater variety of parties and interests; you make it less probable that a majority of the whole will have a common motive to invade the rights of other citizens; or if such a common motive exists, it will be more difficult for all who feel it to discover their own strength and act in unison with each other.
—James Madison, 1787

In many important respects, this famous passage from *Federalist 10* helps explain the underlying "problems" of multiple use management. The move to multiple use was certainly a conscious attempt to extend the sphere of interests directly involved in federal land management decisions. Yet, we have put problems in quotation marks here because it is not at all clear that the gridlock produced by multiple use management is a troublesome phenomenon from a Madisonian perspective. In fact, the logic of Madison's prescription is that the competition among multiple interests would likely produce gridlock, thereby protecting the republic from the tyrannical implications of majority rule.

At the heart of Madison's argument are two premises: first, that government policy should be based on the "community interest" and, second, that the various parties and interests (factions) within society were usually at odds with, if not openly hostile to, the community interest. Madison was not idealistic enough to presume either that the task of defining the community interest would be easy or that the definition of community interest would remain constant over time. Thus, his prescription for extending the sphere can be understood as a kind of community interest "litmus test." On the one hand, if the interactions among various parties and interests led to contention and gridlock, then there was ample reason to believe that a definition of the community interest had not been articulated. If, on the other hand, the various factions did find a common ground, then there was evidence that the common position might be a statement of community interest.

Viewed in this light, the gridlock in contemporary federal land policy may not be as troublesome as it might otherwise seem. As Samuel Hays (1975, 265) has argued, the early conservation movement sought to link natural resource management with the broader community interest (goal) of creating a "highly organized, technical, and centrally planned and directed social organization which could meet a complex world with efficiency and purpose." By the 1960s, this broad social vision was undergoing serious challenge, and in consequence, the community interest to be served by the federal estate was open to redefinition. Subsequent developments in federal land policy, then, could be interpreted as an effort to arrive at a new definition of community interest for the federal estate. And following Madison's logic, the current gridlock simply indicates that a new definition has not yet been articulated.

But whether gridlock is interpreted as a problem or simply as part of the process, the more important question is how we might arrive at a new definition of the community interest to be served by the federal estate. Although we do not presume to have a definitive answer to this question, we believe that there are some general paths worth exploring. To get at these paths, we first need to rephrase our earlier comments about the flaw in the logic of multiple use.

At the heart of the concept of multiple use is a tension between the political goal of the approach and its practical implementation. The political goal is to provide statutory or administrative recognition that the competing uses of the federal estate should be treated as equally legitimate claims. Implementing this goal raises fairly obvious problems. It is simply not possible to manage a specific site simultaneously for timber, watershed, wildlife, grazing, recreation, and wilderness. Thus, determining an appropriate management regime for a specific site requires making choices among these competing uses. As noted earlier, MUSY and FLPMA recognized this tension, but in the kind of "congressional sleight-of-hand" trick that animates Theodore Lowi's (1979) critique, these acts delegate authority for resolving the tension to the land management agencies. Herein lies the beginning of the paths to be explored.

One path, it seems to us, comes directly from Lowi's argument. Thirty years of experience with multiple use affirms two of Lowi's (1979) premises. First, rather than producing a self-correcting system, the interactions among competing groups have created a dysfunctional decision process animated by acrimony and dissatisfaction. Second, true to McArdle's assertion, multiple use has put the agencies in the middle of conflict; but rather than this being a sign of success, the agencies find themselves "demonized" by virtually all federal land user groups. In its own way, then, multiple use has led to a kind of "crisis of public authority" in federal land policy. Moreover, remembering that Article 4, Section 3 of the U.S. Constitution directs Congress to "make all needful rules and regulations respecting the territory or other property belonging to the United States," it could be argued that multiple use fits the test of the *Schechter Poultry v. United States* (1935) case because it represents a delegation of legislative authority to the executive branch "without sufficiently defining the policy or criteria to guide the administrator" (Lowi, 1979, 92–126, 300–301).

One way out of the current policy morass, then, is congressional action. In the mid-1960s, for example, Congress recognized that the public understanding of the federal estate was undergoing a rather dramatic shift. In response, Congress created the PLLRC, which was charged with the task of reviewing existing federal land policy and developing recommendations for subsequent congressional deliberation. Although the PLLRC's final report, *One-Third of the Nation's Land*, generated some controversy (Pyles, 1970), it nevertheless also served as the focal point for federal land policy discussions throughout the 1970s. Indeed, at the time of its adoption, FLPMA was widely hailed as embodying most of the PLLRC's recommendations.

One path, then, might be the establishment of a new commission modeled after the PLLRC. In fact, one of the PLLRC's major recommendations, which received little attention, could serve as the primary charge for a new commission. Noting that they had received "statements from diverse interests who all commended the idea of multiple use," the PLLRC went on to suggest that "it was apparent that they were supporting different basic positions. This confusion permeates public land policy" (PLLRC, 1970, 5). To remedy this situation, the PLLRC recommended adoption of a "dominant use" approach, wherein federal lands with a clearly identifiable "highest primary use" would be managed for that use and any "secondary uses that are compatible with the primary purpose." Thus, a new commission working with the USFS and the BLM might develop dominant use recommendations that would then be codified by congressional action.

At first glance, this approach might seem to be an abandonment of multiple use. Our view, however, is that it is basically consistent with the original intent contained in MUSY. As noted above, MUSY (and FLPMA) recognized that "some land will be used for less than all of the resources." The primary change, therefore, would be to move the decisional arena from the agencies to Congress. At the same time, it is important to note that a congressionally designated dominant use approach has proven to be relatively successful for several categories of the federal estate. For example, from its inception to the present, the National Park Service has proceeded under a dominant use philosophy. And although there have been, and continue to be, arguments over park management, those disputes have not produced the kind of gridlock that characterizes forest and range policy (Freemuth, 1991). Other examples of gridlock-free policy arenas include lands administered by the National Wilderness Preservation System and the Fish and Wildlife Service, and the lands usually overlooked in federal policy discussions, those administered by the Department of Defense (Cawley and Lawrence, 1994).

Obviously, a congressional effort to determine dominant use, especially in the politically charged contemporary arena, would not be expected to produce recommendations in a short time period. Nor would it immediately alter the zero-sum game character of federal land policy discussions. Yet, it would change the dynamics of these arguments. Rather than simply producing a shouting match among the various user groups, a dominant use assessment would focus the discussion on the project of matching land to appropriate uses. In the long run, this approach might produce a clearer picture of the community interest to be served by the federal estate.

There is, of course, a more subtle change embedded in this approach. Moving the decision process to Congress presents a direct challenge to the ongoing progressive contention that land management is best left to trained professionals. Although the experiences over the past thirty years could be interpreted as providing sufficient evidence of the need for such a change, there is another possibility that takes us along a completely different path.

Earlier, we discussed the expert-centered forest management regime that was first implemented during the Pinchot era in the USFS, which has been described by Samuel Hays. It has become apparent that we may be seeing an attempt to offer up a new land management regime with some similar characteristics. That regime is ecosystem management. Consider several definitions of the term.

> The careful and skillful use of ecological, economic, social and managerial principles in managing ecosystems to produce, restore, or sustain ecosystem integrity and desired conditions, uses, products, values and services over the long term. (O'Laughlin, et al., 1993, 239)

> Ecosystem management integrates scientific knowledge of ecological relationships within a complex sociopolitical and values framework toward the general goal of protecting native ecosystem integrity over the long term. (Grumbine, 1994, 27–38)

> All ecosystem management activities should consider human beings as a biological resource. (BLM, 1994)

These definitions resemble what might be termed a "reinvention" of the Progressive Era land management regime. The first two definitions imply the value of using some sort of expert manager who will "integrate" or "skillfully use" an established knowledge base to achieve a goal that apparently has *already* been defined and agreed upon.

All three approaches appear to view the people who live within various ecosystems as another component to be managed rather than as a public to be consulted. These people are to be studied and surveyed to provide social data for a "scientifically sound and ecosystem based" (USFS and BLM, 1995, 1) management framework. If ecosystem management does provide a scientific basis for land use decisions, then it would be an alternative path out of the current policy morass. As democratic theorist Benjamin Barber (1984, 129) has noted, "Where there is certain knowledge, true science, or absolute right, there is no conflict that cannot be resolved by reference to the unity of truth, and thus there is no necessity for politics."

Yet experiences to date suggest that ecosystem management has not yet attained the status of certain knowledge or absolute right. Until ecosystem management is accepted, land managers must recognize that local people who happen to live in a defined ecosystem are frequently skeptical of, even openly hostile to, the approach. This is not merely a theoretical concern. We have argued elsewhere that local community disapproval was a key reason for the failure of the Yellowstone Vision process:

> The federal lands, whether as national parks, national forests, or ecosystems, are owned by the American public. But they are also places in which local communities have developed. In consequence, management decisions are as much about defining the character of those local communities as they are about defining land use practices. It would be misdirected, of course, to allow local desires to dictate national policy. However, it is not only misdirected but ultimately counterproductive to dismiss local concerns as somehow not part of the public discourse over national policy. (Freemuth and Cawley, 1993, 30–31)

Our view, in turn, echoes the sentiment of Wallace Stegner (1989, 169), who asserted: "A place is nothing in itself. It has no meaning, it can hardly be said to exist, except in terms of human perception, use and response."

Conclusion

Roughly thirty years ago, it became clear that federal land policy decisions were first and foremost political problems that required political solutions. At that time, multiple use management seemed to provide an appropriate solution. Over the ensuing years, the fundamental political character of federal land use decisions has become even more pronounced. We have tried to outline here some possible paths that would move us beyond the gridlocked arena of Lowi's interest group liberalism.

But whether this occurs through a congressional commission or ecosystem management, or through some combination of the two, the paths ultimately lead to the same place. We need to recover a positive definition of the word politics and thereby lay the foundation for an active and informed public conversation about the public lands. The goal should not be to *reach* "consensus," as was envisioned by MUSY. Instead, it should be to *build* a new consensus. Such a project requires that public officials be willing to lead a public conversation and that citizens be willing to participate.

NOTES

1. It is important to remember that at the time MUSY was enacted, "wilderness" was an administrative category created by the USFS. Four years later, wilderness became a statutory category with the enactment of the Wilderness Act of 1964.

REFERENCES

Barber, Benjamin. 1984. *Strong Democracy.* Berkeley: University of California Press.
Bureau of Land Management. 1994. "Human Dimensions of Ecosystem Management." Internal working document.

Cawley, R. McGreggor. 1993. *Federal Land, Western Anger: The Sagebrush Rebellion and Environmental Politics.* Lawrence: University Press of Kansas.

Cawley, R. McGreggor, and John Freemuth. 1993. "Tree Farms, Mother Earth, and Other Dilemmas: The Politics of Ecosystem Management in the Greater Yellowstone." *Society and Natural Resources* 6:41–53.

Cawley, R. McGreggor, and Robert M. Lawrence. 1994. "National Security Policy and Federal Lands Policy, or, The Greening of the Pentagon." In William Crotty, ed., *Post-Cold War Policy: The Social and Domestic Context.* Chicago: Nelson-Hall Publishers.

Congressional Research Service (CRS). 1992. *Multiple Use and Sustained Yield: Changing Philosophies for Federal Land Management?* Washington, DC: Government Printing Office.

Culhane, Paul. 1981. *Public Land Politics.* Baltimore: Johns Hopkins University Press.

Freemuth, John. 1991. *Islands Under Siege: National Parks and the Politics of External Threats.* Lawrence: University Press of Kansas.

Freemuth, John, and R. McGreggor Cawley. 1993. "Ecosystem Management: The Relationship Among Science, Land Managers, and the Public." *George Wright Forum* 10:26–32.

General Accounting Office (GAO). 1994. *Ecosystem Management: Additional Actions Needed to Adequately Test a Promising Approach.* Washington, DC: Government Printing Office.

Grumbine, R. Edward. 1994. "What Is Ecosystem Management?" *Conservation Biology* 8:27–38.

Hays, Samuel P. 1975. *Conservation and the Gospel of Efficiency: The Progressive Conservation Movement, 1890–1920.* New York: Atheneum.

———. 1987. *Beauty, Health, and Permanence: Environmental Politics in the United States, 1955–1985.* Cambridge: Cambridge University Press.

Hirt, Paul W. 1994. *A Conspiracy of Optimism: Management of the National Forests Since World War II.* Lincoln: University of Nebraska Press.

Kaufman, Herbert. 1960. *The Forest Ranger: A Study in Administrative Behavior.* Baltimore: Johns Hopkins University Press.

Lowi, Theodore J. 1979. *The End of Liberalism: The Second Republic of the United States.* New York: W. W. Norton and Company.

McArdle, Richard. 1953. "Multiple Use—Multiple Benefits." *Journal of Forestry* 51:325.

McCloskey, J. Michael. 1961. "Natural Resources, National Forests: The Multiple Use-Sustained Yield Act of 1960." *Oregon Law Review* 41:49–79.

O'Laughlin, Jay, James MacCracken, David Adams, Stephen Bunting, Keith Blatner, and Charles Keegan. 1993. *Forest Health Conditions in Idaho.* Moscow: University of Idaho Policy Analysis Group Report No. 11.

Public Land Law Review Commission (PLLRC). 1970. *One-Third of the Nation's Land.* Washington, DC: Government Printing Office.

Pyles, Hamilton K. 1970. *What's Ahead for Our Public Lands.* Washington, DC: Natural Resources Council of America.

Ray, Dixy Lee, with Lou Guzzo. 1993. *Environmental Overkill: Whatever Happened to Common Sense?* Washington, DC: Regnery Gateway.

Stegner, Wallace. 1989. "The Marks of Human Passage." In David Harmon, ed., *Mirror of America: Literary Encounters with the National Parks.* Boulder: Roberts Reinhart.

Stone, Deborah A. 1988. *Policy Paradox and Political Reason.* Glenville, IL: Scott, Foresman/Little, Brown College Division.

United States Forest Service (USFS) and Bureau of Land Management (BLM). 1995. *Upper Columbia River Basin Environmental Impact Statement Purpose and Need: Summary.* Washington, DC: Government Printing Office.

Vig, Norman J., and Michael E. Kraft. 1984. *Environmental Policy in the 1980s: Reagan's New Agenda.* Washington, DC: CQ Press.

PART TWO

PROGRAMS

4

From Localism to Legalism: The Transformation of Federal Forest Policy

GEORGE HOBERG

This chapter examines the transformation of federal forest policy over the past fifty years. As in other western public land policy areas, forest policy has undergone a series of sweeping changes, moving from a traditional policy regime that emphasized rapid timber harvesting and economic development to a modern regime in which environmental values have been brought into greater balance with developmental ones. This transition, which has produced wrenching change within the U.S. Forest Service, occurred in several stages, with the first burst of reform in the mid- to late-1970s followed by a more recent era of dramatic change in the late 1980s and early 1990s.

After a brief overview of federal forest policy, this chapter outlines the traditional timber regime that characterized forest policy from World War II to around 1970. The next section analyzes the transformation of this regime in the 1970s into what I call the "pluralist forest policy regime," tracing the dramatic changes that occurred in the interests, institutions, ideas, and officials guiding forest policy in that period. The analysis then turns to several case studies: the most extreme case of policy change, the Pacific Northwest; the Tongass National Forest in Alaska; and the controversy over below-cost timber sales in the inland West. Finally, some preliminary speculations about the implications of the new Republican majorities in Congress are offered.

I argue that there has been a fundamental change in federal forest policy. Environmental values have become far more important in forest policy decisionmaking. This change is the result of a combination of conditions, the most important of which has been the emergence of a powerful regional and national environmental movement. This movement has been successful in achieving statutory and institutional changes that have broken up the cozy alliance of commodity-oriented Forest Service officials, the timber industry, and regional congressional delegations. New laws require that greater weight be placed on environmental values, courts have been active in forcing a reluctant Forest Service to abide by these new laws, and the nationalization of the forest policy issue has overcome the legacy of localism that promoted a timber-first pattern of forest management.

Before examining the history of forest policy, some general background is in order. Seventy-two percent of U.S. commercial forest land is privately owned, 21 percent is owned by the federal government, and the remaining 7 percent is owned by states, localities, or Indian tribes (Cubbage, O'Lauglin, and Bullock, 1993, 16). Private forested land is regulated by state governments. The overwhelming amount of forests on public lands is controlled by the U.S. federal government as part of the system of national forests under the jurisdiction of the Forest Service, housed within the Department of Agriculture.[1] The total area of the national forests is 191 million acres of land, of which 85 percent is in the eleven western states and Alaska (Wilkinson, 1992, 119). Of the 5.9 billion board feet of timber harvested in 1993, 70 percent came from the West (U.S. Department of Agriculture, 1994, 135).

The central dilemma for federal forest policymakers is how to balance the conflicting uses of Forest Service land. The national forests contain vast tracks of commercially valuable timber, as well as mineral deposits and rangeland that are beyond the scope of this analysis. The national forests also contain spectacular wilderness areas, some of the last tracts of virgin forest on the continent, and an extraordinary diversity of fish and wildlife habitat. These environmental values for the most part directly conflict with the interests in timber harvesting and other extractive activities. Forest Service officials must determine how to allocate land use among these various competing interests.

This conflict of interest in forest land use is complicated by the spatial distribution of interests. Residents of rural communities across the West depend on extractive activities such as logging for their livelihood. Nevertheless, many people in timber-dependent communities also treasure the environmental values of the forests, as do residents of urban areas who rely on these environmental amenities for recreation. And because these forests are owned by the federal government, all Americans have a claim over how they are used, not just those who live in adjacent areas. In the postwar period, local interests were given priority and use focused on timber harvesting. Over time, however, the Forest Service faced increasing pressures from urban and national interests to protect environmental amenities, and USFS discretion was increasingly constrained by statutes, regulations, and court decisions. The remainder of this chapter describes this policy change.

The Traditional Timber Regime

Prior to the dramatic changes of the 1970s, the forest policy regime was characterized by a dominant administrative agency, a strong orientation toward the development of timber resources, and little input from the public.[2] The Forest Service reflected its origins in the Progressive Era: It was given broad discretion to manage public forests, in its expert judgment, to promote the public interest. The 1897 Forest Service Organic Act authorized the Forest Service "to improve and protect the forest within the reservation . . . and to furnish a continuous supply of timber for the use and necessities of the citizens of the United States." The act authorized the Forest Service to manage the national forests "to regulate their occupancy and use and to preserve the forests thereon from destruction."[3]

The Forest Service has a long tradition of professionalism and autonomy (Kaufman, 1960; Steen, 1976; Clarke and McCool, 1985). Historically, it has exhibited a strong pro-timber orientation. This philosophy is perhaps best exhibited in a letter from Forest Service founder Gifford Pinchot, who, despite his association with the utilitarian view of the "greatest good of the greatest number in the long run," viewed timber production as the preeminent objective. According to Pinchot, national forests were to be managed "for the benefit of the home builder first of all" (cited in Wilkinson, 1992, 128–129; see also Clary, 1986; Hays, 1987, 124–126). The agency was dominated by professional foresters trained in silviculture and oriented toward maximizing the long-run sustainable yield of timber products from the nation's forests. This view was particularly dominant in the agency as the demand for national forest timber escalated dramatically after World War II, largely as a result of the postwar boom in housing (Clary, 1986, 159).

Forest policy in this era operated much like the classic iron triangle, with the Forest Service, timber industry, and relevant appropriations subcommittees forming the triad. The interest group environment of the agency was dominated by timber companies that began to depend on trees from federal lands after World War II. Although the voices of organized environmental groups such as the Sierra Club were occasionally heard, environmentalists were largely peripheral to the functioning of the traditional timber regime.

In Congress, regional delegations used the appropriations process to oversee agency activities. Because of the geographically discrete nature of forest resources, there has always been a powerful tendency toward localism in congressional forest policy. Timber sales are an important source of jobs in forested rural areas. Indeed, much of forest policy in this era was focused on stabilizing the economic base of rural communities (Clary, 1986, chap. 5). More important from the congressional perspective, in the early twentieth century Congress provided for counties to receive 25 percent of the receipts for timber sales for use in road and school construction, to compensate localities for the limitations on the taxable land base created by federal ownership (Sample, 1990, 149). This program ties local revenues to timber sales and gives regional members of Congress powerful incentives to maintain and even increase timber sales. Thus, to the extent that Congress had an interest in forest policy, it reinforced the Forest Service's and timber industry's interest in timber harvesting. One of the effects of this policy over the years was to create a strong perception in forest-dependent communities that there was a type of "social contract" between the Forest Service and these communities that guaranteed a sustained flow of timber (Lee, 1990). When environmental restrictions forced reductions in timber harvests in some areas around 1990, these communities felt betrayed.

As in many areas of the administrative state during this era, the courts played virtually no role. Charles Wilkinson and Michael Anderson have argued that "the Forest Service was largely immune from judicial oversight" in this period, with Forest Service decisions "considered protected by an aura of virtual unreviewability, and the few court challenges were routinely dismissed" (Wilkinson and Anderson, 1987, 72).

The dominance of timber interests within this iron triangle was subjected to greater challenges unleashed by the same forces promoting higher timber demand. The wealthier, more mobile postwar population began to place increasing recreational demands on national forests. In response to this growing tension, Congress enacted the Multiple Use and Sustained Yield Act in 1960 to give formal statutory recognition to nontimber uses of national forests (Culhane, 1981, 52–53). The act explicitly charged the agency with protecting the forests for "outdoor recreation, range, timber, watershed, and fish and wildlife purposes." Although the new act was wordier, it did little to restrict the discretion of the agency.[4]

The first major restriction on Forest Service discretion occurred in 1964 with the enactment of the Wilderness Act. Prior to the passage of this act, the Forest Service had the discretion to designate certain areas within its land base as wilderness and thus preserve them from development. In the Wilderness Act, Congress asserted its control over the wilderness designation process. Congress specifically designated a number of wilderness areas and established a process to maintain its continued control over the issue (Wilkinson and Anderson, 1987, chap. 9; Culhane, 1981, 54–55). Although this new statute constrained the Forest Service's discretion by removing certain areas from its multiple-use management mandate, it did not directly affect the essential timber management activities.

These two statutory changes in the 1960s revealed the growing tensions within the traditional timber regime. Although more wilderness was set aside and the agency adopted the rhetoric of multiple use, timber harvesting continued to be the dominant value within the Forest Service (Clary, 1986, 163, 169). The dominant forces in the agency's environment, the timber industry and regional delegations in Congress, reinforced this bias. Advocates of recreation and wilderness preservation became increasingly influential but could do little more than eat away at the edges of the regime. In the 1970s, however, changes in values and institutions produced a sweeping change in every element of the regime.

The Pluralist Forest Policy Regime

The American forest policy regime underwent a profound transformation in the 1970s, in the wake of a larger change in the U.S. policy regime that occurred in other areas around 1970. In the United States, the first wave of environmentalism around 1970 was met with profound changes in the American "policy style." This transformation had five fundamental components: the emergence of an organized environmental movement; the enactment of a battery of new environmental laws and the creation of new government organizations to execute them; expansion of congressional control over policy through increasingly specific statutes; an explosion of judicial scrutiny of administrative action; and increased public participation in policymaking, through new formal procedural avenues in administrative rule making and greater access to courts (Hoberg, 1992; Melnick, 1983; Harris and Milkis, 1989). A new public philosophy of *pluralist legalism* emerged to reflect these changes in relations among citizens, Congress, the courts, and the administrative state. The notion of business capture of regulatory agencies became commonplace, and the perceived solution was to restrict agency discretion through more specific statutory mandates and expand the representation of nonindustry groups through the use of formal, legalistic procedures, monitored by the courts (McCann, 1986).[5]

In the late 1960s and early 1970s, environmental groups became increasingly active and assertive in forest policy. Forest policy did not play as large a role as pesticides or air and water pollution in the wave of environmental reforms of this period, but there was still a notable increase in environmental group presence in the forest policy arena. Traditional groups such as the Sierra Club, the Wilderness Society, and the National Wildlife Federation continued to press for greater wilderness protection and took advantage of the judicialization of environmental policy to pursue their goals.

The key shift in judicial scrutiny of Forest Service behavior occurred between 1971 and 1975. The last gasp of the era of judicial deference was evident in the 1971 case of *Sierra Club v. Hardin,* in which environmentalists challenged the Forest Service's commitment to rapid liquidation of old-growth forests in Alaska's Tongass National Forest. The district court ruled that despite the obvious priority given to timber over other multiple-use values, "Congress has given no indication as to the weight to be assigned each value and it must be assumed that the decision as to the proper mix of uses within any particular area is left to the sound discretion and expertise of the Forest Service."[6]

By 1975 the deferential stance had been abandoned. The development that ultimately undermined the traditional forest policy regime was litigation by environmental groups to halt the environmentally damaging forest practice of clear-cutting. Conservationists found an obscure provision of the original authorizing statute of the Forest Service, the 1897 Organic Act, requiring that harvested trees had to be "dead or matured" and that they had to be marked before being cut.[7] Although these requirements were legislated even before the development of the forestry profession in the United States, the court refused to defer to the Forest Service's interpretation of the statute's meaning and enjoined clear-cutting in the Monongahela National Forest in West Virginia and the Tongass National Forest in Alaska.[8] By outlawing the most common method for harvesting timber, these rulings created a crisis in timber management. Congress was forced to rewrite forest management laws to address the impasse (Le Master, 1984, chap. 4; Wilkinson and Anderson, 1987, 40–41).

In revising the statute, Congress was acting in a political environment far more favorable to environmental interests. The mobilization of environmental groups and more environmentally oriented public opinion elevated environmental protection as a policy objective and downgraded traditional timber interests. The court-imposed clear-cut ban also gave environmentalists and their supporters in Congress a strategic advantage in that the alternative to new legislation was a very pro-environment status quo. The ultimate result was the National Forest Management Act of 1976 (16 U.S.C 472a). NFMA transformed forest policy in two ways. First, it shifted jurisdiction over forest policy from the appropriations committees, dominated by industry and regional interests, to authorizing committees far more sensitive to national environmental constituencies. Appropriations committees continued to be powerful vehicles for the representation of regional interests (Sample, 1990), but they were now more effectively balanced by pro-environment authorizing committees.

Second, NFMA produced profound sustantive and procedural changes in forest policy, through its requirements for forest practice regulations and the creation of a new planning process. Unlike a number of other environmental statutes passed in the 1970s, NFMA did not create any major substantive restrictions on agency discretion. The fundamental task of balancing among multiple uses was still left largely for the agency to decide. The statute did direct the Forest Service to promulgate regulations establishing standards and guidelines for timber management and the protection of other resources. The clear-cutting crisis created by the court rulings was resolved by permitting clear-cutting but requiring the agency to institute forest practices protecting a wide range of resource values, such as water, fisheries, wildlife, soils, and so on.

In developing these standards, the Forest Service imposed a number of restrictions on its own discretion (Wilkinson and Anderson 1987, 119). Perhaps the most famous standard was the language chosen to implement that statute's language for the protection of wildlife. NFMA requires that forest planning "provide for diversity of plant and animal communities based on the suitability and capability of the specific land area in order to meet overall multiple-use objectives" (16 U.S.C. sec 1604 [g][3][B]). The implementing regulations transformed this general guideline into a stringent action-forcing requirement: "Fish and wildlife habitat shall be managed to maintain viable populations of existing native and desired non-native vertebrate species in the planning area" (Wilkinson and Anderson, 1987, 296). To the surprise of many Forest Service officials, this language became the centerpiece of the environmentalists' litigation strategy to stop logging in old-growth forests in the Pacific Northwest to preserve the northern spotted owl and other vulnerable species.

The second major feature of NFMA was the establishment of a planning process, in which the Forest Service is required to prepare long-term, integrated plans for each national forest.[9] This planning approach transformed the forest policy process by dramatically expanding opportunities for public participation, intensifying the role of courts, introducing new government officials representing new values into the policy process, and eventually leading to a change in the scientific knowledge-base underlying forest policy.

Public participation, particularly by environmental groups, was dramatically expanded by the new planning process. The NFMA included required public participation in the "development, review, and revision" of forest plans (Office of Technology Assessment, 1992, chap. 5). In addition to the requirements of the NFMA, the planning process also had to comply with National Environmental Policy Act procedures, which also contained extensive opportunities for public participation. Moreover, the Forest Service created its own process of administrative appeals (Boberz and Fischman, 1992). These new, multilayered requirements forced the agency to pay more attention to environmental group concerns, but they also created a procedural quagmire for the agency. The planning process costs $200 million annually; almost all of the plans have been subjected to administrative appeal, and many aspects of them to court challenges as well (*Economist,* March 10, 1990, 28).

As in many other areas of natural resource policy, courts have come to play a pivotal role in policy formation. In the 1960s, the Forest Service faced an average of one lawsuit per year. By the early 1970s, litigation intensified to an average of two dozen a year, much of which resulted from the implementation of NEPA (Brizee, 1975). The new planning requirements in NFMA and its regulations have created a number of avenues for environmentalists to challenge Forest Service decisions in court and have produced an explosion of litigation. In spring 1991, pending litigation for the agency consisted of 94 cases. Six cases involved regional guides, 15 cases involved forest plans, 7 cases involved other issues under NFMA, and 66 lawsuits challenged timber sales (Office of Technology Assessment, 1992, 100). As is discussed in more detail later in the chapter, in the most extreme case, Federal District Judge William Dwyer has essentially seized control over the management of forests in the Pacific Northwest.

Another change brought about by the new planning process, less recognized but equally important, is a significant shift in the attitudes of Forest Service officials. Although the Forest Service has traditionally been a multidisciplinary agency, the agency was dominated by a mind-set or worldview that emphasized timber production. The Multiple Use and Sustained Yield Act of 1960 was designed to increase the priority given to nontimber values such as recreation and wildlife, but it left so much discretion to the agency that it had little impact. The NFMA planning process required that a broad range of values be extensively analyzed. As a result, the agency needed to assemble greater expertise in these nontraditional areas and therefore had to hire fishery and wildlife biologists.

This restocking of personnel had profound effects on the agency as officials with environmental expertise and ideologies increased in number and eventually made their way up the organization hierarchy.[10] This strengthened perspective within the agency received formal organizational support with the establishment of the Association of Forest Service Employees for Environmental Ethics in 1989, which, among other activities, publishes a regular newsletter, *Inner Voice,* that has a strong environmental bent. Referring to the impact of the NFMA, William Dietrich writes: "Since it was passed the Forest Service has gone from 284 to 688 wildlife biologists, 75 to 236 fisheries biologists, 47 to 206 archeologists, 7 to 84 ecologists. The new disciplines attract enthusiasts from across the United States, many of them more liberal, worldly, and wildlife-oriented than their predecessors" (Dietrich, 1992, 98; see also Office of Technology Assessment, 1992, 165). The culmination of this development was the appointment of Jack Ward Thomas as chief forester by the Clinton administration in 1993, the first time someone not trained as either a forester or an engineer has held the position (Donahue, 1994; Hirt, 1994, 291).

Although these changes in laws, processes, and officials took a long time to develop, they produced a fundamental change in the scientific basis for forest policy. Traditional forestry was based on converting natural forests into faster-growing plantations so as to maximize the long-run sustainable yield of forest products. This paradigm was modified by increasing emphasis on nontimber values in the 1960s and 1970s. By the late 1980s and early 1990s, however, the new science of conservation biology had become increasingly influential within the agency. In June 1992, Chief Forester Dale Robertson announced that "ecosystem management" was the new concept guiding agency decisionmaking, claiming that "the Forest Service is committed to using an ecological approach in the future management of national forests" (quoted in Gerlach and Bengston, 1994). Eight months later, the new Clinton administration officially embraced the concept of "ecosystem management" as its management approach in forestry and other environmental and natural resource policies.[11] It is still difficult to know whether this concept reflects a fundamental departure in agency philosophy or simply another rhetorical innovation (like multiple use in the earlier regime) to mollify agency critics while maintaining traditional priorities. Judging from its application in the Pacific Northwest and elsewhere, as described further on, it does seem to embody the promise of a reorientation of the agency's approach to forest management.

Unfortunately, it is not possible to provide comprehensive data to measure the true extent of policy change as a result of this regime change. However, one indicator of the relative emphasis of Forest Service activities—the level of timber harvests in national forests—does reveal an interesting pattern. The turmoil in forest policy in the early 1970s had quite an impact, depressing harvest levels for several years. Once the crisis was resolved by the passage of the National Forest Management Act, levels began to increase again.

It is striking that the regime changes of the 1970s did not have an immediate impact on this indicator of public policy. Once the 1982 recession ended, the

Reagan administration was able to dramatically increase timber harvests, even though there is considerable evidence that they did so by deliberately manipulating planning techniques for political reasons and playing fast and loose with the new environmental requirements created by the NFMA and other laws (Hirt, 1994, chap. 12).

By 1990, however, this timber binge had ended, and harvest levels have been declining precipitously since then. The 1993 level of 5.9 billion board feet was less than one-half the peak level of 12.7 billion board feet in 1987 and is the lowest level since the early 1950s. By 1995, the level was reduced even further to 3.9 billion board feet, a 33 percent reduction from the 1993 level (USDA, 1996).

It took more than a decade to influence the core activities of the Forest Service, but forest policy has come to reflect the broader pluralist policy regime in the United States. Policy objectives of environmental protection have been given far greater emphasis. Substantive and procedural requirements in statutes, as well as regulations promulgated by the Forest Service, more narrowly constrain the discretion of regulatory officials. Courts have become effective "partners" in many aspects of forest management. Environmental groups, previously peripheral to forest policy, have become powerful players.

This combination of changes in interest groups and institutions, especially jurisdictional shifts in Congress, has produced a significant "nationalizing" trend that has countered the strong pro-timber "localism" that dominated forest policy in the earlier regime. The societal shift in values toward more environmental sensitivity was reflected in changes in agency personnel. New environmentally oriented officials have changed the values of the agency, eventually producing a new paradigm—"ecosystem management"—to guide agency decisionmaking.

Old-Growth Forests in the Pacific Northwest

The most extreme example of these changes in the forest policy regime has occurred in the battle over the old-growth forests in the Pacific Northwest. Environmental groups combined a lobbying strategy to nationalize the issue with a brilliantly successful litigation strategy to bring logging in the region's forests almost to a halt. In developing a response to these challenges, the Forest Service was forced to rely increasingly on the new science of conservation biology, which has revolutionized the ways the forests in the region are being managed. Although these changes were most extreme in this region, they were not isolated to the Northwest. As the subsequent section shows, the Northwest was the crucible for forest policy changes that have spilled over into other regions.

The controversy over old-growth forests in the Northwest did not emerge as a significant policy issue until late 1987.[12] There was an active and reasonably well-balanced forest policy subsystem in place prior to that date, but it was focused on the issue of designation of alpine wilderness areas. A major shift occurred when the Sierra Club Legal Defense Fund (SCLDF) opened its new Seattle office in

January 1987. The SCLDF launched a two-pronged legal strategy that has to be considered one of the most successful legal campaigns in the history of American environmental law.[13] The first prong involved the listing of the spotted owl under the Endangered Species Act. In December 1987, the Fish and Wildlife Service (FWS) issued a decision that listing the spotted owl was not warranted. The agency's own scientists had concluded the opposite, but the report was altered under the directions of Reagan political appointees (General Accounting Office, 1989).

The Sierra Club Legal Defense Fund challenged the agency's decision in district court, and in November 1988 a federal district court vacated the Fish and Wildlife Service's decision as "arbitrary and capricious" and remanded the issue to the agency for reconsideration.[14] In response, the FWS chose to list the owl as "threatened" in June 1990. Although this court ruling turned out to have relatively little practical significance, it signaled the entry of the judicial branch into the old-growth controversy.

The second and far more important prong of the legal strategy was the series of legal challenges to the Forest Service's efforts to comply with the requirements of NEPA and especially to the NFMA in the district court in Seattle. In December 1988, the Forest Service finalized its supplemental environmental impact statement on the spotted owl and issued new regional guidelines for its protection. The SCLDF sued, and in March 1989, Judge William Dwyer, an appointee of Ronald Reagan, ruled that the plan was inadequate and issued his first injunction on timber sales in Washington and Oregon. This injunction, which turned out to be the first of many, was a pivotal event in the history of Northwest forest policy because it shifted the beneficiary of the status quo. Now, for affected timber sales to go forward, the Forest Service either had to comply with the judge's strict interpretation of the law or Congress had to take specific action to change the law as it applied in this case. Success in the judicial arena gave environmentalists new power resources in the executive and legislative arenas.

The Northwest delegation to Congress sought to regain control over the issue by attaching riders to appropriations bills exempting relevant logging activities from lawsuits.[15] The most prominent effort was "Section 318," which, among other things, exempted both BLM and USFS timber sales from ongoing litigation.[16]

In response to this setback, environmentalists revamped their strategy, fighting fire with fire. They reoriented litigation to focus on the constitutionality of Section 318, claiming that by attempting to decide the outcome of particular court cases, Congress had violated the separation of powers. Environmentalists also reconsidered their entire political approach, recognizing that as long as old-growth forests were considered a regional issue, they would continue to lose in Congress. According to Andy Kerr of the Oregon Natural Resources Council, "Expecting the Northwest Congressional delegation to be rational about ending the cutting of ancient forests in the late 1980s is like expecting the delegation from the American South to deal rationally with ending segregation in the late

1950s" (personal interview, Portland, OR, July 20, 1993). Environmentalists understood that in order to succeed politically they would have to nationalize the issue. Public opinion surveys show that there are significant differences between the national and regional publics on these issues, with the national public being consistently more pro-environment (Steel, List, and Shindler, 1992; Timber Industry Labor-Management Committee, 1993).

The timing for the nationalization of the old-growth debate could not have been better, as the environment issue more generally was gaining extraordinary salience nationwide. Emphasis was placed on the fact that the remaining old growth was virtually all in national forests, owned equally by all citizens of the United States. Feature stories appeared in the *New Yorker* and *National Geographic,* network news ran stories about activists sitting in trees in protest, and the issue reached the pinnacle of media exposure when the spotted owl made the cover of *Time* magazine on June 25, 1990.

This successful campaign in the arena of public opinion was supplemented by national interest group mobilization efforts. Groups not only sought to convince lawmakers outside the Northwest that they had electoral incentives to take an interest in the issue, but they also launched a more targeted political campaign to delegitimize the strategy of using appropriations riders to exempt Northwest forests from the application of environmental statutes (Sher and Hunting, 1991, 487–490).

The revamped environmental strategy was extraordinarily successful. In a decision that rocked forest politics and raised eyebrows throughout Congress, in September 1990 the Ninth Circuit Court of Appeals took the dramatic step of striking down key parts of Section 318 as unconstitutional, on the grounds that Congress directed a particular decision in pending litigation without amending the statutes used as the basis for litigation.[17] This decision was a stunning blow to timber interests and their allies in the Northwest congressional delegation because it invalidated their most effective means of insulating timber sales from environmental litigation.

The ruling turned out to be temporary, however; in March 1992, the Supreme Court overruled the Ninth Circuit in a unanimous decision.[18] Nonetheless, by the time the right of members of Congress to "protect their own" through appropriations riders was restored, the use of that tactic in forest policy had been completely delegitimized by the concurrent political campaign by environmentalists to nationalize the issue. Legislators outside the region began taking an interest in the issue, and authorizing committees, whose statutes were being quietly rewritten, began to reassert their jurisdictional interests in the issue.

The focus of the process returned to efforts by the Forest Service and associated agencies to develop a plan for the protection of the spotted owl that could win judicial approval. A haphazard plan put together by the hostile Bush administration was challenged in court, and Judge Dwyer again ruled in favor of environmentalists, chastising the government for "a deliberate and systematic refusal . . . to comply with the laws protecting wildlife." The relevant law was the requirement in the regulations promulgated under the NFMA, discussed earlier, that viable populations of wildlife be maintained. Dwyer ordered the Forest Service to develop "revised standards and guidelines to ensure the northern spotted owl's viability" by March 1992, and enjoined timber sales until they did so.[19]

The Forest Service went back to work. This time it followed proper procedures and in March 1992, adopted a new plan based on the prestigious "Thomas report," setting aside about 8 million acres of old-growth forest for spotted owl habitat. Naturally, the environmentalists sued again. In late May 1992, Judge Dwyer rejected the Forest Service's attempt to adopt the Thomas report as its spotted owl plan. The most striking part of the decision was his ruling that the plan was flawed because it did not adequately address issues related to species other than the spotted owl.[20] Continuing the pattern of previous cases, Dwyer imposed an injunction on timber sales until a satisfactory plan was put in place.

The decision stunned the Forest Service. Not only was the Thomas report, a state-of-the-art scientific document in 1990, ruled inadequate, but the whole objective of the process was redefined by judicial order. The scope of the issue was significantly enlarged, moving beyond the situation of one medium-sized owl to an entire ecosystem. A far more sophisticated analytical process was necessary to address this larger problem, and as a result, the emphasis shifted from protection of particular species to the management of an entire ecosystem.

While these developments in the bureaucratic and judicial arena were unfolding, activity in the congressional arena increased significantly. The focus of action shifted away from efforts by appropriations committees to exempt Forest Service activities from court decisions to efforts by authorizing committees, where environmental groups had far more influence, to develop a substantive legislative solution to the issue. The locus of action during the 102nd Congress (1991–1992) was the House Interior Committee, chaired by George Miller (D-CA), a strong environmentalist. The committee's bill was thwarted, however, by the intervention of House Speaker Thomas Foley (D-WA), the de facto leader of the Northwest congressional delegation (1992 CQ Almanac, 279). Environmentalists had enough power to block appropriations riders, but not enough power to enact their own legislation. On this issue, Congress was deadlocked. Neither side could muster sufficient support to achieve a legislative solution. The result, however, was that the pro-environment status quo imposed in the judicial arena remained in force, demonstrating again the remarkable power of injunction to alter the distribution of influence.

With Clinton's election, the executive arena was transformed. Pro-timber officials were replaced by pro-environmental ones, the most prominent among them being Interior Secretary Bruce Babbitt, previously president of the League of Conservation Voters, and Chief Forester Jack Ward Thomas, the first biologist ever to hold the position. Rather than facing intense pressures from political superiors to water down their proposals to protect wildlife, the Forest Service and Fish and Wildlife Service now confronted pressures to expand protection.

Making good on a campaign promise, the administration held a "forest summit" on April 2, 1993, in Portland, Oregon. The president, vice president, and six cabinet officials spent an entire day around a table listening to short speeches on one regional issue. In his closing remarks, Clinton committed his administration to the development of a plan that would be "scientifically sound, ecologically credible, and legally responsible" (Pryne and Matassa, 1993). The assignment was given to three working groups dominated by representatives of the relevant agencies: ecosystem management assessment, labor and community assistance, and agency coordination.

President Clinton announced his forest plan on July 1, 1993, his face clearly showing strain from the burdens of imposing costs and from the campaign rhetoric of "false choices," a faint and distant memory. The plan calls for an annual harvest level of 1.2 billion board feet, which the scientific work group concluded was the maximum cut permissible under current law. In addition, the plan provides for extensive reserves for spotted owl protection and dramatically expands riparian reserves for the protection of fish habitat. The scientific team assessed the plan's impact on the viability of over 1,000 species. Of the 82 vertebrate species analyzed, the plan is expected to provide an 80 percent likelihood of the maintenance of viable populations of all but 3 species of salamanders. In total, the plan would set aside 80 percent of the remaining old-growth forests for habitat protection purposes. In an attempt to ease the resulting regional unemployment, the plan also provides for a massive $1.2 billion economic assistance package.

The compromise was bitterly attacked from all sides. Industry and labor groups claimed the dramatically reduced cuts would devastate timber-dependent rural communities. Environmentalists harshly criticized the size of the cut, especially the nature of proposed cutting on the old-growth reserves. These areas, rather than being inviolate, would be subjected to some logging for fire or insect salvage and to some thinning of second-growth stands to promote old-growth characteristics.[21]

Although environmentalists did their utmost to act as outraged as the timber industry and loggers, they had in fact achieved a remarkable victory. To put Clinton's plan in proper perspective, one need only go back to 1989. During the debate over Section 318, environmentalists proposed an allowable cut level of 4.8 billion board feet per year. A harvest level they were willing to accept in 1989 is four times higher than the level they consider outrageously high in 1993. This shift by a factor of four in the harvest level indicates the dramatic redistribution of power achieved in this issue area by four years of effective lobbying in Congress, a successful public relations campaign to polish and nationalize the issue, and especially, a brilliant litigation campaign.

Environmentalists were not satisfied, however, and once the plan was finalized in April 1994, they challenged it in court again. This time industry challenged the decision as well, arguing that the process used to develop the plan violated the Federal Advisory Committee Act. In what may be the final action on this policy issue, Judge Dwyer upheld the Clinton forest plan in December 1994, brushing aside the criticisms from both sides.[22]

This case study reveals all the major elements of the transformation of the forest policy regime. It documents the success of a concerted campaign by environmental groups to change forest policy in fundamental ways. Although the groups did not get everything they wanted, no one can question that the case reflects an extraordinary victory for the environmental movement. The environmental strategy can be boiled down to two tactics: nationalization and judicialization. The victory would not have been possible if the issue continued to be constructed in regional terms, as forest policy has traditionally been. This case study offers perhaps the most extreme case of judicial intervention into environmental policymaking. From the time of his first injunction in 1989 to his approval of the Clinton forest plan in late 1994, Judge Dwyer essentially managed Region Six of the U.S. Forest Service.

Environmentalists would respond that Dwyer was merely enforcing the law, and they have a point. The regulations promulgated to implement NFMA "diversity" requirements elevated the status of species protection in the agency's multiple-use equations, forcing the agency into unexpectedly preservationist decisions. As the priority given to nontimber values increased, the expertise of biologists and ecologists increased in importance, as did their influence in the region. The new science of ecosystem management, implied by NFMA viability regulations, began to take shape in the development and implementation of the Clinton forest plan.

The Last Frontier: Alaska's Tongass National Forest

The Northwest region has unquestionably been the centerpiece of forest policy conflict in the past decade, and events there have spilled over into other regions. A pitched battle has been raging over the balance between old-growth forest preservation and timber harvesting in Tongass National Forest in Alaska, the northern end of the band of temperate rain forest that hugs the Pacific coast of North America. Commercial timber harvesting in the area began in earnest in the 1950s. In an effort to create a stable economic base for the region, the Forest Service signed two extraordinary long-term contracts that guaranteed two corporations long-term supplies of timber in exchange for their construction and operation of pulp mills in southeast Alaska. Because of its remoteness, the economics of timber harvesting in the Tongass has always been questionable, and these contracts have involved massive government subsidies to keep the mills operating. The Tongass is the most extreme case of below-cost timber sales, a subject discussed later on. One estimate claims that the Forest Service receives a rate of return of only eight cents on the dollar for timber sales in the region (Grode, 1991, 880).

Environmental controversies in the Tongass began in the 1970s, and the area was involved in some of the early judicialization of forest policy in the early and mid-1970s.[23] In the wake of the NFMA in 1976, the Forest Service completed the Tongass Land Management Plan in 1979, the first plan developed under the act's requirements. In 1980, Congress passed the Alaska National Interest Lands Conservation Act (ANILCA), which set aside vast tracts of Alaska land as wilderness, including 5.4 million acres in the Tongass National Forest. Most of this wilderness was rock and ice, however, leaving much of the region's timber available for harvesting. Although ANILCA did much to protect wilderness, it represented an explicit effort to insulate forestry in the Tongass from the new pluralist forestry regime. The bill guaranteed the industry a timber supply of 4.5 billion board feet of timber for the decade and appropriated $40 million a year to subsidize the industry. In addition, ANILCA exempted the Tongass from the "suitability" requirements of NFMA that provided the basis for environmental regulation of forest practices (McCrackin, 1993, 1147; Grode, 1991, 875).

The Tongass entered the modern forest regime in the 1990s as a result of statutory change and the spillover of the scientific issues from the Pacific Northwest. Throughout the 1980s, environmental group criticism of the forest management in the Tongass escalated. A regional environmental coalition, the Southeast Alaska Conservation Coalition, succeeded in attracting enough supporters from outside Alaska to get Congress to enact the Tongass Timber Reform Act of 1990 (TTRA). The debate pitted congressional environmentalists such as Senator Tim Wirth (D-CO) and Representative George Miller (D-CA) against the Alaska state delegation and other defenders of the timber industry (*Congressional Quarterly Almanac,* 1990, 294–297). An environmentalist in the region noted that success required nationalizing the issue: "We have always had to rely on people outside Alaska" (personal interview, Juneau, AK, July 6, 1994).

The TTRA eliminated many of the special exemptions the Tongass had been given in ANILCA. It repealed the guaranteed timber supply and annual appropriation to subsidize it and eliminated the Tongass's exemption from NFMA's environmental requirements. It replaced the pro-timber statutory directions with a pro-environment direction by establishing one-hundred-foot buffer zones on each side of fish-bearing streams.[24] It also applied a "proportionality" requirement to timber harvesting to prevent companies from taking only the most valuable trees, an environmentally destructive practice known as "high-grading." Although the act did not terminate the long-term contracts as environmentalists had proposed, it did modify them to be more consistent with the competitive short-term sales used elsewhere (McCrackin, 1993, 1148–1150).

Since the enactment of the TTRA, Tongass forest politics has come to resemble those of its counterparts in the Pacific Northwest. Environmentalists have used the courts to challenge the Forest Service's implementation of the new environmental requirements of the TTRA. A federal court has rejected as "arbitrary and capricious" the methodology used by the Forest Service in attempting to comply with the new proportionality requirement that has slowed down timber sales.[25]

Of greater long-term significance, the ecosystem science used in the Pacific Northwest has worked its way north, promising to bring radical change to forest management. The key triggering events were the decisions by Judge Dwyer establishing the binding nature and significance of the "minimum viable populations" provisions of the NFMA regulations. The Forest Service began to consider how the standards and guidelines applied in the Tongass would measure against this standard and realized that they lacked a meaningful strategy. An interagency Viable Population Committee was convened, and the report recommended dramatic changes to forest practices in the area in order to maintain wildlife viability. The report represented such a radical shift from the pro-timber values of the Forest Service in the Tongass that it was suppressed by the Forest Service (Schulte, 1992). A Freedom of Information Act request forced its release, and Congress responded to the controversy by requiring a scientific peer review of the report.

The congressionally mandated peer-review report called for even more protection and urged the adoption of a series of "immediate actions" while a more comprehensive strategy was being developed. Reflecting the spirit of the new science, the report stated: "No scientist is free of values so it is important to state up front that we believe wildlife is an important part of our life and heritage. Within that broad belief we seek to understand the ecology of species and their communities so that they may be perpetuated indefinitely" (Keister and Eckhardt, 1994, 9). No mention is made of jobs or community stability in this ecocentric value statement. Environmentalists seized on the implications of the government reports and filed a formal petition demanding that the agency adopt the "immediate actions" recommended, as well as a more comprehensive, long-term strategy.[26] In addition to this comprehensive ecosystem approach, petitions have also been filed to list two species in the area as threatened, the gray wolf and northern goshawk.

In a dramatic reflection of the shift in professional orientation of the Forest Service, a wildlife biologist, Phil Janik, was appointed as the new regional forester. The seemingly perpetual land-management plan process was transformed by teaming officials from the Tongass region who represented a more conservative view with Forest Service wildlife biologists imported from the Pacific Northwest Research Station.

The Alaska delegation in Congress tried to insulate the Forest Service from the implications of these new studies by using the same process the Northwest regional delegation had—appropriations riders. Senator Ted Stevens pushed through a rider for fiscal year 1994 preventing Tongass officials from acting on the new studies by requiring them to stick to the existing Tongass Land Management Plan.[27] Attempts to attach a similar rider for fiscal year 1995 were defeated, however. After the failure of legislative preemption, the Forest Service denied the environmental petition but proposed an amendment to the Tongass Land Management Plan that incorporated many of the interim measures proposed, including setting aside 600,000 acres of "habitat conservation areas." In yet another striking parallel to the effort that occurred in the Northwest, the Alaska Forestry Association, the industry group, has filed a lawsuit challenging these interim measures.

Another sign of the collapse of the old regime became evident in April 1994, when the Forest Service terminated one of the two major long-term timber contracts that have characterized the region's uneconomical forest policy since the 1950s (Cushman, 1994). Despite the fact that its operation was specified in its contract, the Alaska Pulp Corporation (APC) closed its pulp mill in the region, and the Forest Service responded by canceling the contract altogether. When the Forest Service proposed to offer the timber allocated to APC to others, environmentalists took them to court, claiming that given the contract cancellation, the new timber offer requires a new environmental impact statement that includes a consideration of the alternative of offering less timber. As of February 1995, the case was still pending.

Although the situation in the Tongass is very unsettled, there is little doubt that significant reductions in timber harvesting will result.[28] Forest policy in the Tongass, though late in coming, has been radically transformed in the past five years. A successful effort by local environmentalists to nationalize the issue resulted in statutory changes that brought the Tongass into the modern era of environmental regulation of forestry. Environmentalists continue to use the courts to challenge the way the Forest Service implements these laws, but the new science of conservation biology first applied in the Pacific Northwest has invaded the northern end of the coastal old-growth rain forest. Despite the active resistance of the old guard in the Forest Service, the prowildlife values of biologists appear to be displacing the pro-timber values of traditional foresters.

The Rest of the West: Below-Cost Timber Sales and the Legacy of Localism

The new ecosystem approach has made its presence felt outside the temperate rain forests along the coast. For instance, the Pacific Southwest Region of the Forest Service confronted appeals and litigation by environmentalists over the impact of logging on the habitat of the northern spotted owl's southern cousin, the California spotted owl. Rather than exposing themselves to the injunctions the Pacific Northwest Region had imposed on it, Pacific Southwest officials quickly moved to assemble an advisory group, including timber industry and environmental officials, to propose putting an interim plan in place to protect owl habitat. The plan protects the largest trees in the region and is expected to reduce harvesting by about 25 percent (U.S. Department of Agriculture, 1993). A longer-term, more comprehensive ecosystem management plan is currently in the works.

Another major effort is occurring in the Columbia River Basin in eastern Washington State and Oregon, Idaho, and Montana. The Clinton administration has created the Interior Columbia Basin Ecosystem Management Project, which is developing an integrated ecosystem plan for the region. The central issues in this region are habitat for salmon and other fish and "forest health," a term describing a combination of insect infestation, disease, and fire risk created by management policies over the past fifty years. Environmentalists have pounced on the recent designation of several salmon species as endangered to create the same legal-political dynamic witnessed in the "westside" Northwest and Alaska. Indeed, salmon may become to the inland West what the spotted owl was to the westside forests. In response to a suit by environmental groups represented by the Sierra Club Legal Defense Fund, a federal district court judge in Idaho imposed an injunction on all logging, roading, and mining activities in six national forests in Idaho until the Forest Service formally "consults" with the National Marine Fisheries Service on the threats to the endangered salmon as required by the Endangered Species Act.[29]

Although this recent focus on ecosystem issues reflects the influence of development in the Northwest, the issue of "below-cost timber sales" has vexed the areas outside Washington and Oregon for some time and has been remarkably resistant to reform. Forest Service timber is sold to private firms on a competitive bid basis, providing some role for the market in the timber harvesting process. The problem is that in many areas of the country, the amount recouped from timber sales does not match the amount of money the Forest Service spends preparing the sale and undertaking other activities, such as road building and reforestation, that support the timber harvesting by private companies (O'Toole, 1988; Wolf, 1989). Other than the Pacific Northwest and the Southern Region, the remaining regions of the Forest Service—including the entire West outside of Washington, Oregon, and northern California—routinely lose money (Wilkinson, 1992, 148–150).

The persistence of this striking phenomenon results from both the organizational incentives of the Forest Service and the political incentives of members of Congress. Various statutes specify that some of the receipts from timber sales go right back into Forest Service budgets for various activities, rather than simply going back into the federal treasury. Thus, the resources available to Forest Service bureaucrats depend not just on their annual appropriation from Congress but also on the level of timber sales. The "budget-maximizing" tendencies of bureaucrats thus promote uneconomical timber harvesting (O'Toole, 1988). The real question is why Congress has failed to counter those incentives by imposing requirements prohibiting below-cost timber sales. The answer to that question lies in the enduring localism that continues to influence congressional forest politics. Federal timber sales provide jobs in rural communities, and legislators from those areas are reluctant to terminate the de facto subsidies that exist.

Environmentalists have been concerned about below-cost timber sales because they put upward pressures on harvest levels.[30] Despite their efforts to publicize the issue and push for legislation to remedy the problem, the practice has been remarkably resistant to reform efforts. It survived the "Reagan revolution." Bruce Babbitt, President Clinton's secretary of the interior, pressed for comprehensive reform of federal land management policies to eliminate federal subsidies for grazing, mining, and timber (Egan, 1993). At first, the issue appeared to be attractive because it combined environmental concern with market-based reforms and deficit reduction. But members of Congress from western states, including Democrats, revolted against Babbitt's plans, and they were withdrawn (Taylor, 1993). Efforts by environmentalists in Congress to legislate an end to the practice have been thwarted repeatedly. This is a case where the old politics of localism have triumphed over the new environmental politics; the fact that the practice amounts to a taxpayer subsidy to rural development in the West makes its persistence all the more curious.

The greatest impetus for change has come from within the agency, although the catalyst was concern over environmentally unsustainable harvest levels rather than uneconomical ones, per se. In the late 1980s, forest supervisors in Region One (Montana and northern Idaho) engaged in a revolution of sorts. Concerned that they were being asked to harvest timber at levels well beyond what was environmentally sustainable, the officials wrote a stinging letter to Chief Forester Dale Robertson in November 1989. Referring to "troubling times" within the agency, the letter stated: "Congressional emphasis and our traditional methods and practices continue to focus on commodity resources. We are not meeting the quality land management expectations of our public and our employees" (quoted in Wilkinson, 1992, 151; Hirt, 1994, 285–286). Their superior, Regional Forester John Mumma, defied the annual timber targets implied in congressional appropriations bills, claiming that meeting them would violate congressional laws designed to protect environmental values. As a result, he was attacked by the area's congressional delegation and was eventually forced by his superiors to resign in 1991 (U.S. Congress, 1992; Wilkinson, 1992, 152).

Although the old guard in the Forest Service hierarchy won that battle, they lost the war. With the election of the Clinton administration, the new leadership of the Forest Service was more sympathetic to the concerns of the forest supervisors. Despite the absence of congressional action to reduce uneconomical timber sales, Assistant Secretary of Agriculture Jim Lyons announced the agency's intention to bring an end to the practice. Harvesting levels in the mountain West have been reduced. At the same time, supply pressures caused by the more dramatic decrease in Pacific Northwest timber harvests have pushed up the value of timber from national forests farther east, increasing the price the Forest Service can get for its timber and dramatically reducing the number of below-cost sales.[31]

Reversing the Winds of Change

Over the past twenty-five years, environmentalism has been in the ascendent on western public lands, including the Forest Service. Not surprisingly, the change of values represented in land management has provoked opposition from those who have benefited from traditional policies. The "Sagebrush Rebellion" in the 1970s represented a response to this change, but it was diffused by the Republican dominance of the presidency in the 1980s. With the election of Clinton in 1992 and Babbitt's subsequent threat to reverse some of the legacies of the past, which Charles Wilkinson calls the "lords of yesterday," the anti-environmental movement has intensified (Kriz, 1994). This grassroots movement has various manifestations and labels, including the "Wise Use" and "property rights" movements, but its core is an alliance of workers and local communities dependent on resource extraction and the resource-based corporations.[32] With the Republican sweep of the Congress in the 1994 election, these interests have gained considerable influence.

One striking indication of the new political reality is the change in committee leadership. The Alaska state delegation, at only three in number, dominates committees with jurisdiction over the Forest Service. The House Resources Committee leadership has transferred from Representative George Miller (D-CA), a strong environmentalist, to Representative Don Young, a Republican from Alaska. The Subcommittee on Forests and Public Lands Management has gone from environmentalist Bruce Vento (D-MN) to conservative James Hansen (R-UT). The Senate Energy and Natural Resources leadership has transferred from J. Bennett Johnston (D-LA), a conciliator on many environmental issues (excluding those of oil and gas) and a strong force behind the Tongass Timber Reform Act, to Alaska Republican Frank Murkowski. Murkowski has hired Mark Rey, the leading forest industry lobbyist for the past five years, to help him reform forest policy. The Subcommittee on Forests and Public Land Management is chaired by Idaho Republican Larry Craig, a prominent supporter of the region's timber industry (replacing Dale Bumpers [D-AR]).

The Senate Appropriations Committee is now chaired by Oregon Republican Mark Hatfield, who has replaced Democrat Robert Byrd. Its Subcommittee on the Interior, birthplace of riders to exempt timber activities from environmental requirements, is in the hands of Washington state Republican Slade Gorton (Alaskan Senator Ted Stevens is also on Gorton's subcommittee). The average League of Conservation Voter score on environmental policy proposals for the outgoing chairs of these committees and subcommittees is 55 percent; for incoming chairs it is 15 percent.[33]

It is premature to assess the significance of this dramatic political change for federal forest policy. But the winds of change have clearly reversed direction. The principal goal of the property rights movement—to require compensation to property owners whose assets are reduced by government regulatory action—so-called "regulatory takings"—has been included in the House Republicans' Contract with America. The committees chaired by both Young and Murkowski are beginning the process of amending the Endangered Species Act to restrict its powers (Connelly, 1995). There are indications that in a different effort that has received less attention, Republicans will also seek to change the NEPA and the

National Forest Management Act, including the provisions of the NFMA that have been used by the courts to halt logging until the government has prepared adequate species preservation plans.

Just as Ronald Reagan did in the early 1980s, Republicans in Congress seem to have misinterpreted their mandate and to have added to it a desire to cut back on environmental protection. Republican efforts during the 104th Congress to rewrite environmental laws, including those related to forest policy, have been thwarted by public opposition. As of March 1996, no major changes to environmental statutes have been made, and none seem likely as long as a Democrat is in the White House. With the path toward statutory change apparently blocked, Republicans have returned to the less visible appropriations process to influence forest policy.[34] In recent years, environmentalists have been able to rely on nationalizing the issue and appealing to the jurisdictional interests of authorizing committees to defeat these, but with the new Republican majorities and sympathetic authorizing committee chairs, environmental requirements are far more vulnerable to this strategy.

The Republicans' most important success in this regard occurred with the attachment of a rider to the 1995 Recissions Act. Originally understood as an effort to facilitate the harvesting of fire or insect-damaged trees, the rider has turned out to be far more sweeping, opening up areas of old-growth forests that had been protected in the Clinton forest plan and insulating many timber sales from citizen appeals and environmental reviews. Industry groups have begun waging an aggressive litigation campaign of their own, and their first major success was a federal district court opinion that significantly expanded the mandate of the rider beyond what it seemed to have intended. The rider, which has been castigated as "logging without laws" by environmentalists, has been a major source of controversy behind the scenes in the negotiations between the White House and Congress on the details of budgetary compromise for fiscal year 1996. The Republicans are intent on maintaining the new provisions, whereas the Clinton administration is pressing for either an outright repeal or substantial changes to limit the effects of the provisions. A decision had still not been made at the end of March 1996 (Kriz, 1996).

At least until January 1997, when the term of office ends for the current Clinton administration, environmentalists will still have some defense against these challenges to the new environmentally oriented forest policy. But the new composition of Congress has strengthened the hand of hardliners within the Forest Service, and the Clinton administration may be forced into concessions in its effort to preempt more radical changes in law and policy.

Conclusion

This chapter has shown that there have been substantial changes in the regime of federal forest management over the past twenty-five years, although different elements of the regime have changed at different times. Change began with environmental group pressures, litigation, and statutory change in the 1970s. Evidence for the short-term impact of these changes is limited, as trends in harvest levels suggest that logging was still the dominant interest of the Forest Service (Sample, 1990; Office of Technology Assessment, 1992; Hirt, 1994, chap. 12). Real policy change seems to have been delayed until 1990, and it resulted from a combination of circumstances.

First, there was the remobilization of environmental interests, particularly the construction of the issue as national rather than regional. This change was critical to the success of environmental groups because polls have shown that nationwide publics are more environmentally oriented on forest issues than are local regional populations that are dependent on timber harvesting for jobs and tax revenues. The second reason for the post-1990 changes was the success of environmentalists, through the courts, in forcing the Forest Service to live up to the environmental requirements created by the NFMA and its implementing regulations. The third reason was change within the Forest Service itself, as officials there became more environmental in orientation. This development was absolutely critical because it created a semblance of an alliance between environmentalists and at least some officials within the agency. Finally, the emergence of a new philosophical approach, called ecosystem management, and a scientific basis for the approach, in the form of conservation biology, provided an essential foundation for a forest policy that places more emphasis on habitat preservation than on logging. These more recent developments show the limitations of partial regime change in changing the real distribution of power over public policy.

Recent political developments suggest that this new environmental era in forest policy may be exceptionally short-lived. Opponents of this new approach now dominate Congress and threaten to dismantle the pluralist forest policy regime. Environmentalists are quick to point out that the 1994 election was not about dismantling the environmental laws that have taken twenty-five years to develop. But the change in Congress does seem to suggest a frustration with government, and the century-old battle over the role of government in environmental and natural resource issues in the West is likely to be renewed. Because of the dramatic changes in recent years and the impact that logging reductions have had in some areas, forest policy may be particularly vulnerable to a political backlash.

NOTES

1. There are also significant federal holdings of forest on Bureau of Land Management lands in Oregon. These are considered beyond the scope of this analysis.

2. For comprehensive histories of U.S. forest policy, see Hirt (1994); Steen (1976); and Clary (1986).

3. Cited in U.S. Office of Technology Assessment 1992, 60. For a concise overview of the U.S. Forest Service, see Wilkinson (1992, chap. 4).

4. For instance, it defines "multiple use" as "the management of all the various renewable surface resources of the national forest so that they are utilized in the combination that will best meet the needs of the American people; making the most judicious use of the land for some or all of these resources or related services over areas large enough to provide sufficient latitude for periodic adjustments in use to conform to changing needs and conditions; that some land will be used for less than all of the resources; and harmonious and coordinated management of the various resources, each with the other, without impairment of the productivity of the land, with consideration being given to the relative values of the various resources, and not necessarily the combination of uses that will give the greatest dollar return or the greatest unit output." As a Ninth Circuit Court of Appeal decision stated, the statute "breathe[s] discretion at every pore," *Perkins v. Bergland,* 608 F.2d 803 (9th Cir. 1979).

5. This new doctrine reflects a move away from "interest group liberalism," a term Lowi has used to describe the American policy process (Lowi, 1979).

6. *Sierra Club v. Hardin,* 325 F.Supp. 99 (D. Alaska 1971), at 123.

7. The case was actually originated by turkey hunters concerned about the impact of clear-cuts on wild turkey habitat in the Monongahela National Forest (Clary 1986, 190).

8. *West Virginia Division of the Izaak Walter League of America, Inc., v. Butz,* 522 F.2d 945 (4th Cir. 1975); *Zieske v. Butz,* 406 F. Supp. 258 (D. Alaska 1975).

9. This planning requirement was originally established by the Forest and Rangeland Renewable Resources Planning Act of 1974, but the act was fundamentally revised by NFMA before it could be fully implemented.

10. See also Brown and Harris (1993). This shift in the 1970s and 1980s intensified the conflict between the "traditionalists" and "stewards" that had already existed in the agency (Alexander, 1989) and dramatically shifted the balance away from the stewards.

11. On conservation biology and its implications for environmental policy, see Grumbine (1994).

12. A thorough account of the spotted owl controversy, focusing on the administrative and interest group aspects, can be found in Yaffee (1994).

13. There was a third prong to the SCLDF legal strategy involving the lands managed by the Bureau of Land Management in Oregon, but it will not be addressed here.

14. *Northern Spotted Owl v. Hodel,* 716 F.Supp. 479 (W.D.Wa. 1988).

15. As Sher and Hunting (1991) document, appropriations riders were an attractive and proven mechanism that members of Congress could use to override the implementation of environmental statutes when they had harsh local consequences.

16. Public Law No. 101–121, sec 318, 103 Stat. 701, 745–50 (1989). For a detailed discussion of the events surrounding the first "timber summit" and the enactment of Section 318, see Balmer (1990) and Johnston and Krupin (1991).

17. *Seattle Audubon Society v. Robertson,* 914 F.2d 1311 (9th Cir. 1990).

18. *Robertson v. Seattle Audubon Society,* 112 S.Ct. 1407 (1992). The Supreme Court ruled that appropriations riders did indeed amend the relevant statutes and therefore did not violate the separation of powers.

19. *Seattle Audubon Society v. Evans,* 771 F.Supp. 1081 (W.D. Wash. 1991). The decision was upheld on appeal, *Seattle Audubon Society v. Evans,* 952 F.2d 297 (9th Cir. 1991).

20. *Seattle Audubon Society v. Moseley,* U.S. District Court, Western District of Washington, C92–479WD, May 28, 1992; July 2, 1992.

21. See, for instance, the extensive coverage in the *Seattle Times, Seattle Post-Intelligencer,* or *Portland Oregonian* on July 2, 1993.

22. *Seattle Audubon Society et al. v. Lyons,* No. C92–479WD, Order on Motions for Summary Judgment re 1994 Forest Plan, U.S. District Court, Western District of Washington, December 21, 1994. In February 1995, the main environmental coalition represented by the Sierra Legal Defense Fund announced that it would not appeal Dwyer's decision. Both industry and more extremist environmental groups are appealing, however.

23. *Sierra Club v. Hardin,* 325 F.Supp. 99 (D. Alaska 1971), at 123. *Zieske v. Butz,* 406 F. Supp. 258 (D. Alaska 1975).

24. In another example of the influence of courts on policy development, this statutory stream buffer requirement had its origins in a court case in which a group of fishermen and natives received a temporary restraining order to prevent logging within one hundred feet of streams from a federal judge ("Tongass Timber Reform Act: Legislative History," *U.S. Congressional Code and Administrative News,* 1990, 8:6236).

25. *Wildlife Society, Alaska Chapter v. Barton,* No. J93–0001-CIV, U.S. District Court of Alaska, April 14, 1994.

26. Natural Resources Defense Council and Sierra Club Legal Defense Fund, Petition with Request for Stay to the Regional Forester of the Alaska Region, USDA Forest Service, June 24, 1994.

27. In addition to the viable populations study, the rider was also targeted at the so-called "Pac-fish" plan that was emerging in the Pacific Northwest. The report called for a three-hundred-foot stream buffer rather than the one-hundred-foot buffer in the TTRA, and consideration was being given to applying it to the Tongass.

28. Personal interviews with Tongass-area environmentalists and Forest Service officials (Juneau, AK, July 6, 1994).

29. *Pacific Rivers Council v. Thomas,* Civil No. 94–0159-S-DAE, Order Granting Injunctive Relief and Denying Summary Judgment, U.S. District Court, Idaho, January 12, 1995.

30. The issue is not straightforward for environmentalists, however. Apparently, one of the reasons that Forest Service accounts routinely show losses is that the agency allocates money appropriated for timber sales to environmental management activities (confidential interviews, Washington, DC, 1995).

31. Personal interview, Al Sample, Pinchot Institute (Washington, DC, February 15, 1995).

32. For a detailed, if polemical, account of the wise-use movement, see Helvarg (1994).

33. These figures are tabulated for the 1991–1992 years (League of Conservation Voters, 1992).

34. *Robertson v. Seattle Audubon Society,* 112 S. Ct. 1407 (1992).

REFERENCES

Alexander, Thomas. 1989. "Timber Management, Traditional Forestry, and Multiple-Use Stewardship: The Case of the Intermountain Region, 1950–85." *Journal of Forest History* 33:21–35.

Balmer, Donald G. 1990. "United States Federal Policy on Old-Growth Forests in Its Institutional Setting." *Northwest Environmental Journal* 6:331–360.

Boberz, Bradley, and Robert Fischman. 1992. *Sustaining the Forests: Reinventing the Forest Administrative Appeal Process.* Washington, DC: Environmental Law Institute, December.

Brizee, Clarence. 1975. "Judicial Review of Forest Service Land Management Decisions." *Journal of Forestry* 73:424–425, 516–519.

Brown, Greg, and Charles Harris. 1993. "The Implications of Work Force Diversification in the U.S. Forest Service." *Administration and Society* 25:85–113.

Clarke, J. N., and D. McCool. 1985. *Staking Out the Terrain: Power Differentials Among Natural Resource Management Agencies.* Albany: State University of New York Press.

Clary, David A. 1986. *Timber and the Forest Service.* Lawrence: University Press of Kansas.

Connelly, Joel. 1995. "Now, the Act Is in Danger." *Seattle Post-Intelligencer,* January 16:A1.

Cubbage, Frederick W., Jay O'Lauglin, and Charles S. Bullock III. 1993. *Forest Resource Policy.* New York: John Wiley and Sons.

Culhane, Paul. 1981. *Public Lands Politics.* Baltimore: Johns Hopkins University Press.

Cushman, John. 1994. "U.S. Moves on Two Fronts to Reshape Logging Rules." *New York Times,* April 15:A14.

Dietrich, William. 1992. *The Final Forest.* New York: Simon and Schuster.

Donahue, Bill. 1994. "Jack Ward Thomas: Tough New Top Forester." *American Forests* (July/August) 100:13–16.

Egan, Timothy. 1993. "Sweeping Reversal of U.S. Land Policy Sought by Clinton." *New York Times,* February 24:A1.

General Accounting Office. 1989. *Endangered Species: Spotted Owl Petition Beset by Problems.* (GAO/RCED–89–79). Washington, DC: General Accounting Office.

Gerlach, Luther P., and David N. Bengston. 1994. "If Ecosystem Management Is the Solution, What's the Problem?" *Journal of Forestry* 92 (August):18–21.

Grode, Jim. 1991. "The Tongass Timber Reform Act: A Step Towards Rational Management of the Forest." *University of Colorado Law Review* 62:873–898.

Grumbine, R. Edward, ed. 1994. *Environmental Policy and Biodiversity.* Washington, DC: Island Press.

Hanson, Christopher. 1995. "Gorton Prepares to Push Changes in Logging Curbs." *Seattle Post-Intelligencer,* January 11:A1.

Harris, Richard, and Sidney Milkis. 1989. *The Politics of Regulatory Change.* New York: Oxford University Press.

Hays, Samuel P. 1987. *Beauty, Health, and Permanence: Environmental Politics in the United States, 1955–1985.* Cambridge: Cambridge University Press.

Helvarg, David. 1994. *The War Against the Greens.* San Francisco: Sierra Club Books.

Hirt, Paul. 1994. *A Conspiracy of Optimism: Management of the National Forests Since World War Two.* Lincoln: University of Nebraska Press.

Hoberg, George. 1992. *Pluralism by Design: Environmental Policy and the American Regulatory State.* New York: Praeger.

Johnston, Bryan, and Paul Krupin. 1991. "The 1989 Pacific Northwest Timber Compromise: An Environmental Dispute Resolution Case Study of a Successful Battle That May Have Lost the War." *Willamette Law Review* 27:613–643.

Kaufman, Herbert. 1960. *The Forest Ranger.* Baltimore: Johns Hopkins University Press.

Keister, A. Ross, and Carol Eckhardt. 1994. *Review of Wildlife Management and Conservation Biology on the Tongass National Forest: A Synthesis with Recommendations.* Corvallis, OR: Pacific Northwest Research Station.

Kriz, Margaret. 1994. "Shoot-Out in the West." *National Journal,* October 14:2388–2392.
_____. 1996. "Timber!" *National Journal,* February 3: 252–257.
League of Conservation Voters. 1992. *National Environmental Scorecard, 1992.* Washington, DC: Earth Works Press.
Lee, Robert G. 1990. "Social and Cultural Implications of Implementing a Conservation Strategy for the Northern Spotted Owl." University of Washington, Seattle.
Le Master, Dennis. 1984. *Decade of Change: The Remaking of Forest Service Statutory Authority During the 1970s.* Westport, CN: Greenwood Press.
Lowi, Theodore. 1979. *The End of Liberalism.* New York: Norton.
McCann, Michael. 1986. *Taking Reform Seriously.* Ithaca: Cornell University Press.
McCrackin, Karen. 1993. "*Tenakee Springs v. Franzel* and the Tongass Timber Reform Act." *Environmental Law* 23:1143–1164.
Melnick, R. Shep. 1983. *Regulation and the Courts: The Case of the Clean Air Act.* Washington, DC: Brookings Institution Press.
O'Toole, Randal. 1988. *Reforming the Forest Service.* Washington, DC: Island Press.
Pryne, Eric, and Mark Matassa. 1993. "Clinton Not in Favor of Changing Environment Laws or Halting Suits." *Seattle Times,* April 3:A1.
Sample, V. Alaric. 1990. *The Impact of the Federal Budget Process on National Forest Planning.* New York: Greenwood Press.
Schulte, Brigid. 1992. "Tongass Wildlife Report Suppressed." *Anchorage Daily News,* December 27:A1.
Sher, Victor, and Carol Sue Hunting. 1991. "Eroding the Landscape, Eroding the Laws: Congressional Exemptions from Judicial Review of Environmental Laws." *Harvard Environmental Law Review* 15:435–491.
Steel, Brent, Peter List, and Bruce Shindler. 1992. "Oregon State University Survey of Natural Resource and Forestry Issues." Corvallis, Oregon, January 15.
Steen, Harold K. 1976. *The U.S. Forest Service: A History.* Seattle: University of Washington Press.
Taylor, Andrew. 1993. "President Will Not Use Budget to Rewrite Land-Use Laws." *CQ Weekly Report* (April 3):833–834.
Timber Industry Labor-Management Committee. 1993. "The Endangered Worker: A Labor Perspective on Timber Issues." Press Package. Washington, DC, May 26.
U.S. Congress. House. 1992. Committee on Post Office and Civil Service, Subcommittee on the Civil Service. *The Directed Reassignments of John Mumma and L. Lorraine Mintzmeyer.* 102d Cong., 1st Sess., Serial No. 102–27. Hearing, September 24, 1991.
U.S. Department of Agriculture. 1993. *California Spotted Owl Sierran Province Interim Guidelines Environmental Assessment.* San Francisco: Pacific Southwest Region, U.S. Forest Service.
_____. 1994. *Ecosystem Management—1993 Annual Report of the Forest Service.* Washington, DC: USDA Forest Service.
_____. 1996. *Report of the Forest Service—Fiscal Year 1995.* Washington, DC: U.S. Department of Agriculture.
U.S. Office of Technology Assessment. 1992. *Forest Service Planning: Accommodating Uses, Producing Outputs, and Sustaining Ecosystems.* Washington, DC: Government Printing Office, February.
Wilkinson, Charles F. 1992. *Crossing the Next Meridian: Land, Water, and the Future of the West.* Washington, DC: Island Press.

Wilkinson, Charles, and H. Michael Anderson. 1987. *Land and Resource Planning in the National Forests.* Washington, DC: Island Press.

Wolf, Robert E. 1989. "National Forest Timber Sales and the Legacy of Gifford Pinchot: Managing a Forest and Making It Pay." *University of Colorado Law Review* 60:1037–1078.

Yaffee, Steven Lewis. 1994. *The Wisdom of the Spotted Owl.* Washington, DC: Island Press.

5

Politics and Public Rangeland Policy

Proposals to reform the management of livestock grazing on public rangelands have encountered considerable resistance from advocates of the status quo, despite increasing concern about the ecological condition of federal lands among environmentalists. Like other natural resource issues, including water (Ingram, 1990; McCool, 1987), energy development (Rosenbaum, 1993; Jones and Strahan, 1985), agricultural commodities (Browne, 1988), timber harvesting (Clary, 1986), and hardrock mining (Wilkinson, 1992), public range policies were originally developed within a distributive policy context to encourage industrial growth and provide economic opportunity (Culhane, 1981).

Each of these policy areas has also spawned a protective subgovernment that restricts participation in policy decisions to public agency administrators, legislators, and interest group representatives with shared programmatic concerns. Groups such as the National Cattlemen's Association have had an important economic stake in the retention of subsidies and other program benefits (Arrandale, 1983). These subgovernments maintain a low degree of visibility within the media and the general public and a high degree of stability over time. Closed systems of governance of this sort provide a classic example of distributive policymaking, in which benefits are provided for a relatively small number of individuals while program costs are spread across all U.S. taxpayers.

How can we account for the continuing political strength of the range policy subgovernment in the face of opposition from both environmental groups and advocates of greater efficiency in government? This chapter provides a discussion of policy decisions affecting grazing programs administered by the BLM and the Forest Service over the past thirty years and an analysis of why fluctuations in policy occur. Key factors considered here include the impact of shifting political coalitions over time and the strategic manipulation of both short-term circumstances, such as media events or the publication of evaluative studies on range program operations by policy actors on both sides, and larger sociopolitical forces, such as fluctuating economic conditions or election outcomes.

The Range Policy Subsystem

Livestock grazing has been regulated on federal lands since 1906 by the U.S. Forest Service, a practice begun under the initiative of its first chief, Gifford Pinchot. Early efforts to cut back on livestock use and to levy grazing fees to enhance conservation objectives were controversial but ultimately successful because of the ability of field rangers to contain disputes at the local level (Dana and Fairfax, 1980; Graf, 1990). Pinchot's political skills, coupled with agency success in projecting an image of professionalism in the application of scientific forestry to resource management decisions, led to the development and retention of considerable organizational autonomy, enabling the Forest Service to manage its administrative tasks with relatively little interference from elected officials (Wilkinson, 1992).

Forest Service regulation was largely confined to land within forested and mountainous terrain, and the larger area of public rangelands within western states remained substantially unregulated until 1934. In that year, the enactment of the Taylor Grazing Act by Congress provided access for livestock operators to lands administered by the Grazing Service (later renamed the Bureau of Land Management) within the U.S. Interior Department. The law called for the issuance of permits to ranchers, allowing them to graze a certain number of cattle, horses, or sheep on a given parcel of land over a period of time (up to ten years), depending on existing rangeland conditions. The actual number of animals was determined by considering historic use patterns as well as estimates of available forage provided through BLM range surveys. Each permittee was also assessed a grazing fee for each animal unit month, or AUM.

The original goal of this law was to enhance economic stability for western ranchers through the creation of organizational arrangements to more efficiently manage the use and distribution of livestock. Congressional sponsors clearly intended that an ostensibly regulatory law would not adversely affect industry interests. Grazing fees were kept to a minimum, prior users received priority attention in the allocation of leases, and local advisory boards were given real decisionmaking authority (Culhane, 1981; Klyza, 1991). This exemplified a "dominant use" approach to land management that effectively excluded the consideration of noneconomic goals (Arrandale, 1983).

Perhaps the most widely cited example of industry influence occurred in the mid-1940s when Clarence Forsling, the newly appointed director of the Grazing Service, proposed to treble grazing fees based on the results of a range economics study. This seemingly audacious act provoked the wrath of Senator Pat McCarren (D-NV), a persistent critic of the Interior Department and a staunch supporter of privatization. An investigation of the Grazing Service was carried out, and in apparent retribution for staking out an overly independent position on the fee issue, Congress slashed its 1947 budget to 53 percent of its 1945 level (Foss, 1960; Voigt, 1976). This had the effect of reducing the already under-manned Grazing Service staff by 66 percent and placed the agency in the embar-rassing position of relying on grazing fee monies derived from range users to pay the salaries of its field administrators (Culhane, 1981). Shortly thereafter, President Harry S. Truman acted to create the Bureau of Land Management by merging the Grazing Service with the General Land Office.

In short, the Taylor Grazing Act offers a classic example of how Congress can create the statutory underpinnings of a dominant subgovernment. Ranchers were able to exercise disproportionate influence over decisions because of require-ments for operator input through grazing advisory boards, close political ties be-tween stock-growers associations and the two interior committees of the U.S. Congress (later renamed the House Resources Committee and the Senate Energy and Natural Resources Committee), and a tradition of managerial decentraliza-tion (Voigt, 1976; McConnell, 1966). From the 1930s through the 1950s, these ad-visory boards took advantage of a chronically understaffed and politically weak BLM to successfully resist efforts to reduce livestock numbers on rangelands that were deteriorating from overgrazing and to slow efforts to raise grazing fees to levels that more closely approximated the economic value of the resource (Foss, 1960).

Public Range Policymaking Since 1960

Events and key policy decisions pertaining to public rangeland management from 1960 through 1994 are summarized in Table 5.1. In the early 1960s, the subgov-ernment was clearly in control of the policy agenda. This is demonstrated by a review of congressional hearings on proposed grazing fee hikes in 1963, which re-vealed the stark imbalance of political forces. A glance at the roster of participants shows a sizable number of ranchers (over 100), western legislators, and governors testifying about the deleterious economic effects that a fee hike would wreak on western communities. A single state wildlife organization offered token support for the notion that the existing fee structure was an unjustifiable subsidy to a rel-atively small number of beneficiaries from a much larger base of U.S. taxpayers (U.S. Congress. Senate, 1963).

However, the winds of change in the larger policy environment were beginning to stir. Growth in the number and popularity of environmental organizations could be observed, along with a corresponding rise in the diversity of issues cov-ered. Adding to a sense of optimism among environmental leaders was the eco-logically friendly tone toward natural resource policymaking adopted by the Kennedy administration and subsequently maintained by President Lyndon Johnson. A key move was the appointment of Stewart Udall, an individual with strong conservationist views, as secretary of the interior.

TABLE 5.1   Chronology of Events Leading to Public Range Policy Decisions

1960	Election of John F. Kennedy as U.S. president and his subsequent appointment of Steward Udall as interior secretary.
1964	Enactment of the Classification and Multiple Use Act giving the U.S. Bureau of Land Management (BLM) temporary authority to manage public rangelands under multiple-use management principles.
	Establishment of the Public Land Law Review Commission (PLLRC) to provide a comprehensive review and evaluation of public land policies including range management and grazing fees.
	Publication of a study by the U.S. Bureau of the Budget titled *Natural Resource User Charges,* which concluded that the federal government should receive a fair price from public land resource use including livestock grazing.
1996	Publication of the *1966 Western Livestock Grazing Survey* by the Departments of Agriculture and the Interior (USDA/DI), which provided cost data for grazing on both public and private lands to aid in the development of a grazing fee.
1968	A new grazing fee schedule was proposed by USDA/DI, which recommended a formula requiring average total costs on public lands to equal the average total costs on private lands, with the increases to be phased in over a ten-year period.
1970	Publication of the final report by the PLLRC, titled *One Third of the Nation's Land,* which recommended legislation establishing fair market value as the basis for determining grazing fees.
	Under pressure from Congress and livestock associations, USDA/DI officials announced a moratorium on fee increases from the 1969 level.
1974	A federal court decision, *Natural Resources Defense Council v. Morton,* provided a key victory for environmentalists by requiring BLM to conduct site-specific environmental impact statements (that can be more easily challenged) rather than a massive impact statement covering its entire grazing program in the western United States.
1975	A second moratorium on grazing fee increases was imposed by USDA/DI.
1976	Enactment of the Federal Land Policy and Management Act, which gave statutory recognition to BLM and its multiple-use mission, increased the importance of environmental criteria in public land decisionmaking, and again froze grazing fees at existing levels.
1977	A USDA/DI grazing fee study analyzed seven fee alternatives and recommended a formula that adjusted fees according to rates charged on private sector rangelands.
1978	Congressional reaction to the 1977 study resulted in a fourth moratorium on grazing fee increases.

(continues)

TABLE 5.1   *(continued)*

1978	Enactment of the Public Rangelands Improvement Act (PRIA), calling for greater emphasis on maintaining or improving the ecological health of public rangelands and establishing a new fee formula for a seven-year trial period, which incorporated the base price of $1.23 per animal unit month from the 1966 study with adjustments for the production costs of livestock operators and beef prices.
1980	Election of Ronald Reagan as president and his subsequent appointments of James Watt as interior secretary and Robert Burford as BLM director. Secretary Watt attempted to reorient range management decisionmaking by deemphasizing environmental goals in favor of resource production goals.
1986	In response to the expiration of the trial period for the PRIA fee formula, President Reagan issued Executive Order No. 12548, which called for its continued use for an indefinite period of time.
	A USDA/DI grazing fee study analyzed an array of fee alternatives and recommended changes in methods of calculating appraised value of ranches adjacent to public lands and the production costs incurred by permittees.
1992	Election of Bill Clinton as president and his subsequent appointment of Bruce Babbitt as interior secretary. Secretary Babbitt identified public land reform as his top policy priority.
1993	Publication of a USDA/DI study on incentive-based grazing fees, which recommended that the fee formula not include either beef prices or production costs but rely strictly on the forage value index, a reasonably good indicator of fair market value.
	Secretary Babbitt unveiled a new legislative package titled Rangeland Reform '94, which was debated and subsequently filibustered to death in the Senate in November. He then announced an intention to achieve his policy goals through administrative changes.
1994	Republicans gained control of Congress in the midterm elections and selected supporters of existing range policies to chair the House Natural Resources Committee and the Senate Energy and Natural Resources Committee.
	Secretary Babbitt announced his intention to drop efforts to change the grazing fee formula.

Both Congress and Secretary Udall attempted to respond to public concerns affecting federal land management, including increasing demands for recreation, the desire for a wilderness policy that would result in the withdrawal and preservation of large tracts of scenic land, and an end to the view that extractive users such as miners, ranchers, and loggers had a superior claim to resource use.

BLM and Incremental Policy Change

The enactment of the Classification and Multiple Use Act (CMU) in 1964 represented a small but significant victory for BLM officials and Interior Secretary Udall, who became convinced that multiple-use management techniques should be applied to public rangelands as well as national forests. The statute gave BLM temporary authority to manage rangeland resources under multiple-use management principles. Although this shift was not particularly monumental in scope, it did offer a source of encouragement to agency administrators seeking the same type of decisionmaking autonomy based on range science that the Forest Service had long since achieved (Fairfax, 1984) and to environmental groups that were beginning to appreciate the ecological significance of rangeland reform.

Congressman Wayne Aspinall (D-CO), the powerful chairman of the House Interior Committee, was clearly opposed to any policy shifts that compromised the privileged position held by "traditional conservationists." However, he was somewhat mollified by a separate provision of the bill that established the Public Land Law Review Commission, a nineteen-member body that included twelve individuals from the House and Senate interior committees. The PLLRC was charged with the responsibility of reviewing public land policies to determine whether changes were needed and what direction such changes might take (Fairfax, 1984; Cawley, 1993). According to PLLRC member Paul Gates (1980), Aspinall believed that the study would ultimately provide a persuasive set of policy recommendations that would effectively counter criticisms of public land programs advanced by fiscal conservatives and conservationists.

Although early 1960s range reform efforts were largely motivated by the desire of BLM officials and Secretary Udall to attain a firmer legal basis for agency action, including a multiple-use mandate, other policy actors sought change for economic reasons. In 1964, the U.S. Bureau of the Budget issued a report dealing with natural resource user charges that concluded that the sale or lease of federally owned resources should follow pricing or fee setting guidelines that approximate fair market value. Ideally, fees would be established through appraisal or competitive bidding, taking comparable fees charged by state government or the private sector into account. This foreshadowed a major theme that would emerge in the arguments of range reform advocates—that grazing permits on BLM lands had been underpriced and that fees should be raised to ensure that the government receive a fair rate of return.

Meanwhile, a task force consisting of analysts from the U.S. Departments of Agriculture and the Interior (USDA/DI) undertook a major research project to provide information about the costs of ranching operations on public and private lands. The results of this project, issued in a report titled the *1966 Western Livestock Grazing Survey*, were used in the preparation of a new grazing fee formula that was unveiled by the two departments in November 1968. In the proposed fee levels, prior approaches that had been based on the price of livestock were rejected in favor of the principle that average total costs incurred by ranchers operating on public lands should equal those of private sector ranchers. Since the subsequent increase in charges per AUM to meet this new standard was quite pronounced, USDA/DI officials proposed that the ensuing financial burden on permittees be eased somewhat by phasing in the fee increases gradually over a ten-year period (Backiel and Rogge, 1985).

The Empire Strikes Back

The political fallout from the proposed fee increase was both immediate and predictable. Both the House and Senate interior committees scheduled hearings in early 1969 to allow feedback from affected constituents. Testimony from western legislators, livestock associations, and individual ranchers was overwhelmingly negative. A frequent claim was that many small ranchers would be unable to afford fee increases and would be forced off the land with negative ripple effects on the economies of nearby communities. Another point of contention was the interpretation of "reasonable" compensation for public land use found in the language of the Taylor Grazing Act. An increase of this magnitude was surely incompatible with the statutory goal of a stable livestock industry; hence, policy moves in the direction of fair market value were seen not only as ill conceived but also as illegal. A smaller coalition of groups, including BLM and Forest Service spokesmen and representatives from wildlife and environmental organizations, argued in favor of the proposed fee hike, citing the unfairness of existing fee structures.

Under pressure from Congress, USDA/DI officials imposed a moratorium on fee increases in 1970 (the first of four delays initiated during the 1970s), citing difficult economic times in the cattle industry and drought conditions in the West. On a related front, several range policy bills requiring that the BLM give greater weight to environmental criteria in land management decisions were defeated in the early 1970s because of opposition from livestock associations and western legislators. Members of the pro-grazing coalition were beginning to recognize the importance of competing groups within the range policy arena but were not "cowed" by the initiation of reform legislation.

Environmentalists and Range Policy Reform

Discouraged by the unfavorable policy outcomes emanating from both executive agency and legislative venues, environmentalists led by the Natural Resources Defense Council (NRDC) turned to the courts to regain political momentum. And, in 1974, they succeeded. In *Natural Resources Defense Council v. Morton*, environmental lawyers made strategic use of the National Environmental Policy Act to force an alteration of the BLM's administrative procedures. After the agency filed a draft environmental impact statement covering its entire grazing program in the western United States, NRDC attorneys filed suit, arguing that the BLM could not adequately address local impacts arising from overgrazing or other poor management practices.

The NRDC's main argument revolved around the need for a site-specific EIS to provide necessary information for land use decisions. Federal District Judge Thomas Flannery agreed with this position. He and other parties recognized that the decision had important implications for the BLM, which stood to gain additional funding and manpower to implement the edict (which eventually called for the preparation of 144 EISs by 1988) as well as additional political leverage that could be used by field administrators to negotiate livestock reductions or other contentious issues with ranchers (Nelson, 1985).

Having received a temporary boost from the *NRDC v. Morton* decision, environmentalists and other range reform advocates turned their attention to legislative activities. Considerable debate ensued and in 1976 Congress enacted the Federal Land Policy and Management Act. This was widely known as the BLM's organic act, putting into place the multiple-use management scheme coveted by agency officials. Much to the disdain of traditional constituency groups, the new law amended the Taylor Grazing Act by replacing the provision identifying livestock grazing as the predominant use of public rangelands with a much broader set of policy goals. FLPMA requires that

> Public lands be managed in a manner that will protect the quality of scientific, scenic, historical, ecological, environmental, air and atmospheric, water resource and archeological values; that, where appropriate, will preserve and protect certain public lands in their natural condition; that will provide food and habitat for fish and wildlife and domestic animals; and that will provide for outdoor recreation and human occupancy and use.

Other features of this statute include the incorporation of planning requirements prior to resource allocation decisions and an opportunity for public participation through testimony on resource management plans and judicial review (Coggins, 1983).

Although these sections were clearly welcomed by environmental groups, other parts of FLPMA were designed to allay the fears of traditional constituencies by reaffirming the need for extractive uses of the public lands. The law did not abolish either the permit system or the grazing advisory boards. In addition, an additional moratorium on fee increases was mandated. However, environmentalists were generally satisfied by the removal of structural advantages embedded within the Taylor Grazing Act (such as the dominant use clause) that had proven to be beneficial to livestock producers (Cawley, 1993).

The dust had scarcely cleared with the passage of FLPMA when Congress enacted yet another policy affecting the BLM's administration of public rangelands in 1978. The Public Range Improvement Act (PRIA), like FLPMA, contained sections to satisfy divergent constituencies. Environmentalists generally applauded the inclusion of a key section assigning greater management priority to the improvement of range conditions. This goal was to be achieved through a series of actions, including the continuous monitoring of rangeland quality, the utilization of this information in the preparation of allotment management plans (AMPs), increased funding for the rejuvenation of damaged lands, and the Experimental Stewardship Program, designed to offer incentives or rewards to permittees who demonstrated sound resource management techniques (*Congressional Quarterly Almanac,* 1978, 716–718).

Although these program changes were well received by reform advocates, it was equally evident that a gap remained between the promise of better rangeland management practices and the likelihood of effective implementation. For example, statutory adoption was not accompanied by a corresponding increase in the funds or personnel needed to make a sizable dent in rangeland improvement projects (Durant, 1987; Hamilton, 1987). In addition, ranchers were placated by certain policy provisions such as an adjusted grazing fee formula that kept fees lower than the amount charged on comparable private lands by factoring in livestock prices and production costs (Backiel and Rogge, 1985). Assurances that permittees would receive security of tenure were also made, a promise that enhanced the property value of private ranches adjacent to public lands (Borman and Johnson, 1990). Finally, Congress accepted a last-minute amendment by Senator James McClure (R-ID) that called for a "phased-in approach" to any reductions in livestock deemed necessary for the reconstruction of healthy rangelands.

Political Resistance to Range Reforms

Perhaps the most visible form of discontent over public land-use changes occurred in the late 1970s as Interior Secretary Cecil Andrus began to implement FLPMA through a combination of intensive management initiatives and livestock reduction plans. Irate ranchers contacted friendly state lawmakers in western states to propose legislation calling for the transfer of BLM and Forest Service lands to the states, a legally questionable but symbolically powerful message that became popularly known as the Sagebrush Rebellion (Culhane, 1984; Francis, 1984).

The Sagebrush Rebellion epitomized the clash in values between ranchers and other traditional beneficiaries of public lands policy and environmentalists (with an occasional assist from ideological conservatives). In 1980, Ronald Reagan, a self-proclaimed sagebrush rebel, was elected president, and he promptly rewarded his sizable core of western supporters by selecting James Watt as the new interior secretary and Robert Burford as the new BLM director. Both men were determined to reverse the direction of range policy by moving away from the "environmental excesses" of the Carter administration toward a "good neighbor" policy that placed greater emphasis on the economic health of extractive industries such as ranching (Fairfax, 1984).

Early policy initiatives such as privatization of public lands and land swaps between the BLM and the Forest Service set off fire alarms in Congress and were subsequently rebuffed. Thereafter, Secretary Watt (and his successors William Clark and Donald Hodel) essentially wrote off the possibility of attaining desired changes within the legislative arena and sought to influence policy through administrative decisionmaking. The BLM's budget was repeatedly slashed and a pro-grazing orientation was maintained through personnel policies that emphasized the elimination or transfer of people in environmental positions (such as that of wildlife biologist) in order to increase the number of positions geared toward maximizing commodity production (Durant, 1992).

Despite a philosophical orientation toward land management that was quite compatible with the policy preferences of the traditional range policy subgovernment, there was relatively little legislative activity during Reagan's two terms in office or during the administration of President George Bush from 1989 to 1993. An executive order issued by President Reagan in 1986 continued the grazing fee formula established under PRIA for an indefinite period of time. And President Bush's interior secretary, Manuel Lujan, continued along the same policy path, although the BLM director, Cy Jamieson, did tilt slightly in the direction of increased recreational use on public lands.

Range Reform, Part Two: Rhetoric or Reality?

A renewed effort to revamp public range laws was launched in the late 1980s within the House Interior Committee. Bills calling for a dramatic increase in grazing fees were pushed by Representatives Mike Synar (D-OK) and Buddy Darden (D-GA), with considerable support from other nonwestern legislators. Members of the range reform coalition, including the NRDC and the National Wildlife Federation, sought to interpret range policy within the larger context of deficit politics, arguing that an end to grazing subsidies made sense on both economic and ecological grounds. A move toward fair market value would not only eliminate unfair advantages enjoyed by public land permittees but would produce additional fee revenues that could be used for rangeland improvement projects. Reform advocates also directed attention to environmental quality problems such as the loss of habitat for wildlife (other than coyotes) and the link between overgrazing on public rangelands and subsequent damage to riparian areas.

Supporters of the status quo, including the Bush administration and members of the pro-grazing coalition, were vehemently opposed to these bills, suggesting that the true purpose of the legislation was not "true reform" but rather the virtual elimination of livestock grazing on public lands. Moreover, they argued, a careful analysis of nonfee costs incurred by ranchers operating on public lands indicated that the characterization of grazing fees as a subsidy was misleading since the amount and quality of forage on public rangelands was not comparable to more lush pastures associated with privately owned ranches. In addition, more expensive private sector leases were often accompanied by improvements such as fences and stock ponds, which were not found on BLM or Forest Service lands (Obermiller, 1991). Several western legislators led by Representative Ben Campbell (D-CO) cosponsored a rival bill that called for a much smaller fee increase while maintaining the basic formula established under the PRIA.

Reform advocates received a political boost in 1992 with the election of Bill Clinton as president. Environmentalists were elated when Clinton selected Bruce Babbitt as interior secretary and James Baca as BLM director. Both men had held elective office in a western state, had wrestled with the intricacies of public land issues, and were known to favor change that would overturn the entrenched resource development privileges held by "the lords of yesterday" (Wilkinson, 1992). Proposed legislation was soon developed that combined substantially higher grazing fees associated with the Synar and Darden proposals with a partial rebate for permittees that subsequently demonstrated good environmental management practices. As before, the new proposal encountered fierce resistance from western senators, led by Pete Domenici (R-NM).

Under pressure, the Clinton administration dropped the grazing fee proposal from the 1994 budget act when several western Democrats threatened to vote against the closely contested package (Knickerbocker, 1993). The proposal was then introduced as a separate piece of legislation, but the pro-grazing coalition held firm against the bill. In an effort to break the legislative gridlock, Secretary Babbitt threw his support to a compromise bill sponsored by Senator Harry Reid (D-NV) that maintained most reform provisions but called for a lower ceiling on fee increases. Once again, the Clinton administration's efforts were unsuccessful. The bill was defeated in November 1993 after the Senate waged a successful filibuster.

Conceding that a legislative solution was unlikely to work, Secretary Babbitt adopted an administrative approach focusing on consensus building among affected parties to achieve desired policy goals (Kenworthy, 1994). The product of these efforts was a new package entitled *Rangeland Reform '94*. Again, the emphasis was on reform that combined fee increases for permittees with a rebate for evidence of good environmental stewardship. An additional part of the package was the creation of a new multiple-use advisory board (to replace rancher-dominated grazing advisory boards). Babbitt argued that the advice offered by the newly constituted boards should be given considerable weight by public land managers, particularly when they worked out implementation details such as how individual allotment plans would mitigate livestock impacts on riparian areas (Babbitt, 1994).

To date, there has been only one attempt to test the ideas contained in the reform package. The opportunity arose early in 1994 when Babbitt accepted an invitation from Governor Roy Romer (D-CO) to meet with a statewide task force consisting of ranchers, local environmentalists, and a university professor. Eight meetings were held. The main goal was to determine whether groups with disparate policy interests could establish a good working relationship over time that would lead to agreement on a host of sticky range-management issues. The result was a tumultuous but ultimately successful process that ultimately produced a compromise report acceptable to the participants (Babbitt, 1994).

Can a project like this one be replicated elsewhere? And even if consensus is achieved on how range management issues are to be resolved within a given jurisdiction, can we assume that the implementation of these agreements will occur without subsequent reliance upon litigation or political end runs by affected interests? Both environmentalists and ranchers are skeptical about whether a multiple-use board can work as planned. Livestock operators fear the prospect of boards stacked with nonlocal environmentalists with little understanding of range management issues, whereas reform advocates worry about the ability of local conservationists to persist in their efforts to achieve ecologically sound management practices in the face of hostile community pressure. Preliminary results have been encouraging, but it is difficult to predict whether the Colorado experience can be transplanted to other western states, particularly to states that are less urbanized and more economically dependent upon natural resource industries.

Explaining Policy Change

How can we make sense of the evolution of events and policy decisions? Recent analyses of policy change by Paul Sabatier and Hank Jenkins-Smith (1993) and by Frank Baumgartner and Bryan Jones (1992) provide three key variables that can be used to explain fluctuations in public range policymaking. One particularly useful explanation focuses on shifts in the political coalitions favoring or opposing existing programs. For example, changes in either the leadership or the demographic composition of key congressional committees with jurisdiction over public range policy issues may well lead to greater support for legislative reforms. A second factor is the strategic use of information by the grazing reform coalition to alter the existing policy image, which in turn contributes to change-oriented behavior by public officials. Third, major external factors such as fluctuating economic conditions or the emergence of a new governing coalition with differing policy priorities can produce programmatic shifts.

Shifting Political Coalitions

At the outset of the 1960s, the range policy arena was dominated by the pro-grazing coalition, which consisted primarily of livestock associations, federal legislators and governors representing western states, and, occasionally, BLM and Forest Service officials. The coalition has maintained this core of regional support within government over time (especially in the Senate) and has gradually expanded its organizational base as well. Among the more visible new participants are umbrella groups such as the Public Lands Council and the Wise Use Movement, which represent the interests of ranchers, miners, loggers, and energy companies operating on federal lands. Other allies include several natural resource economists who are based at western state universities and state banking associations operating within public land states.

The stability of congressional support is less evident, particularly within the House of Representatives. However, between 1960 and 1992, the House Interior Committee and its public lands subcommittee did manage to retain a predominately western membership base that hovered around 50 percent for the parent committee and the subcommittee. A strong regional base of support became particularly important for the pursuit of coalition goals, in light of shifts in the policy preferences of Democratic representatives holding committee leadership positions from the mid-1980s through the midterm congressional elections of 1994.

During this period, legislators who chaired the House Natural Resources Committee such as Morris Udall (D-AZ) and George Miller (D-CA) espoused pro-reform policy positions. Similar views were expressed by individuals heading the public lands subcommittee, notably, John Seiberling (D-OH) and Bruce Vento (D-MN). An important consequence of this shift, coupled with the energetic efforts by committee members Synar and Darden to push grazing reform legislation, was the increasing willingness of nonwestern legislators on the committee and in the parent chamber to disregard regional programmatic objectives in favor of national economic and resource conservation objectives. Bills calling for an increase in grazing fees were adopted by the House of Representatives annually between 1990 and 1994, but in each case the Senate refused to follow suit.

A similar pattern of geographical overrepresentation is found within the Senate Energy and Natural Resources (formerly Interior) Committee. The average proportion of western state members declined from approximately 70 percent for the 1960 to 1972 period to 50 percent from 1976 to 1992, but its subcommittee percentage held steady at 70 percent. However, unlike their House counterparts, committee leaders have steadfastly maintained a prodevelopment philosophy. Thus, until recently, public land controversies were characterized by a growing rift between an increasingly reform-oriented House of Representatives and a Senate that remained wedded to the preservation of existing benefits.

However, growth in the number of grazing reform advocates has been more pronounced. Original members included wildlife organizations and the Bureau of the Budget as well as Interior Secretary Stewart Udall, whose tenure spanned the Kennedy and Johnson administrations. By the end of the 1960s, environmental organizations such as the Sierra Club, the Wilderness Society, and the NRDC had joined the National Wildlife Federation in pushing for change. More recent participants within the coalition include congressional leaders within the House Natural Resources Committee (discussed earlier) and, to a lesser extent, Interior Department and Forest Service officials whose support for range reform is largely tied to the policy preferences of differing presidential administrations.

The passage of grazing reform bills in the House of Representatives suggests that the deference formerly shown to the policy goals of the western livestock industry has declined. Why has this occurred? What are the most important factors related to support or rejection of legislative initiatives? A summary of the demographic and partisan makeup of legislators supporting grazing policy changes in both chambers in 1992 is presented in Table 5.2.

The data indicate that the House is more supportive of grazing reform than the Senate, although part of the gap can be attributed to differences in statutory language. But there are clearly sharp distinctions between proponents and opponents of reform proposals that can be linked to both regional and partisan factors. As expected, western legislators are significantly more likely to vote against these bills than legislators representing other regions. And if we break down the western region further to compare lawmakers from the Pacific Coast and Rocky Mountain states, the results are equally striking. Members of the House and the Senate from the interior West are clearly united against policy proposals perceived to work against state economic interests.

Table 5.2 also indicates that in both chambers, Democrats are far more likely to support grazing reform legislation than Republicans. This is consistent with the oft-stated generalization that legislators will be more responsive to party leaders if their own constituency interests aren't affected and if the issues under consideration are not high-profile bills resulting in strong appeals from multiple groups. Other factors contributing to a pro-reform vote include a higher proportion of state residents belonging to an environmental organization and a greater degree of dependence on livestock production as a source of state economic health.

Economic and Political Effects

Even if we acknowledge the continuing political effectiveness of the pro-grazing coalition in protecting key program benefits, it is also true that proponents of grazing reform have succeeded in changing other aspects of range policy. Why has this occurred? Socioeconomic conditions have probably had some impact on policy, but it is difficult to say how much. Members of the pro-grazing coalition consistently pointed to economic hardship as a reason to hold the line during the 1970s when Congress and federal land management agencies imposed several moratoriums on grazing fee hikes. In a similar vein, reform advocates cited mounting federal deficits as ample justification for scaling back or eliminating subsidies contained within federal programs during congressional debates leading to House (but not Senate) approval of grazing fee increases in 1992 (U.S. Congress. Senate, 1992).

In contrast, grazing program advocates have always contended that proposed fee hikes would economically cripple smaller ranches dependent upon forage in nearby federal lands. But there is little evidence to indicate that the western livestock industry suffered from serious financial setbacks as the result of past increases. Moreover, the conditions resulting in lower beef prices affect livestock operators on private and public lands alike. Since the most controversial aspect

TABLE 5.2   Congressional Support for Grazing Fee Increases, 1992

	House of Representatives[a]		Senate[b]	
	% favor	(N)	% favor	(N)
Overall Votes	75	(423)	47	(94)
Region				
West	55	(91)	5	(22)
Other	80	(332)	58	(74)
Subregion				
Pacific	66	(65)	25	(8)
Rocky Mountain	21	(19)	0	(16)
Party ID				
Democrat	92	(251)	62	(53)
Republican	49	(171)	26	(43)
Membership in Environmental Groups[c]				
Low	70	(201)	37	(46)
High	79	(222)	54	(50)
Livestock Production[c]				
Some	63	(208)	4	(23)
Little	87	(215)	59	(73)

[a]Voting patterns on a bill offered by Representative Sidney Yates (D-IL) to increase grazing fees on public lands from $1.86 per animal unit month to $3.45 by fiscal year 1996.

[b]Voting patterns on a motion offered by Senator Robert Byrd (D-WV) to defeat an amendment calling for an increase in grazing fees from $1.86 per animal unit month to $2.40. A vote for this motion was considered to be pro-reform, since the amount of the suggested increase was far lower than competing proposals.

[c]Data obtained from Bob Hall and Mary Lee Kerr, *1991–92 Green Index* (Washington, DC: Island Press).

SOURCE: Data were obtained from *CQ Almanac, 1992* (Washington, DC: Congressional Quarterly, Inc., 1993).

of fee formulas revolves around the disparity between prices per AUM charged by private-sector ranches and the federal land management agencies, it appears unlikely that undecided legislators from nonpublic land states would be persuaded by appeals of this sort (Davis, 1995).

Changes in governing coalitions offer a more promising explanation for range policy shifts. Although presidents rarely get involved in the details of public land policy, their ability to appoint top officials and to shape the general outline of the federal budget is critically important (Davies, 1984). The selection of pro-environmental interior secretaries by Presidents Kennedy, Carter, and Clinton contributed to the enactment of the Classification and Multiple Use Act of 1964, to the implementation of the conservationist provisions of FLPMA in the late 1970s, and to range reform initiatives undertaken in the 1990s.

An equally dramatic shift in the direction of policies favored by the pro-grazing coalition accompanied the appointment of Interior Secretaries James Watt, William Clark, and Donald Hodel by President Reagan and the appointment of Manuel Lujan by President Bush. All favored the maintenance of existing programs and saw little need to add new statutory initiatives. Moreover, in each case, secretarial preferences for a procommodity development slant in program management decisions were reinforced by budgetary and staffing recommendations submitted to the OMB.

Strategic Use of Information

Shifts in governing coalitions have certainly influenced the course of policy decisions, but they only represent part of the puzzle. Perhaps the most intriguing political characteristic of legislative debates dealing with public rangeland programs has been the consistent use of technical information by both coalitions in an effort to gain short-term tactical advantage in winning over policy brokers as well as undecided members of Congress.

The first blows were struck by members of the minority coalition in the mid-1960s with the Bureau of the Budget study and the survey of public land permittees. Both reports were designed to move the policy debate in the direction of an economically rational grazing fee formula based on fair market value and were relied upon heavily by the authors of the USDA/DI task force in their proposed fee increase of 1968 (Backiel and Rogge, 1985). Legislators' use of technical information was also reflected in other range policy decisions, notably in key substantive sections of FLPMA. Congress went along with the PLLRC recommendations originally offered in 1970 to enfranchise the BLM with an organic act and a multiple-purpose management philosophy (Congressional Quarterly, 1977).

Other provisions incorporated within both FLPMA and PRIA illustrate the strategic use of technical information as a political resource to win over policy brokers in subsequent political battles. Environmentalists and their legislative allies seized an opportunity to publicize evaluative reports on range management issued by the General Accounting Office (GAO) that had concluded that much of the land under BLM's jurisdiction was in fair to poor shape (U.S. General Accounting Office, 1977). They subsequently called for policies to elevate the importance of environmental criteria in management decisions and increased funding to administer new range-improvement programs.

Both laws reflect an effort by Congress to accommodate these concerns. FLPMA gave the BLM the authority to recommend lands under its jurisdiction for inclusion within the National Wilderness Preservation System and to prepare a long-range plan for the management and protection of California desert lands. In like fashion, PRIA provided additional monies to restore the quality of deteriorating public rangelands.

Since that time, comprehensive studies have been conducted by USDA/DI researchers in 1977 and again in 1986, 1992, and 1993 to assess range-management costs and to evaluate fee alternatives other than the PRIA-based formula (Backiel and Rogge, 1985; Cody, 1993). These studies, along with a series of reports issued by the GAO over the past fifteen years, have been frequently cited by members of the grazing reform coalition in congressional hearings as evidence justifying the need for policy change (U.S. Congress. House, 1991). Indeed, many of the proposals contained within Secretary Babbitt's *Rangeland Reform '94* report were drawn from a 1993 study entitled *Incentive-Based Grazing Fee System* (U.S. Department of the Interior, 1993).

Political uses of information include efforts to alter policy definition and image as well as the development of programmatic alternatives (Baumgartner and Jones, 1992). Reform advocates such as Representative Synar and environmental groups like the Wilderness Society have attempted to portray public land permitholders as corporate entities with few ties to the land or community who reap sizable profits from subsidized grazing programs (U.S. Congress. House, 1991).

Spokespersons for the pro-grazing coalition continue to insist that such studies are flawed because of a failure to consider key differences between privately owned ranches and those that operate on a combination of public and private lands. And in a recent oversight hearing conducted by the Senate Energy and Natural Resources Committee, western legislators brought in consultants to counter the methodology used by the GAO in reaching conclusions about the need for reform (U.S. Congress. Senate, 1992).

In addition, range program supporters have also attempted to hold their ground in the battle over policy symbols. Testimony offered in hearings on range-reform bills includes references to "the need to maintain a way of life" from opponents of change, along with the depiction of grazing reform advocates as "environmental elitists." Coalition members also suggest that declining numbers of public land ranchers would not result in the restoration of ecologically healthy grasslands with abundant wildlife but would instead produce an increase in residential development, including "ranchettes and coffee bars" (U.S. Congress. Senate, 1992).

Conclusions

A number of public-range policy changes have been initiated since 1960 with mixed results. Although reform advocates have managed to push for the adoption of policies that may yet result in more ecologically sensitive range-management practices, the overall package of program benefits favored by subgovernmental participants remains intact. FLPMA and PRIA, enacted in the late 1970s, contained several programmatic gains for environmentalists, such as the requirement that administrators consider ecological criteria in the preparation of resource management plans, range-improvement funding, and greater opportunities for public involvement in administrative decisionmaking. However, from the vantage point of the pro-grazing coalition, these changes, though distasteful, could be tolerated since the political quid pro quo was the preservation of their primary policy goal—the new grazing fee formula within PRIA that favored livestock interests.

How can we account for fluctuations in range policy over time? The stability of the dominant coalition and its ability to make tactical adjustments in reaction to changing circumstances has created a rather formidable hurdle in the path of range-reform advocates. Contributing to the preservation of program benefits are two key aspects of coalitional influence—agenda control and regional solidarity. Both the House Natural Resources Committee and the Senate Energy and Natural Resources Committee have managed to retain control over public land issues despite a larger trend in Congress to divide program jurisdiction on many issues with an array of standing committees and subcommittees.

Issue control within these committees is reinforced by geographical overrepresentation. Western senators and representatives remain firm in their support of existing policies despite a growing rift between the chambers in their respective actions on reform legislation. This is particularly true of legislators from the interior West, where a greater percentage of rural communities remain economically dependent on extractive land-use industries. From the mid-1980s through the mid-1990s, some cracks could be found in the political support base of commodity interests within the House Natural Resources Committee because of pro-environment committee leaders and individual legislators with a reform-oriented policy agenda. However, the Republicans gained control of both the House and the Senate in the congressional midterm elections of 1994, resulting in the ascendancy of staunch grazing-program supporters to committee chair positions in both chambers.

The ability of the pro-grazing coalition to adapt in response to differing policymaking circumstances is shown by its use of both conciliatory and hardball tactics. Coalition members have demonstrated flexibility whenever the decision to offer a concession on secondary policy goals has contributed to their primary policy goal of preserving a favorable fee structure. Western senators, however, have reacted more strongly to serious challenges by threatening to withhold support for major legislation (such as the 1994 Budget Bill) until references to a major fee increase were deleted and by conducting a filibuster to kill a policy package containing grazing policy reforms in November 1993.

Policy shifts favored by environmentalists can be attributed to the emergence of new governing coalitions and, to a lesser extent, to fluctuating economic circumstances. But the analysis also indicates that the strategic manipulation of information by members of both coalitions is at least as important in explaining policy decisions over time as the more broad-based and visible external factors are. Overall, the prognosis for more fundamental shifts in public-range policy is rather bleak. The failure of the Clinton administration to obtain its range reform objectives in 1993, coupled with the election of a Congress in 1994 that is likely to favor the retention of existing grazing programs, led Secretary Babbitt to abandon his efforts to seek fee formula changes through the legislative process. By 1996, his policy sights had been narrowed to include objectives that can be achieved administratively, namely, the pursuit of changes in the structure of grazing advisory boards to reflect environmental as well as commodity-oriented concerns. His efforts to meet with ranchers and livestock associations across western states to extol the virtues of locally centered consensus decisionmaking based on the Colorado experiment will continue.

Can a scaled-back effort to achieve limited reforms work? A best-case scenario for Secretary Babbitt begins with the presupposition that ranchers and urban environmentalists will recognize the legitimacy of competing views and buy into a new process for making range-policy decisions. The carrot for livestock operators would be the reduction of uncertainty rooted in ongoing proposals to alter grazing programs that has hampered their access to capital from lending institutions in recent years. And a decision to accept admittedly modest programmatic changes here could be utilized by grazing policy supporters as political leverage to justify moving other, more onerous reform proposals off the policy agenda.

However, the effort to make even modest changes in public-range policy faces formidable political hurdles. First, the access to capital argument has been devalued by the decision to abandon reform proposals linking grazing fee rates to fair market value. Second, strong presidential support has been lacking on this issue. Finally, members of the pro-grazing coalition remain quite vocal in their opposition to the substitution of multiple-use councils for grazing advisory boards at the local level. The applicability of the Colorado experiment in range reform to conditions in other western states is limited because of Colorado's relatively large environmental constituency and its lesser economic dependence on extractive natural resource industries.

REFERENCES

Arrandale, Tom. 1983. *The Battle for Natural Resources.* Washington, DC: CQ Press.
Babbitt, Bruce. 1994. "Remarks to the Society of Range Management." *Land and Water Law Review* 29 (2):399–405.
Backiel, Adela, and Lee Ann Rogge. 1985. *Federal Grazing Fees Administered by the Bureau of Land Management and the Forest Service.* Washington, DC: Congressional Research Service, February 21.
Baumgartner, Frank, and Bryan Jones. 1992. *Agendas and Instability in American Politics.* Chicago: University of Chicago Press.
Borman, Michael, and Douglas Johnson. 1990. "Evolution of Grazing and Land Tenure Policies on Public Lands." *Rangelands* 12 (August):203–206.

Browne, William P. 1988. *Private Interests, Public Policy, and American Agriculture.* Lawrence: University Press of Kansas.

Cawley, R. McGreggor. 1993. *Federal Land, Western Anger: The Sagebrush Rebellion and Environmental Politics.* Lawrence: University Press of Kansas.

Clary, David. 1986. *Timber and the Forest Service.* Lawrence: University Press of Kansas.

Cody, Betsy. 1993. *Grazing Fees: A Primer.* Washington, DC: Congressional Research Service, November.

Coggins, George Cameron. 1983. "The Law of Public Rangeland Management IV: FLPMA, PRIA and the Multiple Use Mandate." *Environmental Law* 14, 1:1–132.

Congressional Quarterly. 1977. *Congress and the Nation, Volume 4.* Washington, DC: Congressional Quarterly, Inc.

_____. 1981. *Congress and the Nation, Volume 5.* Washington, DC: Congressional Quarterly, Inc.

Culhane, Paul. 1981. *Public Lands Politics.* Baltimore: Johns Hopkins University Press.

_____. 1984. "Sagebrush Rebels in Office: Jim Watt's Land and Water Policies." In Norman Vig and Michael Kraft, eds., *Environmental Policy in the 1980s.* Washington, DC: CQ Press.

Dana, Samuel T., and Sally Fairfax. 1980. *Forest and Range Policy.* New York: McGraw-Hill.

Davies, J. Clarence. 1984. "Environmental Institutions and the Reagan Administration." In Norman Vig and Michael Kraft, eds., *Environmental Policy in the 1980s.* Washington, DC: CQ Press.

Davis, Charles. 1995. "Public Lands Policy Change: Does Congress Support It?" *Journal of Forestry* 93 (June).

_____. Forthcoming. "Legislative Support for Public Land Policy Reforms." *Journal of Forestry.*

Durant, Robert. 1987. "Public Lands, the BLM and the Reagan Administration." *Public Administration Review* (March/April):180–189.

_____. 1992. *The Administrative Presidency Revisited: Public Lands, The BLM and the Reagan Revolution.* Albany: State University of New York Press.

Fairfax, Sally. 1984. "Beyond the Sagebrush Rebellion: The BLM as Neighbor and Manager in the Western States." In John Francis and Richard Ganzel, eds., *Western Public Lands.* Totowa, NJ: Rowman and Allanheld.

Foss, Phillip O. 1960. *Politics and Grass.* Seattle: University of Washington Press.

Francis, John. 1984. "Environmental Values, Intergovernmental Politics and the Sagebrush Rebellion." In John Francis and Richard Ganzel, eds., *Western Public Lands.* Totowa, NJ: Rowman and Allanheld.

Gates, Paul W. 1980. *Pressure Groups and Recent American Land Policies.* Ithaca: Department of History, Cornell University.

Graf, William L. 1990. *Wilderness Preservation and the Sagebrush Rebellions.* Savage, MD: Rowman and Littlefield.

Hall, Bob, and Mary Lee Kerr. 1991. *1991–1992 Green Index.* Washington, DC: Island Press.

Hamilton, Michael. 1987. "Deregulation and Federal Land Management in the 1980s: Introducing Atrophy in Bureaucracy." In Phillip O. Foss, ed., *Federal Lands Policy.* Westport, CT: Greenwood Press.

Ingram, Helen. 1990. *Water Politics.* Albuquerque: University of New Mexico Press.

Jones, Charles O., and Randall Strahan. 1985. "The Effect of Energy Politics on Congressional and Executive Organization in the 1970s." *Legislative Studies Quarterly* 10 (May):151–178.

Kenworthy, Tom. 1994. "For Love of the Land." *Washington Post National Weekly Edition,* February 21–27.

Klyza, Christopher McGrory. 1991. "Framing the Debate in Public Lands Politics." *Policy Studies Journal* 19 (3–4):577–585.

Knickerbocker, Brad. 1993. "Babbitt Wades into the Debate on Western Land." *Christian Science Monitor,* May 4.

McConnell, Grant. 1966. *Private Power and American Democracy.* New York: Knopf.

McCool, Daniel. 1987. *Command of the Waters.* Berkeley: University of California Press.

Nelson, Robert H. 1985. "*NRDC v. Morton:* The Role of Judicial Policymaking in Public Rangeland Management." *Policy Studies Journal* 14 (December):255–264.

Obermiller, Frederick. 1991. "Elements of the 1991 Federal Grazing (Fee) Debate." Testimony presented to the U.S. House Committee on Agriculture in Burns, Oregon, August 19.

Rosenbaum, Walter. 1993. "Energy Policy in the West." In Zachary Smith, ed., *Environmental Politics and Policy in the West.* Dubuque, IA: Kendall/Hunt.

Sabatier, Paul, and Hank Jenkins-Smith, eds. 1993. *Policy Change and Learning: An Advocacy Coalition Approach.* Boulder: Westview.

U.S. Congress. House. Committee on Interior and Insular Affairs. 1991. *BLM Reauthorization and Grazing Fees.* 102d Cong., 1st sess. Hearings held on March 12 in Washington, DC. Washington, DC: GPO.

U.S. Congress. Senate. Committee on Interior and Insular Affairs. 1963. *Public Land Review.* 87th Cong., 2d sess. Hearings held May 6 and 7. Washington, DC: GPO.

_____. Committee on Energy and Natural Resources. 1992. *Grazing Management and Grazing Fee Issues.* 102d Cong., 2d sess. Hearings held on September 3 in Casper, Wyoming. Washington, DC: GPO.

U.S. Department of the Interior, Bureau of Land Management, and U.S. Department of Agriculture, Forest Service. 1993. *Incentive-Based Grazing Fee System.* A report from the Secretaries of Interior and Agriculture. Washington, DC: GPO.

U.S. General Accounting Office. 1977. *Public Rangelands Continue to Deteriorate.* Washington, DC: General Accounting Office.

Voigt, William, Jr. 1976. *Public Grazing Lands: Use and Misuse by Industry and Government.* New Brunswick, NJ: Rutgers University Press.

Wilkinson, Charles F. 1992. *Crossing the Next Meridian: Land, Water, and the Future of the West.* Washington, DC: Island Press.

6

Reform at a Geological Pace: Mining Policy on the Federal Lands, 1964–1994

CHRISTOPHER MCGRORY KLYZA

In May 1994, with an oversized check for $10 billion in the background, Interior Secretary Bruce Babbitt signed patents transferring 1,800 acres of public lands in Nevada to Barrick Goldstrike Mines for less than $10,000. Under the 1872 Mining Law, which governs hardrock mining policy on the public lands, individuals or private firms can purchase mineral-bearing lands for $2.50 or $5.00 per acre. This law, the subject of serious reform efforts since the 1970s, allows extremely valuable mineral deposits—like Barrick's—to go from public to private ownership for a minimal fee. To Babbitt, who called the transfer "the biggest gold heist since the days of Butch Cassidy," the 1872 Mining Law is outdated and badly in need of reform. Indeed, Babbitt had been delaying signing the lands over to Barrick in hopes that Congress would pass such reform legislation in 1994. A federal judge ruled that Babbitt could wait no longer, though, and ordered him to patent the land to Barrick by June 20th (Christensen, 1994a).

Both the House and the Senate passed mining reform legislation in 1993, but the bills were quite different. The House bill featured an 8 percent royalty on miners' gross revenue (minus smelting costs), the elimination of patenting of land, environmental standards for mining operations, the creation of an Abandoned Locatable Minerals Mine Reclamation Fund to finance cleanups, and a provision allowing the secretary of the interior to declare certain lands unsuitable for mining. The Senate bill sought less far-reaching change: a 2 percent royalty on net value of the minerals, retention of patenting but charging market value for the surface land, and only requiring mining operations to meet widely varying state environmental and reclamation standards. The Conference Committee had worked on and off since June 1994, but by the end of the session, efforts to reach an agreement within the committee had collapsed, as both representatives and senators felt they could compromise no more (Benenson, 1993).

Why does a law that is over one hundred and twenty years old continue to be the basis for mining policy on the public lands? Why has it been so difficult to reform the 1872 Mining Law? In the following chapter, these questions will be at the center of an overview of public lands mining policy since the mid-1960s. In order to understand current mining policy, we must begin with an examination of how the 1872 law came into being.

History and Legislation

In 1848, gold was discovered in California, an area of land that belonged to Mexico although it had been occupied by U.S. troops since 1846. Thus, mining policy began in something of a sovereign vacuum since Mexico was about to surrender the region and the United States did not yet control it. Even when California became a state, there was no federal mechanism for the transfer of mineral lands to private citizens or companies. Miners did not wait for government action. Instead, they created order themselves by establishing mining districts with mining codes governing how minerals would be developed. These districts and codes were extralegal property rights systems, that is, they were systems of property rights enforced and respected by other miners yet there was no governmental authority. As the mineral rushes spread to other western states, so did the legal precedent affecting mining districts and mining codes (Ellison, 1963; Leshy, 1987).

The discovery of gold in 1848 initiated debate over federal mining policy. Some people—especially those from the West—argued for the status quo since maintaining it would help settle the region and develop minerals the country needed. Others argued that these miners were trespassers and that the gold and silver they were taking belonged to the federal government. At the very least, they felt, the federal government should receive some money for these minerals. This debate continued, on and off, through 1866.

During the 1860s, the major method of mining shifted. Early California mining was almost exclusively placer mining, which was done primarily in and along riverbeds and streambeds. Miners sought to recover gold or silver that had been eroded from larger deposits. Quartz, or lode, mining is based on removing minerals from hardrock. Usually, miners discovered a surface lode and then were forced to tunnel to follow the lode underground to recover minerals. After placer mines were played out, the more capital-intensive quartz mines became more important. Investors wanted more secure property rights before committing funds to such projects. This led western senators to shepherd the first federal mining law through Congress in 1866.

The law, which only applied to quartz claims, essentially adopted and legitimized the extralegal property rights system developed in the mining codes. Free and open access to minerals on the public lands would continue, in accordance with local customs. Miners could file claims in local federal land offices (later county courthouses) and had the option to buy (or patent) mineral lands for $5 per acre, if they had followed local customs and spent $1,000 in labor and improvements on developing the land. Any such claims and patents would now have the authority of the federal government behind them (Swenson, 1968).

Four years later, a similar law was passed dealing with placer mining. Claims could be for 160 acres, and patents could be purchased for $2.50 per acre. And finally, the 1872 Mining Law combined and codified the 1866 and 1870 laws. However, it did make a number of significant changes. It stipulated that only "valuable" mineral deposits on the public lands were covered by the Mining Law, reduced maximum placer claims to 20 acres, increased quartz claims (from 200 to 1,500 feet in length), and required $100 of work annually to maintain a claim, dropping the $1,000 development requirement. The 1872 Mining Law has remained substantially unchanged since its enactment (Swenson, 1968).

There are four main reasons the 1872 Mining Law took the shape it did, three of which continue to strongly shape mining policy. First, the dominant idea about how government and society should interact at that time was economic liberalism, which embraced the belief that government should play a minimal role in the economy and in society. If and when it did act, government should help in facilitating the "release of energy." This idea is at the core of Mining Law, which legitimized existing private practices. The other two ideas that have served to guide public lands politics since the late 1800s—technocratic utilitarianism and preservationism—were both in their infancy in the United States at this time and did not significantly influence the mining policy debate.

Second, a national administrative state was practically nonexistent in the 1860s and 1870s. The federal government did not have the capacity, even if it had the desire, to implement a more involved regulatory mining policy. Early mining policy, like most early natural resources policy, was administered by the military. The army was the only potential governmental administrative actor in California and the rest of the West during the mineral rushes from 1848 through the 1860s. The military was charged with administering these programs not because of its expertise but rather because of the lack of alternatives. The two oldest minerals-related agencies, the U.S. Geological Survey (USGS) and the Bureau of Mines, did not yet exist, and the General Land Office, a land disposal agency staffed almost wholly by clerks, did not have offices in much of the West. Not only were there no specific agencies to administer minerals policy, but the national government itself was not yet capable of handling administrative responsibility. The building of a national administrative state capable of administering national programs was only beginning in the 1880s. This lack of state capacity left the federal government with few alternatives in hardrock mining policy (Skowronek, 1982).

Third, the extralegal property rights system developed by the miners in the various mining codes they established was another factor of crucial importance to the mining laws passed in the 1860s and 1870s. The federal laws accepted these existing property rights schemes, incorporating them into federal law. Therefore, even though the miners were technically trespassers, the property rights systems that they developed have fundamentally shaped hardrock mining policy for over one hundred years.

A fourth and final factor shaping the 1872 Mining Law was the failure of a federal lead-leasing program in the Midwest in the 1820s and 1830s. This failure, repeatedly cited in debates over mining policy, essentially ruled out a leasing system or government-run minerals development program (Swenson, 1968).

The legacy of the first three factors in shaping the 1872 Mining Law remains clear in the 1990s. First, the idea of economic liberalism was institutionalized in the mining policy regime at its inception, leading to a privatized policy pattern for mining, that is, government policy has been—with some exceptions—to allow the private sector to make mining policy. Private individuals and firms search for minerals, make claims, and decide when and whether to develop minerals on the public lands. The lack of state capacity at the inception of mining policy continues today, revealing itself in a fragmented executive branch, discussed more fully later on. And finally, the legitimation of the extralegal property rights system affects mining policy when miners argue that they have a right to the minerals on public lands and that their claims are property rights entitling them to compensation if the government does not want the claims developed for any reason.

In the early 1900s, as part of the general conservation movement, public attention began to focus on fuel resources—coal, oil, gas—located on the public lands. Coal lands were not covered by the 1872 Mining Law, but oil lands were. After the withdrawal of nearly 150 million acres of public lands, and after much debate between presidents and members of Congress, the Mineral Leasing Act was passed in 1920. It established a system for private companies to lease public oil, oil shale, coal, and fertilizer or chemical (phosphate, potash, sodium, sulfur) lands and to pay the government a royalty (typically 12.5 percent) for these resources. The leasing program was the first significant change in mining policy since 1872, and it established a differential system for mining metals and energy minerals on the public lands that continues today. It should also be noted that in 1917 Congress passed a law giving the secretary of agriculture the authority to use a leasing system for hardrock minerals on acquired lands. Such a system is still in place on these acquired lands (Leshy, 1987).[1]

Since the passage of the Mineral Leasing Act of 1920, there have been four minor adjustments to the 1872 Mining Law. The Multiple Mineral Development Act of 1954 dealt with hardrock mineral claims that were being leased for oil. Just one year later, Congress passed a law designed to reduce mineral claims of questionable value. The Common Varieties Act of 1955 removed common varieties of "sand, stone, gravel, pumice, pumicite, cinders, and clay" from the functioning of the 1872 act. These minerals would be sold based on regulations established by the secretaries of agriculture and the interior. Another 1955 act, the Surface Resources Act, restricted the surface use of mineral claims to uses required for mining purposes in an effort to prevent fraudulent claims. And lastly, the Federal Land Policy and Management Act of 1976 required that all mineral claims made under the 1872 Mining Law be recorded with the BLM, centralizing information on claims. Prior to FLPMA, claims only had to be recorded in county courthouses. The act also reaffirmed the interior secretary's power to regulate mining on these claims to protect "unnecessary and undue degradation of the lands" (Leshy, 1987).

Institutions

Since hardrock mining policy is essentially a privatized policy realm, it is not surprising that the federal government has limited capacity in mining policy. The executive branch is characterized by fragmentation in this policy realm, a characteristic that has only increased in the last thirty years. Mining responsibility is centralized in one committee in both the House and Senate, so fragmentation is less of an issue there.[2] Of greater significance has been the changing composition of the House Natural Resources Committee and the power of western senators to block passage of legislation reforming the 1872 Mining Law.

The Executive Branch

In the executive branch, the one word that best describes hardrock mining policy is fragmentation. There are five agencies in the Interior Department with substantial mining responsibilities: the Bureau of Land Management, the Bureau of Mines, the Minerals Management Service, the Office of Surface Mining and Reclamation, and the U.S. Geological Survey. Indeed, minerals management is fragmented and falls under the purview of two different assistant secretaries, the assistant secretary of land and minerals management (minerals management) and the assistant secretary of water and science (collection of mineral data and aiding the private sector in the orderly development of domestic minerals). This lack of a coordinated administrative capacity for mining policy has been an issue since the mid-1800s and was the focus of significant policy debate in the 1970s and 1980s (National Archives and Records Administration, 1993).

Only three of these five agencies play a significant role in hardrock mining policy. The BLM, created by the 1946 merger of the General Land Office and the Grazing Service, is the primary manager of minerals on federal lands, including the 270 million acres the BLM manages, lands managed by other federal agencies, and the 300 million acres on which the government controls mineral rights. The agency administers leases for minerals developed under the Mineral Leasing Act and is the agency of record for mining claims under the 1872 Mining Law.

The Bureau of Mines and the USGS are primarily research-oriented agencies. The Bureau of Mines, created in 1910, researches and collects data on economics, supply and demand (especially regarding national security), safety, and environmental problems associated with the extraction of nonfuel minerals both in the United States and throughout the world. The USGS, established in 1879, is one of the oldest scientific agencies in the country. Among its numerous responsibilities is the investigation and assessment of mineral resources in the country. Prior to the 1980s, its Conservation Division administered mineral leases on the public lands. None of the three agencies is particularly strong, and each has close ties to industry and the mining academic community.

The Minerals Management Service, created in 1982, administers leases on the Outer Continental Shelf and manages all royalty and mineral revenue functions on the public lands. Since hardrock minerals are not leased and involve no royalties, the agency has no responsibility in this policy realm. If the 1872 Mining Law is reformed, however, this agency could be in charge of collecting the newly charged royalties. The Office of Surface Mining and Reclamation, established in 1977, deals exclusively with coal surface mining.

This fragmentation is made even clearer when a particular aspect of mining policy is examined. For example, under the Reagan administration, the major actors on strategic minerals policy were the Department of the Interior (including the BLM, the Bureau of Mines, the Minerals Management Service, the Office of Minerals Policy and Research Analysis, and the USGS), the Department of Commerce, the Department of Defense, the Federal Emergency Management Agency (FEMA), the General Services Administration (GSA), the Annual Materials Plan Steering Committee, the Committee on Materials, and the Cabinet Council on Natural Resources and Environment. The working group for Reagan's 1982 minerals report included many more actors, including the nine cabinet Departments of Agriculture, Commerce, Defense, Energy, the Interior, Justice, State, Transportation, the Treasury, as well as the Central Intelligence Agency (CIA), the Council of Economic Advisers, the EPA, the FEMA, the GSA, the National Security Council (NSC), the OMB, the Office of Policy Development, the Office of Science and Technology Policy, and the U.S. Trade Representative.

If the sheer number of executive branch agencies involved in strategic minerals policy is not enough evidence of fragmentation, a vivid example is supplied by the government's lack of knowledge about how many of its acres had been withdrawn from entry under the 1872 Mining Law. The differing figures contained in Interior Department and Office of Technology Assessment studies (discussed later) underline the confusion. Despite numerous proposals to address this fragmentation, no progress has been made (Anderson, 1988).

Congress

Changes in Congress affecting mining policy in the last thirty years have been complicated (see Table 6.1). In the House of Representatives, there has been an increase in the number of members from western states serving on the Interior and Insular Affairs/Natural Resources Committee.[3] In 1964, fewer than one-half of the members were from the West; in 1994, nearly two-thirds were from the West. Even more dramatic has been the increase in western Republicans on the

TABLE 6.1 Western Members on the Congressional Interior Committees

Year	House Total Members/Republicans	Senate Total Members/Republicans
1964	16 of 33/5 of 14	14 of 17/6 of 6
1974	19 of 40/8 of 19	9 of 13/4 of 6
1984	19 of 39/12 of 14	9 of 20/6 of 11
1994	24 of 37/12 of 15	9 of 20/6 of 9

SOURCES: *Congressional Quarterly* (Washington, DC: 1965); Michael Barone, Grant Ujifusa, and Douglas Matthews, *The Almanac of American Politics, 1974* (Boston: Gambit, 1974); Michael Barone and Grant Ujifusa, *The Almanac of American Politics, 1984* (Washington, DC: National Journal, 1983); Barone and Ujifusa, *The Almanac of American Politics, 1994* (Washington, DC: National Journal, 1993).

committee; the proportion has grown from less than one-third to four-fifths. What effect has this increase in western representation had on mining policy?

Despite this rise in western membership, the House Natural Resources Committee is not the servant of the mining industry and other commodity groups. There are three sometimes overlapping reasons for western membership on this committee. The traditional reason has been for House members to help an industry that is important in their own district. The increase in western membership, though, has been driven by two new factors. Representatives from the urban West have sought membership to achieve environmental protection goals, either to accommodate constituent desires or their own policy goals, or both. Conservative Republicans have gained membership as public lands issues have taken on greater importance. In much of the rural West, the fight against changes to the 1872 Mining Law, increased grazing fees, reduced logging, and so on have taken on ideological characteristics identified with conservatism. The advent of the Sagebrush Rebellion and the Wise Use Movement underscores the increased importance of these issues in the rural West.

In general, the House Interior/Natural Resources Committee has become increasingly concerned with environmental protection on the public lands in the past thirty years. This is due to the continued Democratic dominance of the House and the rise of environmentalists on the committee. A look at the major chairs of the committee illustrates this point. In the 1960s, Wayne Aspinall, representing western Colorado, was a strong friend of mining and other commodity interests.

In the 1970s and 1980s, Morris Udall of Arizona was a friend to environmentalists, though he worked to help the mining industry so important in his state. He was succeeded by another pro-environmental legislator, George Miller, from the San Francisco Bay area, who led the committee until the Republican takeover of Congress. Since 1994, the House Natural Resources Committee has been chaired by Alaskan Don Young, a strong advocate of developmental interests.

There have also been significant changes in the Senate, though of a different kind. Western membership has fallen from its previous level of over 80 percent to less than 50 percent. There has been a parallel decline in western Republicans, whose representation has dropped from 100 percent in 1964 to 66 percent in 1994. This change in composition can primarily be explained by the change in jurisdiction. When the Senate Committee on Interior and Insular Affairs became the Senate Committee on Energy and Natural Resources, it became an attractive committee for senators from Louisiana (oil), Kentucky (coal), and New Jersey (energy prices paid by consumers).

The policy preferences of the Senate committee have not followed those of its House counterpart. Under the guidance of Henry Jackson, the Senate Interior Committee was environmentally oriented in the 1960s and 1970s. In the 1980s and 1990s, however, the committee has adopted a less environmental perspective. From 1980 to 1986, with Republican control of the Senate, James McClure of Idaho chaired the committee. Generally, he and the committee were favorably disposed to mining and commodity interests during this period. In 1986, Bennett Johnston of Louisiana became committee chairman. He was moderate on the environment and was a real friend to oil, but less so to mining. In 1994, he was succeeded by Frank Murkowski of Alaska, a close supporter of mining interests.

In summer 1994, a conference committee tried to work out a compromise on Mining Law reform legislation passed by the House and Senate. However, in September, conference committee efforts to work out a compromise between the House and Senate bills were abandoned in the midst of speculation that Senate Republicans might filibuster against any agreement that they found unacceptable. It might well be that this is the characteristic of greatest importance in Congress regarding mining policy; that is, the filibuster has been the chief tool of those fighting for mining interests and fighting to lessen the changes to the 1872 Mining Law. Even if the House overwhelmingly passes significant reform of the law (as it did) and even if the Senate favors such reform, only a handful of western Republicans (and Democrats, too) could block such change for many years.

Since the Republicans gained control of both the House and the Senate in November 1994, it appears that a window of opportunity for reform has closed. Two Alaskans friendly to mining, Don Young in the House and Frank Murkowski in the Senate, now head the natural resource committees. The House committee, renamed the Resources Committee, has forty-two members, of which twenty-four are from the West. Of the twenty-five Republicans, seventeen are from the West. In the Senate, ten of eighteen committee members are from the West, including eight of the eleven Republicans. Given these changes, it is unlikely that any significant reform of the 1872 Mining Law will occur soon.

The Courts

The courts have played a major role in interpreting the 1872 Mining Law since its passage. Indeed, legal scholar John Leshy counts more than two hundred Supreme Court decisions addressing the Mining Law. Among the most impor-

TABLE 6.2   Urbanization in the West, 1960–1990

	Percent Urban	
Location	1960	1990
Nation	69.9	75.2
West	77.6	86.3
Rocky Mountains	67.1	79.7
Pacific	81.1	88.6

SOURCES: U.S. Bureau of the Census, 1964, 1993.

tant issues that the courts have addressed are the determinations on what a valuable mineral is and on when a valid claim can be made (before or after such a discovery). These decisions have added a significant body of common law—both at the state and federal level—to the statute, but there have been no recent decisions that have fundamentally altered the law (Leshy, 1987).

Social and Economic Conditions

One of the greatest changes in the West over the last thirty years has been in its population profile. In 1960, the population of the thirteen western states was slightly over 28 million, or 15.7 percent of the national total. In 1990, the population of the West had risen to nearly 53 million and accounted for over 21 percent of the nation's population. Even more significant than this near doubling of population in thirty years and the increased growth of the West relative to the rest of the country is the dramatic increase in urbanization in the western states. Although in 1960 the West as a region was more urbanized than the national average (indeed, in terms of urbanization it was second only to the Middle Atlantic region), that urbanization was concentrated in California. The Rocky Mountain states were slightly less urbanized than the nation (see Table 6.2).

In 1990, the West as a whole was the most urbanized region of the country, and even the Rocky Mountain states exceeded the national average, with nearly 80 percent of their population living in urban areas. This increase in urbanization has been the most dramatic in Alaska (+29.6 percent), Nevada (+17.9 percent), and Arizona (+13 percent). By 1990, six of the western states had populations that were over 80 percent urban and five of the six most urban states in the country were in the West (California, 93 percent; Hawaii, 89 percent; Nevada, 88 percent; Arizona, 87 percent; and Utah, 87 percent) (U.S. Bureau of the Census, 1964, 1993).

In addition to these general demographic trends within the region, there have been important subtrends. Of great interest to mining and natural resources policy is the growth of tourist and second-home meccas throughout the West, exemplified by such towns as Aspen, Jackson, Kalispell, Moab, Santa Fe, and Telluride. As these towns grow and the type of people who live in them change, views toward mining and the general political picture change as well. Also of interest are the population booms and busts that the general trends mask. From the early 1970s through the early 1980s, the energy boom helped bring people and prosperity to the rural West. That boom, like many in the West, ended in a bust by the middle 1980s, with many of the people who had been attracted by the jobs and a growing economy moving on again.

The economic and social bust was a deep one for the rural West, especially. In 1986, for example, Idaho, Montana, and Wyoming all declined in overall population. In the early 1990s, the Rocky Mountain states were experiencing a boom, as Idaho, Utah, and Nevada each demonstrated significant economic growth. In addition, movement within the West changed. In 1988–1989, for instance, California had net positive migration from all but two of the other ten contiguous western states. In 1992–1993, California had ceased to become the destination state; it had net negative migration to each of the other ten western states. This current population shift is being driven by unhappy Californians seeking a better quality of life (Brownridge, 1989).

These demographic trends in the West had three significant effects, all of which are discussed more fully later on. First, as population and urbanization increased, the economy shifted farther away from reliance on mining and other natural resource–based industries. Second, the demographic trends contributed to the rise of environmentalism in the area. And finally, both of these changes led to the rise of politicians who were willing to fight for the environment, even if it meant alienating natural resources industries.

In terms of economics, the two key trends have been the decline in the relative importance of the mineral, timber, and ranch businesses and the rise of alternative economic activities that rely on increased environmental protection, namely tourism and recreation. Even in 1960, mining (including non-hardrock mining workers, who were far more numerous than hardrock mining employees) accounted for over 5 percent of the nonfarm workforce in only three western states—New Mexico, Utah, and Wyoming. As Table 6.3 indicates, these figures had declined or remained the same by 1990 (U.S. Bureau of Mines, 1961, 1992).[4] Despite the declines in employment, mineral production remains a regionally important industry. Indeed, in 1992 it was a $9 billion industry.

Some of the decline in employment has been due to increased mechanization and technological developments. For instance, there has been a new gold rush in the West, especially in Nevada, based on leachate mining, which is less labor-intensive than past methods. U.S. gold output has increased tenfold in the last twelve years, but employment has declined by roughly one-half. In 1993, 10.6 million ounces of gold were mined in the United States, three times the amount mined per year during the California gold rush in the 1850s. As the data in Table 6.4 demonstrate, the claims patented and acres transferred into private ownership over the last thirty years have fluctuated, with no clear pattern of decline or resurgence apparent, although the new gold rush is pushing those figures up in

TABLE 6.3   Mining Employment and Value of Nonfuel Mineral Production, 1960–1990

| State | 1960 | | 1990 | |
	Employment[a]	Production (in thousands of $)	Employment[a]	Production (in thousands of $)
Alaska	1,845 (1)	14,282	3,470 (3)	576,620
Arizona	15,813 (2)	415,718	12,400 (1)	3,065,448
California	18,370 (3)	430,857	9,000 (3)	2,779,799
Colorado	11,464 (2)	162,460	19,500 (1)	386,192
Hawaii	695 (1)	9,254	—	106,095
Idaho	3,645 (1)	57,441	3,900 (1)	399,761
Montana	7,300 (1)	102,415	6,300 (1)	567,684
Nevada	4,599 (3)	80,285	14,321[b]	2,610,876
New Mexico	11,665 (2)	208,277	6,520 (3)	1,097,550
Oregon	2,027 (1)	54,419	1,600[b]	237,406
Utah	14,163 (2)	287,730	8,602 (1)	1,334,010
Washington	2,729 (1)	68,163	3,800[b]	473,229
Wyoming	4,161 (2)	63,981	18,300[b]	910,848

[a]Employment figures vary in what types of mining they include: (1) includes all mining, (2) includes all non-petroleum mining, and (3) includes all nonfuel mining.
[b]Distinctions among types of mining are not reported.
SOURCES: U.S. Bureau of Mines, 1961, 1992

TABLE 6.4   Mining Activities on the Public Lands, 1964–1991

Year	Claims Patented	Acres	Total Claims Received	Cumulative Claims	Existing Valid Claims
FY1964	61	9,912	—	—	—
FY1974	41	2,614	—	—	—
FY1984	363	8,797	142,091	1,935,541	1,427,782
FY1991	274	3,965	78,053	2,741,025	1,113,368

SOURCES: U.S. Department of the Interior, 1965, 1975, 1985, 1992.

the 1990s (Egan, 1994a; U.S. Department of the Interior, 1965, 1975, 1985, 1992).[5] Overall, then, mining remains a locally important industry—it pays good wages, is a significant contributor to local property taxes, and is one of the few economic options in rural areas in the West. Even where it is still important, though, mining is subject to booms and busts.

A good example of a mining bust can be illustrated by examining Leadville, Colorado, in the 1980s. The town had been a mining community since its birth. In 1981, the Climax Molybdenum Company employed 3,200 people with a payroll of $80 million and was responsible for 85 percent of the county's property tax base. The next year Climax laid off 600 workers, and the mine soon closed. Unemployment rose to over 30 percent and the county population declined by one-third. Some analysts have likened the resource-based industries of the West to neocolonialism. In other words, mining and other commodity corporations based outside of the region milk the region of its resources without returning much, discarding plants and communities when the market or supplies dictate (Farling, 1989; Voynick, 1989).

As the commodity industries have declined, they have been replaced by other industries. By 1994, tourism, broadly defined, was the fastest-growing industry in the West. It is the largest private employer in seven of the eleven western states. For instance, fewer than 50,000 people work in hardrock mining throughout the West, less than the 60,000 who work in the ski industry in Colorado. This tourism and recreation boom has led to significant changes in the West, especially in the inland rural West. These tourists are changing the culture and economics of small towns, driving up the cost of living and leading to conflicts between the old-timers in traditional industries like cattle ranching, mining, and timber harvesting and the newcomers, who are more likely to be attracted to outdoor recreation and the environment. In addition, many of the tourists have decided to stay, further changing the nature of the communities. The economic picture for mining is therefore one of transition throughout the West (Egan, 1994b).

The rise of environmentalism throughout the country, which began in the 1960s, has had significant effects on public lands mining. Prior to this rise, the environmental focus on mining usually involved a small minority that might be opposed to a mining operation in a particular scenic area. Following the rise, some began to question almost all aspects of mining. Environmental groups became concerned with air pollution, water pollution, toxic waste, landscape transformation and reclamation, and location of future mines. A significant portion of society began to question a worldview based on humans as rulers over nature. Most important, the perception that mining was the highest and best use of the land was increasingly challenged (Dunlap and Mertig, 1992; Marston, 1989; Sale, 1993).

Some in society thought the benefits of mining needed to be weighed against its costs in each particular setting. As environmentalism and the demand for outdoor recreation rose, conflicts over mining increased. Some environmentalists began to focus on the 1872 Mining Law, which they argued was outdated. They found allies among fiscal conservatives who thought the government should earn royalties from its hardrock minerals. (These reform efforts are discussed further later in the chapter.)

Environmentalism also invaded the rural West as urban and eastern refugees moved in. This changed the political dynamic for land management in these towns and often raised the local level of conflict as well. A 1980 Council on Environmental Quality report on public opinion on the environment found that although 64 percent of those in the Rocky Mountain region supported environmental protection, 7 percent were unsympathetic, the highest level in the country. Towns that had once fully supported mining could no longer offer such unquestioning support. For example, Crested Butte, originally a mining town, became a ski town once mining pulled out. When AMAX Corporation wanted to open a new molybdenum mine outside of town, the community strongly and successfully opposed it. In addition, new local environmental groups, such as the Southern Utah Wilderness Alliance, have formed to challenge commodity use of the public lands.

Environmentalism generated a counterresponse, based most strongly in the West. It began in the mid-1970s with the Sagebrush Rebellion, a movement by a number of western states to have the federal lands transferred to the states. This movement, though quite popular among grazing interests, was not supported by mining (perhaps because the industry was more comfortable with the federal status quo). The rebellion faded with the election of Ronald Reagan, a declared sagebrush rebel. A related initiative—privatization—arose during the first Reagan term. This effort to sell off significant portions of the public lands was mainly supported by economists both within and outside of the administration. The program went so far as to identify 5 million acres of Forest Service land for potential disposal before public opposition killed it. Again, mining interests were not particularly active in this initiative (Cawley, 1993; Graf, 1990).

The latest, and still very active, counterresponse to environmentalism is the Wise Use Movement. This movement accepts federal ownership but argues that these lands should be managed to maximize commodity production. Among the items relating to mining on the Wise Use agenda are opening all public lands, including wilderness areas and national parks, to the provisions of the 1872 Mining Law and the recognition of private possessory rights to mining claims on federal lands. Among the various Wise Use groups, People for the West! is most involved in mining issues, working to retain the basic structure of the 1872 Mining Law. Much of the funding for this group comes from the mining industry. The Wise Use Movement seeks to paint environmentalism and public lands policy reforms as a war on the West, focusing on the mythology of the small prospector when it comes to mining (Deal, 1993).

This array of demographic, economic, and sociological change throughout the West over the last thirty years is reflected in the political arena, to which we now turn.

Policy and Political Changes

In the early 1960s, mining policy was dominated by subgovernments. Government policy, essentially a privatized mining policy, had been set in 1872 by the Mining Law. The federal involvement that did exist was cooperative and involved the mining industry (often represented by the American Mining

Congress [AMC]), friendly members of Congress in the House and Senate Interior Committees, and relevant government officials in the BLM and USGS.

As the changes discussed earlier occurred, the characteristics of mining policy changed. The privatized, nearly invisible policy of the early 1960s (and before) became a more visible and conflictual policy arena as environmental groups sought access to the policy process. Environmental groups have used a variety of tactics to increase the visibility of mining policy. They have undertaken policy analysis, have offered testimony to Congress, and have used the courts to further their cause. They have used the media in an effort to make more people aware of the issues related to mining and have attempted to shift the arena of policymaking from a region in which mining is an important industry (the West) to one where it is not (the nation). This has moved the policymaking process to outside the subgovernment, making policy more visible and competitive. Part of the environmental strategy has been to help members of Congress from outside the West in their efforts to reform the 1872 Mining Law, people such as Senator Dale Bumpers of Arkansas and Representative Nick Rahall of West Virginia.[6]

Currently, the groups most involved in mining policy are the AMC and the Mineral Policy Center. The AMC, founded in 1897, is the main trade organization of the mining industry (it does not represent oil and gas producers, though). In recent debates over reforming the 1872 Mining Law, the AMC has opposed any leasing system and has sought to limit any royalties or environmental amendments. The Mineral Policy Center was founded in 1988 by former Secretary of the Interior Stewart Udall and others with the express purpose of reforming the Mining Law. Although the center does not have many members (approximately 1,000), it serves as the point group for environmentalists working to change the law. In the 104th Congress, the AMC opposed the House bill and supported the Senate bill; the reverse was true for the Mineral Policy Center. I now turn to an examination of how the policy process has worked on three main issues affecting hardrock mining.

Current Issues

Land Access and Withdrawal

Since the mid-1960s, one of the major issues regarding mining on the public lands has been the withdrawal of certain lands from the functioning of the 1872 Mining Law. The primary and most significant cause for withdrawal of these lands is the Wilderness Act, passed in 1964. Lands preserved under this law are protected from mechanized vehicles, human habitation, and most commodity development, although mining is at least technically allowed. The first wilderness legislation, introduced in 1956, made no exception for mining; all lands declared wilderness were to be closed to the workings of the 1872 Mining Law. Over the next eight years, however, mining interests represented by the AMC, state mining groups, state mining agencies, and individual mining companies won an exemption for mining: Entry under the 1872 Mining Law in wilderness areas would be allowed through December 31, 1983, and mining on valid claims could continue after that date (Allin, 1982; Baker, 1985).

Despite this legislative success, there has been almost no mining in wilderness areas. Although claims could be developed, the secretary of agriculture was empowered to develop regulations covering the mining, and mined areas had to be restored to as full an extent as possible. The theoretical difficulties of mining in wilderness soon became clear in reality. In 1966, Kennecott Copper announced plans to develop an open-pit copper mine in the Glacier Peak Wilderness in Washington state. The Agriculture and Interior Departments announced their opposition, the Forest Service indicated that it would place tight restrictions on the mine and related activities, local opposition groups formed, and eventually the Washington congressional delegation withdrew its support. Kennecott soon capitulated, announcing in 1967 that it would not develop the deposit (Leshy, 1987).

The amount of public land made unavailable to mining rose appreciably over the next three decades. The 1964 Wilderness Act established 9 million acres of wilderness. By 1990, that figure had risen to nearly 100 million acres (although approximately 60 million acres of national park and national wildlife refuge lands were already closed to mining). In addition to this acreage, large areas of land were closed during the 1970s and 1980s for wilderness study. The Forest Service undertook two wilderness reviews (Roadless Area Review and Evaluation I and II [RARE I and RARE II]) in 1971 and 1977. While these studies were being conducted, and in the subsequent legislative efforts to designate lands, much of the land was managed as designated wilderness.

In 1976, FLPMA directed the BLM to begin a wilderness review of its lands, leading to the creation of millions of acres of more wilderness study areas. These BLM lands are under legislative review for wilderness designation, with nearly 7 million acres in the California desert alone being designated wilderness. Furthermore, in 1976 Congress passed legislation banning mining that had been allowed in six units of the national park system.

In addition to these Forest Service and BLM lands withdrawn for wilderness and wilderness review, hundreds of millions of acres of federal land in Alaska were withdrawn pending congressional determination of new national parks, wildlife refuges, and wilderness areas there. This led the mining industry to complain that it was being locked out of the public lands. At about the same time, the industry, and others, began to claim that the United States was facing a strategic minerals crisis due to import vulnerability, a crisis that could be resolved by opening up more of the public lands to mineral development.[7]

This decline of free access and concern over the supply of strategic minerals were the focal points in mining industry public lands political efforts from the mid-1970s through the 1980s. The amount of land removed from free access had increased from 17 percent in 1968 to between 34 percent and 42 percent in the mid-1970s. Additionally, access was severely restricted on 6 to 16 percent of the land. However, of those lands closed to mining, only one-third were closed for environmental and cultural reasons; the remainder were closed to create Indian reservations (53 million acres), military reservations (23 million acres), water and power projects (12.7 million acres), and the like. These different data were generated by different government reports, resulting in a lack of agreement on the amount of land actually exempted from mining activities. Industry sources cited the most restrictive figures; environmentalists cited the least restrictive figures (U.S. Office of Technology Assessment, 1979; Wilkinson, 1992).

Congress took up the issue of mineral vulnerability and access with vigor in the late 1970s and early 1980s. The House Interior Committee's Subcommittee on Mines and Mining, chaired by Representative Jim Santini of Nevada, was the center for action. In 1977, Santini delivered a letter to President Carter, signed by forty-two other representatives, advocating the development of a comprehensive minerals policy in the executive branch. The President ordered a major interagency review of nonfuel minerals policy, which was not well received by Santini's subcommittee in 1979.

The following year, the subcommittee printed a report on the policy implications of United States minerals vulnerability. Among its recommendations were the continuation of the Mining Law exemption in wilderness areas through the year 2000 and a general effort by the Interior Department to make more land open for mineral access. In October 1980, the National Materials and Minerals Policy, Research and Development Act was passed. It was not a document of much substance; rather, it was a general bill advocating a more coherent and coordinated minerals policy in the United States (Carter, 1977; U.S. Congress. House, 1980).

In late 1980, two major events affecting mining access to the public lands occurred: Ronald Reagan was elected president and the Alaska National Interest Lands Conservation Act became law. Reagan, along with the new Republican Senate (the Energy and Natural Resources Committee was chaired by James McClure of Idaho, a friend of mining), promised better times for mining interests. This is amply demonstrated in the words of the new interior secretary, James Watt: "We must allow the private sector the opportunity to explore the mineral potential on public lands. . . . We cannot have a healthy policy unless we have access to public lands." ANILCA permanently removed over 100 million acres from mining, but at least its passage temporarily resolved the public lands access issue in Alaska (New York Times, March 3, 1981).

Secretary Watt used his powers to open more land to the Mining Law and advocated allowing wilderness areas to remain open to the Mining Law through 2003. Furthermore, he claimed that the Wilderness Act not only allowed but mandated the development of minerals in wilderness areas. Because of strong opposition to his proposals, Watt altered his strategy in February 1982. On national television, he supported the withdrawal of all wilderness and wilderness study areas from the 1872 Mining Law through 2000, allowing only presidential exceptions. In the year 2000, the entire wilderness system would be reevaluated. Environmental groups attacked this proposal as antiwilderness due to the presidential loophole and the need to reauthorize all wilderness in 2000 (Shabecoff, 1982).

In April 1982, President Reagan submitted his minerals report and program to Congress (as directed by the Materials and Minerals Policy, Research and Development Act of 1980). One of the four major themes was the need for increased access to the public lands for mining, a policy that supported Watt's proposal. At hearings on the report, Watt testified that

> for various reasons, the Federal Government has refused proper access to our public lands owned by all the American people that could stimulate the industry and allow us to meet many of our strategic minerals and materials needs. . . . We think that if we are going to prepare for national defense, improve the quality of life in America, and enhance our environment as well as create jobs, we have got to change that, and we are in an aggressive manner doing that (U.S. Congress. Senate, 1982, 32).

Neither Watt's proposals nor the president's report led to the adoption of legislation, but the National Security Minerals Act became law in 1984. Like the National Materials and Minerals Policy, Research and Development Act, it had little substance. It created a National Critical Materials Council within the Executive Office of the President through 1990 to coordinate policy in this arena. More concretely, from 1980 to 1985 the BLM reclassified 200 million acres of public lands, opening approximately 30 million to the operation of the mining laws.

By 1985, the strategic minerals issue had begun to dissipate. The fears of resource cartels and a Soviet resource war lessened. Indeed, by the early 1990s the Soviet Union had collapsed and South Africa had begun a transition to majority rule. In addition, as more lands were designated wilderness, many of the areas closed to mining during the wilderness review process were released for potential mining. By 1996, approximately 400 million acres of public lands had been opened to hardrock mining.

In retrospect, the public lands component of the strategic minerals issue is best viewed as an economic issue rather than as a national security issue. The depressed mining industry saw the issue as a vehicle to gain increased access to the public lands, previously unavailable areas could hold new mineral sources that could help revive the industry. This interpretation is further supported by noting that the key congressional leaders involved in the effort to open more of the public lands, notably Santini (NV) and McClure (ID), were from mining states (Leshy, 1987).

Pollution and Land Degradation

Since its inception, mining has had environmental impact. Among its most significant effects in the United States have been the alteration of watercourses for placer mining, air pollution (especially from smelting), water pollution, land sub-

sidence, contamination of land with hazardous materials, and large-scale alteration of the landscape from hydraulic mining and the creation of large pit mines.
During the 1960s, all of these problems except hydraulic mining remained significant. As the environmental movement blossomed through the 1960s, attention
focused on the environmental problems related to mining activities (Smith, 1987).

Among the general environmental laws passed throughout the 1970s and
1980s, mining has been most affected by the Clean Air Act, the Clean Water Act,
and the Comprehensive Environmental Response, Compensation, and Liability
Act (the Superfund). The Clean Air Act treated mining no differently than other
industries in the country, and the act has had its greatest effect on smelter emissions and wind-blown hazardous dust from tailings piles (Leshy, 1987).

The biggest water pollution problem for mining has been acid drainage from
tailing piles. As water drains through rock waste dumps, it becomes acidic and
leaches minerals out of the crushed rock, which can lead to serious surface water
pollution (up to 10,000 stream miles have been contaminated by mining operations in the West) and the pollution of groundwater aquifers. This water pollution is addressed in two ways. Any current discharges of mine-processing waters
onto federal lands or into public waters requires a permit under the Clean Water
Act. This has helped decrease acid mine drainage by one-third since the early
1970s. The second approach focuses on hazardous waste laws, discussed later on
(Wilkinson, 1992; Egan, 1994a).

Another water-related mining effect is groundwater supply. In Nevada, for instance, the Barrick Goldstrike Mine has pumped out enough water to lower the
water table under its open pit by 1,200 feet in order to make it dry enough to
mine. A University of Nevada hydrologist has estimated that current mines in the
area will have created a 1 million acre-foot groundwater deficit by the time they
have shut down, though the mines and the state dispute this estimate. If such de-
watering occurs, it will have significant ramifications on ranching and other land
uses in the arid region (Thompson, 1994).

A July 1993 report by the Mineral Policy Center estimated that cleaning up
abandoned hardrock mines could cost $71.5 billion. There are approximately
558,000 abandoned mines, the vast majority of which pose no health or environmental threats. Those sites that do pose such threats, such as the fifty-two
mining sites on the Superfund national priority list (most in the West), could be
quite expensive to clean up. For example, in the San Juan Mountains of Colorado,
Galactic Resources, a Canadian company, went bankrupt, leaving a major toxic
waste and water pollution problem at its Summitville mine. This problem may
cost from $100 to $350 million to clean up (Egan, 1994a).

Thus far, the mining industry has been successful in preventing mine wastes
from being regulated as hazardous wastes under the Resource Conservation and
Recovery Act (RCRA). This is of great importance since the mining industry gen-
erates 30 billion tons of solid waste per year, second in the nation only to agriculture. This success, however, has led to greater reliance on the Superfund to deal

with mining waste problems. The contamination of water and soil by acid mine drainage—by heavy metals, arsenic, and mercury—can be a significant threat to public health and wildlife.

An increase in the number of Superfund sites is likely, both from old abandoned mines and from newer mines. The latter are often more technologically sophisticated than the older mines, and companies make a greater effort to control wastes better than they did in the past. Even so, newer mines are much larger and employ techniques that pose a threat to environmental quality. For example, gold mining typically employs cyanide leaching, meaning that cyanide is poured over large piles of ore, leaching out the gold. This results in cyanide runoff and a poisonous lake when the mining is done. In addition, using this new method requires mining four tons of rock to obtain one ounce of gold (Smith, 1987; Wilkinson, 1992).

An example of the complexities of dealing with mining and pollution is Kennecott's open-pit copper mine in Bingham Canyon, Utah. Contamination around this site began one hundred and thirty years ago and continues to the present. The EPA had planned to put the area on its Superfund national priorities list, which would have meant the agency would have been in charge of the cleanup. Kennecott, however, has sought to maintain control and direct the cleanup itself, to serve as a model of environmentally sensitive mining. The company has estimated the cleanup will cost $200 million. Perhaps the chief reason Kennecott wants to maintain control is because there is still a great deal of wealth to be had from the mine, and the company would prefer to operate without EPA interference. Kennecott had spent $85 million by 1993 and spent another $80 million in 1994 alone. This money is intended for cleaning up problem areas, building a state-of-the-art facility to hold and monitor the acid leach-water, and reclaiming land with new soil and new plants.

The EPA and Kennecott differ most strongly on cleaning up the contaminated groundwater. The EPA plan would cost $2.2 billion. Kennecott's plan, relying on the rocks in the ground to do much of the cleaning, would only cost $102 million. Negotiations between the EPA and Kennecott are proceeding, but the EPA remains skeptical. The agency's regional director of hazardous waste management has said, "One has to look very closely at this so-called voluntary cleanup. It wasn't until we started the process of listing [for Superfund] that the cleanup work was started." Kennecott has countered by stating that it "has already spent more on cleanup than has ever been spent on a mining superfund site." As of 1996, it is unclear whether an agreement will be made or the site will be put on the Superfund list (Christensen, 1994b).

The 1970s also generated a push for mining regulation based on federal land management authority. Although some have argued that the 1872 Mining Law granted the federal government wide-ranging regulatory authority over mining, the government has been hesitant to make use of this ambiguous authority. The ambiguity was cleared by FLPMA in 1976, which required the secretary of the interior to "prevent unnecessary or undue degradation of the lands" under the 1872 Mining Law. Forest Service authority to regulate surface activities related to mining can be traced back to the 1897 Organic Act and to the agency's first set of regulations in 1912. Both agencies adopted new regulations, the BLM in 1981 and the Forest Service in 1974.

Generally, the regulations require notification before undertaking activities that could disrupt the surface. If the disruption is significant, a plan of operations must be filed, reclamation (and a bond) may be required, and general environmental standards must be met. The regulations have no provisions for fines or penalties. Enforcement of the regulations by both agencies thus far has been weak and inconsistent. The best way to protect land from environmental damage due to mining is still to withdraw the land from the provisions of the 1872 Mining Law (Leshy, 1987; Wilkinson, 1992).[8]

Since the BLM and the Forest Service adopted mining regulations, the National Environmental Policy Act has been deemed applicable to mining law operations on federal lands. Agencies have sometimes avoided environmental impact statements by ruling that mining actions do not have a significant effect on the environment. In addition, NEPA does not apply if a patent has been applied for, since the government does not have discretion on this point, though related actions (e.g., road building for access, acquisition of land for waste disposal) may require an EIS (Leshy, 1987).

The final arena of mining regulation is the states. Since its enactment, the 1872 Mining Law has recognized the authority of the states to regulate hardrock mining. Over the last one hundred years, hundreds of state laws have been passed dealing with location, maintenance, and operation of mining claims on federal lands. More recently, some states have used their regulatory authority for environmental concerns. Such environmental regulation varies greatly from state to state, however (Leshy, 1987).

In conclusion, there are a variety of laws in place to deal with the variety of environmental effects related to mining. Laws dealing with air, land, and water pollution are the most firmly established and have had the greatest effect. The current legal and regulatory framework established under the 1872 Mining Law is less effective when the overall benefits and costs related to mining operations and general land use planning are considered. Open-pit mines and leach mining create massive changes in the landscape, problems that are difficult to address under the current system.

Other laws, such as the Endangered Species Act, may have significant effects on mining. They have often made hardrock mining on the public lands more expensive, further hurting the economic condition of the domestic mining industry. These laws, together with the withdrawal of lands from mining, have greatly contributed to the erosion of the free access philosophy that underlay the 1872 Mining Law. In general, the mineral industry has become more conscientious about its activities because of the enactment of environmental laws in the 1970s and 1980s and the corresponding rise in public support for environmental protection. Nevertheless, the political battle over specific environmental regulations contained within mining reform proposals continues, as the recent failure of the congressional conference committee shows (Leshy, 1987).

Reform of the Mining Law

Efforts to reform the Mining Law of 1872 began less than ten years after its passage, with the first Public Lands Commission in 1879–1880. Such reform efforts have continued up to the present, growing most serious in the 1970s. The first major recent push for reform came as a result of a study conducted by the Public Land Law Review Commission. The study, which began in 1964, considered a host of options for reforming the 1872 Mining Law, ranging from a leasing system to a return to a true free-access system. The final report proposed modifications of the existing policy, but this recommendation did not reflect a consensus within the PLLRC or the nation.

Through the mid-1970s, Congress considered bills based on the PLLRC proposal as well as a leasing system. The chance for passage of a leasing bill seemed best after the election of Jimmy Carter, who supported such an approach. In addition, Henry Jackson, chair of the Senate Energy and Natural Resources Committee, also supported leasing. The efforts came to an end when one-time leasing supporter Morris Udall (AZ), chair of the House Interior and Insular Affairs Committee, announced that he now opposed the leasing plan because of the economic difficulties the mining industry was experiencing. It should also be noted that for the first time, environmental concerns entered into the debate over mining law reform (Leshy, 1987).

Reform moved to the back burner with the rise of the strategic minerals issue in the late 1970s and the election of Ronald Reagan in 1980. During this period, three general mining laws were passed, each seeking to make mining policy more coherent and to stimulate the industry. These laws—the Mining and Minerals Policy Act of 1970; the National Materials and Minerals Policy, Research and Development Act of 1980; and the National Critical Materials Act of 1984—were chiefly symbolic and had little significant effect on mining policy.

Congress returned to the reform effort in 1987. In 1990, the House included a one-year moratorium on the granting of mining patents on federal lands as part of its fiscal year 1991 interior appropriations bill. The Senate had considered such a proposal, but it was defeated in a 48–50 vote. The moratorium was dropped in conference after this Senate opposition. The same pattern was repeated the next year: The House passed a moratorium on patenting in the appropriations bill, the Senate rejected such a moratorium (46–47), and the moratorium was dropped in conference. This time, however, all parties agreed that reform of the 1872 Mining Law would be seriously considered the next year in the relevant committees (Congressional Quarterly, 1990, 1991).

A reform bill did make it out of the House Interior and Insular Affairs Committee in 1992, but Congress adjourned before the bill could be fully debated and voted on. The main provisions of the bill were an 8 percent royalty on hardrock mineral receipts, an end to patenting of land (i.e., the government would maintain ownership), a $25 per acre annual rental fee for claims, a directive to the BLM and Forest Service to review their lands and withdraw lands not suitable for mining, and the creation of an abandoned mine reclamation fund. A similar reform bill was not voted out of the Senate Energy and Natural Resources Committee, so serious reform failed again.

Minor reform occurred, however, through the interior appropriations bill. Senator Harry Reid (D-NV) offered a proposal in amendment form that was approved by the Senate. It required miners to pay fair market value for land they wished to patent, called for land to revert to the government if it was not mined, and mandated strict compliance with environmental and reclamation laws. This reform package was dropped in conference because opponents thought the reforms were not significant enough and would hurt the chances of enacting legislation containing more significant reforms. A provision that was accepted by conferees and became part of the law was a new annual $100 fee that miners would pay to keep their claims active. This replaced the requirement that $100 worth of mining work had to be done to keep a claim active, a practice that often scarred the land for no real purpose (Congressional Quarterly, 1992).

In early 1993, the Clinton administration attempted to reform the 1872 Mining Law through the budget process, by including a 12.5 percent royalty on hardrock minerals in its budget proposal. Clinton dropped the proposal, along with efforts to increase grazing fees and eliminate below-cost timber harvests, in the face of strong pressure from western members of Congress. As described in the chapter introduction here, reform measures passed both the House and Senate in 1993 but died in conference in September 1994 (Congressional Quarterly, 1993).

Throughout these efforts to reform the Mining Law, the mining industry and its supporters advanced the same set of arguments. From their perspective, with the imposition of a significant royalty, substantial limitation to free access, and the institution of environmental regulations, the costs of mining in the United States would increase, potentially causing major problems in the mining industry. These problems could lead to the closure of mines and the potential loss of thousands of jobs. Western politicians added the symbolic argument that any such reform was an attack on the small prospector and the character of the West generally. For instance, a recent study done for the mining industry argued that an 8 percent royalty (as proposed by the House) would lead to the loss of approximately 7,000 jobs in Nevada alone (Congressional Quarterly, 1993).

Conclusion

Efforts to reform the 1872 Mining Law will continue, and as the failure of such reform in 1994 demonstrates, reform will be difficult. A number of factors are responsible. First and foremost is the institutionalized idea of economic liberalism and the privatized policy pattern that it spawned. The mining policy realm has been based on this idea for over one hundred and twenty years; shifting that idea, and shifting foundations, will be difficult indeed. A second and related problem is that the industry has significant political power, which it can use to block reform. The third problem is that of property rights: How will existing valid claims be dealt with? Will claim holders be compensated? If so, where will the money come from? If not, there will be great conflict over the violation of rights. A fourth concern is that any major reform will disrupt the already fragile mining industry. This may have effects on local communities, which often rely on mining for jobs and taxes. A final factor frequently mentioned is the contention that changes will hurt the small independent miner. Although many analysts conclude that the small prospector plays a negligible role in U.S. mining today, supporters of the 1872 Mining Law use the prospector for symbolic reasons. They view mining reform—and other public land reforms—as part of a war on the West. In speaking against the latest reform effort, Senator Alan Simpson of Wyoming claimed: "This is not about money. We are defending our Western heritage." All of these factors making reform difficult are exacerbated by the fact that mining interests are fighting a defensive battle. And those seeking to prevent change almost always have the upper hand in American politics (Egan, 1994a; Leshy, 1987).

Despite these difficulties, the 1872 Mining Law needs to be reformed. A Republican Congress, however, makes this reform less likely in the near future. Although reform efforts collapsed in the fall of 1994, progress was made. The House, especially, has strongly supported such reform. As discussed earlier, the rise of environmentalism and the shifting demographics and economics of the West suggest a shifting context for mining policy, a context that favors reform.

The 1872 Mining Law also has a number of serious shortcomings that need to be addressed. It does not deal with environmental issues. This gap is becoming more noticeable as cyanide leachate mining continues to expand. Also of concern to environmentalists are the thousands of unpatented claims in national parks and wilderness areas and the abuse of the law when vacation homes are established on public lands. The current system cannot address certain problems such as some large-scale development (due to size limits on claims), the nuisance of small prospector claims (often made for speculative reasons), and the lack of pre-discovery protection under the law.

With the resurgence of gold mining, more attention will be focused on the lack of royalties the public receives for resources on its lands. In the 1990s, it is estimated that $4 billion per year of hardrock minerals is extracted from public lands, with no royalty or lease fee, and that companies are trying to patent federal land holding $34 billion worth of minerals (Egan, 1994a; Wilkinson, 1992).

In addition, the changes that have occurred over the last thirty years will strongly shape reform efforts. The most important social trends have been the near doubling of the population in the West and the dramatic increase in urbanization accompanying it, the growth of tourist and second-home meccas, and the rise of environmentalism, both in general and within the region. There has also been a relative decline in the economic importance of the mineral industry within the West and a rise in economic activities relying on increased environmental protection. Finally, in the political realm, environmental groups have opened the mining policy subsystem, and countermovements to environmentalism have risen under the guise of the Wise Use Movement. Generally speaking, these trends favor the forces of reform.

Thus, it seems reform will come, but when? As George Julian, a chief congressional opponent of the 1866 Mining Law wrote in 1883, the "misfortune of this legislation is heightened by the probability of its continuance; for it is not easy to uproot a body of laws once accepted by a people, however mischievous their character. . . . [This] wretched travesty [of a law may be] permanently engrafted upon half a continent." Thus far, Julian has been right, at least regarding the longevity of the 1872 Mining Law (Leshy, 1987).

NOTES

1. These minerals bring in substantial revenues in certain places. For instance, in fiscal year 1984, the federal government collected royalties of over $2 million from lead mines and $1.5 million from zinc mines in Missouri.

2. There is some fragmentation in the legislative branch, though. For example, four committees in the House—Armed Services; Banking, Finance, and Urban Affairs; Interior and Insular Affairs; and Science and Technology—held hearings or produced reports on the strategic minerals issue. The latter two committees appeared to play a coequal role in developing legislation. In the Senate, jurisdiction over the issue was shared by the Committee on Commerce, Science, and Technology and the Committee on Energy and Natural Resources.

3. The West is defined to include thirteen states: Alaska, Arizona, California, Colorado, Hawaii, Idaho, Montana, Nevada, New Mexico, Oregon, Utah, Washington, and Wyoming.

4. The employment figures for nonfuel mining include those industries involved in mining many minerals that were not mined under the 1872 Mining Law, such as stone, sand and gravel, and phosphate rock. In some states, these industries employ the bulk of miners. Mineral production figures were obtained from the U.S. Bureau of Mines, 1961, and were compiled from tables on state mineral production and from the U.S. Bureau of Mines, 1992. As with employment, nonfuel minerals include the minerals just mentioned, which generate much more value than hardrock minerals in some states.

5. Current valid claims cover roughly 25 million acres. Since the 1870s, 65,000 patents have been issued, covering 3.2 million acres. Cumulative claims are all claims received since 1976, when FLPMA required claims to be submitted to the BLM. "Existing valid claims" is defined as cumulative claims minus claims rejected, abandoned, or patented since they were filed.

6. In general, radical environmentalism has not played a major role in mining policy. Although firmly in favor of drastic reforms to hardrock mining law, radical groups have focused their attention on endangered species and wilderness protection, which has en-

tailed more frequent clashes over forestry, grazing, and certain types of recreation (e.g., off-road recreational vehicles, or ORVs).

7. The minerals considered strategic included chromium, cobalt, columbium, manganese, nickel, and the platinum-group metals.

8. In fiscal year 1984, the BLM reviewed 523 mining operation plans (plans that are submitted to the BLM for operations in areas under wilderness review or in any area in which disturbance exceeds 5 acres during the year), and in fiscal year 1991, the agency reviewed 445 such plans (U.S. Department of the Interior, Bureau of Land Management, 1985, 151; U.S. Department of the Interior, Bureau of Land Management, 1992, 93). One estimate has suggested that reclaiming the mining landscape would cost $11 billion.

REFERENCES

Allin, Craig W. 1982. *The Politics of Wilderness Preservation*. Westport, CT: Greenwood Press.

Anderson, Evan W. 1988. *The Structure and Dynamics of U.S. Government Policymaking: The Case of Strategic Minerals*. New York: Praeger.

Baker, Richard A. 1985. "The Conservation Congress of Anderson and Aspinall, 1963–1964." *Journal of Forest History* 29:104–119.

Barone, Michael, and Grant Ujifusa. 1983. *The Almanac of American Politics, 1984*. Washington, DC: National Journal.

_____. 1993. *The Almanac of American Politics, 1994*. Washington, DC: National Journal.

Barone, Michael, Grant Ujifusa, and Douglas Matthews. 1974. *The Almanac of American Politics, 1974*. Boston: Gambit.

Benenson, Bob. 1993. "House Easily Passes Overhaul of the 1872 Mining Law." *CQ Weekly Report* 51:3191–3192.

Brownridge, Dennis. 1989. "The Rural West Is Actually Very Urban." In Ed Marston, ed., *Reopening the Western Frontier*. Washington, DC: Island Press.

Carter, Luther. 1977. "Minerals and Mining: Major Review of Federal Policy Is in Prospect." *Science* 198 (November 25):809–811.

Cawley, R. MacGreggor. 1993. *Federal Land, Western Anger: The Sagebrush Rebellion and Environmental Politics*. Lawrence: University Press of Kansas.

Christensen, John. 1994a. "Babbitt Attacks Mining's Gold Heists." *High Country News*, May 30.

_____. 1994b. "Can a Copper Firm Restore a Blasted Ecosystem?" *High Country News*, May 30.

Congressional Quarterly. 1965. *CQ Almanac, 1964*. Washington, DC: Congressional Quarterly.

_____. 1990. "Art, Owls, Oil Drilling Argued in Interior Bill." *CQ Almanac, 1989*. Washington, DC: Congressional Quarterly.

_____. 1991. "Moratorium on Mining Claims Defeated." *CQ Almanac, 1990*. Washington, DC: Congressional Quarterly.

_____. 1992. "Mining Law Reform Is Stymied Again." *CQ Almanac, 1991*. Washington, DC: Congressional Quarterly.

_____. 1993. "Overhaul of Mining Law Advances." *CQ Almanac, 1992*. Washington, DC: Congressional Quarterly.

Deal, Carl. 1993. *The Greenpeace Guide to Anti-Environmental Organizations*. Berkeley: Odonian Press.

Dunlap, Riley, and Angela G. Mertig, eds. 1992. *American Environmentalism: The U.S. Environmental Movement, 1970–1990*. Philadelphia: Taylor and Francis.

Egan, Timothy. 1994a. "New Gold Rush Stirs Fears of Exploitation." *New York Times*, August 14.

_____. 1994b. "New Feud on the Range: Cowman vs. Tourist," *New York Times*, September 18.

Ellison, Joseph. 1963. "The Mineral Land Question in California, 1848–1866." In Vernon Carstensen, ed., *The Public Lands*. Madison: University of Wisconsin Press.

Farling, Bruce. 1989. "Butte Comes out of the Pit." In Ed Marston, ed., *Reopening the Western Frontier*. Washington, DC: Island Press.

Graf, William L. 1990. *Wilderness Preservation and the Sagebrush Rebellion*. Savage, MD: Rowman and Littlefield.

Leshy, John. 1987. *The Mining Law: A Study in Perpetual Motion*. Baltimore: Johns Hopkins University Press.

Marston, Ed, ed. 1989. *Reopening the Western Frontier*. Washington, DC: Island Press.

National Archives and Records Administration. 1993. *U.S. Government Manual 1993/1994*. Washington, DC: Government Printing Office.

Sale, Kirkpatrick. 1993. *The Green Revolution*. New York: Hill and Wang.

Shabecoff, Phillip. 1982. "Bill Would Bar Wilds Drilling," *New York Times*, February 25.

Skowronek, Stephen. 1982. *Building a New American State: The Expansion of National Administrative Capacities, 1877–1920*. New York: Cambridge University Press.

Smith, Duane. 1987. *Mining America: The Industry and the Environment, 1800–1980*. Lawrence: University Press of Kansas.

Swenson, Robert W. 1968. "Legal Aspects of Mineral Resource Exploitation." In Paul W. Gates, *History of Public Land Law Development*. Washington, DC: Government Printing Office.

Thompson, Ernie. 1994. "Gold Mines Are Sucking Aquifers Dry." *High Country News*, June 13.

U.S. Bureau of the Census. 1964. *Statistical Abstract of the United States: 1964*. Washington, DC: Government Printing Office.

_____. 1993. *Statistical Abstract of the United States: 1993*. Washington, DC: Government Printing Office.

U.S. Bureau of Mines. 1961. *Minerals Yearbook, 1960*. Washington, DC: Government Printing Office.

_____. 1992. *Minerals Yearbook, 1990*. Washington, DC: Government Printing Office.

U.S. Congress. House. 1980. Committee on Interior and Insular Affairs. *Report on U.S. Minerals Vulnerability: National Policy Implications*. Washington, DC: Government Printing Office.

U.S. Congress. Senate. 1982. Committee on Energy and Natural Resources. *Hearing on the President's National Materials and Minerals Program and Report to Congress*. Washington, DC: Government Printing Office.

U.S. Department of the Interior, Bureau of Land Management. 1965. *Public Land Statistics, 1964*. Washington, DC: Government Printing Office.

_____. 1975. *Public Land Statistics, 1974*. Washington, DC: Government Printing Office.

_____. 1985. *Public Land Statistics, 1984.* Washington, DC: Government Printing Office.
_____. 1992. *Public Land Statistics, 1991.* Washington, DC: Government Printing Office.
U.S. Office of Technology Assessment. 1979. *Management of Fuel and Nonfuel Minerals in Federal Land: Current Status and Issues.* Washington, DC: Government Printing Office.
Voynick, Stephen. 1989. "Bust Trounces a Once Tough Town." In Ed Marston, ed., *Reopening the Western Frontier.* Washington, DC: Island Press.
Wilkinson, Charles F. 1992. *Crossing the Next Meridian.* Washington, DC: Island Press.

7

Energy on Federal Lands

DAVID HOWARD DAVIS

During the 1970s and early 1980s, the most dynamic and controversial issue with respect to federal lands was energy. Americans debated, even fought, over the topic in Washington, in western state capitals, and literally in the field. They disputed drilling for oil on the North Slope of Alaska, access to national parks, how to manage strip mining, the correct price for coal, whether ownership should be private, cleaning up plutonium, and tearing down hydroelectric dams. In the 1970s, the driving force was the so-called energy crisis, and during the early 1980s, it was the Reagan Revolution. Since then, the pendulum has swung the other way; the debate on energy is quiescent, most of the issues having been resolved for the present.

Four factors may explain the evolution of energy policy on federal lands: (1) interest groups, (2) political partisanship, (3) bureaucratic routines, and (4) economics. The first, a favorite of political scientists for forty years and perhaps since as far back as *Federalist No. 10* in 1787, focuses on the clash of interest groups. In this case, the conflict almost always divides into the environmentalists versus business. The polarization between these groups characterized the Environmental Decade of the 1970s and has continued into the 1990s. Most generally, greater prosperity, leisure time, and educational levels in the post–World War II boom enticed millions of Americans to venture beyond mere materialism and try camping, hiking, traveling, and just contemplating nature. The boom also pumped out the millions of tons of soot, pesticides, and ozone that prompted people to worry about pollution. Widespread popular attention broke down the tight subgovernments between federal agencies, congressional committees, and industries. In the National Environmental Policy Act, the Clean Air Act, and the Clean Water Act, Congress included avenues for the public to participate in decisionmaking.

Another common form of interest group behavior is found in the "NIMBY" (not in my back yard) syndrome. The typical scenario occurs when a company wants to establish a toxic dump, a municipality wants to start a landfill, or a utility wants to build an electric generating plant. Threatened by this disturbance, neighbors rally in opposition. The rhetoric employed concerns saving the natural environment; underneath, the objective is to keep the facility out of their own locality. In an opportunistic fashion, the neighbors link the threat to broad values, but behind most clashes is a more parochial concern. The remoteness of most federal lands means the NIMBY syndrome is less common in such issues than in other environmental disputes, with the notable exception of efforts to site high-level nuclear waste repositories.

The second factor, political partisanship, is another old favorite of political scientists. In its most simple form, it maintains that Republicans favor business, industry, and ranchers more than Democrats do. For example, President Eisenhower's secretary of the interior, Douglas McKay, was known as "Give Away McKay" for his eagerness to dispose of federal land, and he offers a rather vivid contrast to interior secretaries with strong environmental values such as Stewart Udall, who served Democratic Presidents Kennedy and Johnson.

However, partisanship is more complex. Basic partisanship is filtered differently by different presidential administrations. The Republican administrations of Richard Nixon and Ronald Reagan took very different tacks from a philosophical perspective. Although Nixon won election in 1968 on a conservative southern strategy, his private beliefs within the environmental policy arena were more moderate. Reagan, however, viewed environmental programs as an unwanted extension of the regulatory state. In like fashion, partisan differences can be found within Congress. For example, western Democrats are more likely to oppose restrictions on developmental activities on public lands than are Democrats in other regions.

The third factor, bureaucratic routines, means (in its narrower scope) that the Bureau of Land Management, the Forest Service, and other agencies follow established procedures and jurisdictions, much as Max Weber described seventy-five years ago. The negative side of this is that bureaus may overconform and be too rigid in making policy decisions. In its broader sense, bureaucratic routines mean the desire of the national government to plan and to maintain control, even when it shares jurisdiction with states or Indian tribes.

Although Washington's yearning to plan has lessened since the glory days of the New Deal and the World War II mobilization, the desire to plan remains a strong force. Many in the West bridle at the arrogance of "the Feds." The desire of federal bureaus to maintain control in delegated programs should not be blamed entirely on them, but should also rest on Congress, which, during the Environmental Decade of the 1970s, passed many laws like the Clean Air Act, the Clean Water Act, and the Surface Mining Control and Reclamation Act, acts that explicitly required Washington-based officials to make the big decisions and the state governments to implement them. The specificity and length of environmental laws (often 100–300 pages) lead to agency decisions that are overly legalistic.

The fourth factor is the impact of the national and international economy. Prior to the 1970s, energy development on the western public lands was less pronounced, largely because U.S. energy producers had an ample supply of fuel from both domestic and international sources. But things began to change in the early 1970s because of decisions made by political leaders in the Middle East. When the Organization of Petroleum Exporting Countries (OPEC) imposed a sixfold price rise for crude oil in 1973 and doubled it again in 1979, demand escalated for oil produced within the United States. Furthermore, the Arab core of OPEC announced it would boycott the United States because of its support for Israel during the Yom Kippur War.

The pressure to develop energy resources from the federal lands was immense. Energy producers were particularly interested in drilling in national forests and rangelands for more oil, but they also saw opportunities to extract more coal and natural gas from known reserves. For a few years, it also appeared that oil shale deposits in Colorado and Wyoming might be profitably mined despite adverse environmental impacts.

In short, understanding energy policy changes since 1970 differs from studying other policy areas because of the disproportionate impact of international events on policy decisions, above and beyond the influence of more common factors such as partisanship, interest group actions, and bureaucratic routines. Consequently, it is appropriate to begin the analysis in the early 1970s, with actions taken by the Nixon administration to resolve energy supply problems in the United States.

The Nixon Administration Confronts the "Energy Crisis"

The 1973 debate over building the Trans-Alaska Pipeline was a turning point for both the environmental movement and energy. The 1968 discovery by Arco of a superfield of oil on the North Slope seemed like a godsend in view of the declining supplies in the lower forty-eight states and the uncertain politics of the Middle East. The technical problems of building a pipeline eight hundred miles across the Arctic tundra and mountains could be solved, albeit at a high cost.

Eight oil companies—Arco, Sohio, British Petroleum (BP), Humble (now Exxon), Mobil, Phillips, Union, and Ameranda Hess—joined to build the pipeline to the port of Valdez, whence tankers would take it to the west coast. At first, they persuaded the U.S. Department of the Interior (DOI) to give them a right-of-way over the federal land, arguing that the government had such authority under the 1920 Mineral Leasing Act. When they realized that this was not possible because of insufficient statutory authority, they banded together to urge Congress to pass a special law. Joined by the chief industry association, the American Petroleum Institute, the oil companies collectively lobbied Congress (Berry, 1975).

Environmentalists feared that building the pipeline would ruin the state's delicate ecological balance. Because the ground was permanently frozen and the crude oil was hot when it flowed out of the well, the pipeline had to be raised above the ground. The environmentalists sued in court, arguing that the DOI could not give permission to drill without violating the National Environmental Policy Act (a law passed in reaction to environmental damage from leaks and fires from federal leases in the Santa Barbara Channel in 1968). Meanwhile, thousands of pipes sat rusting in the Arctic cold.

Members of Congress who favored the industry introduced a bill authorizing construction, which declared in the legislation itself that the pipeline met the criteria of NEPA. This was an evasion of the National Environmental Policy Act. Six environmental groups opposed to the pipeline assembled in Washington to coordinate their fight, agreeing for the first time to work cooperatively. The Environmental Defense Fund took the lead, with the Wilderness Society, the Friends of the Earth, the Sierra Club, and the Audubon Society following. This teamwork set the pattern for many future coordinated lobbying projects.

The outcome of this legislative battle was the enactment of the Federal Land Right-of-Way Act, which accommodated the interests of both industry and environmentalists. The new law allowed construction to go forward, but the pipeline had additional valves and alarms to minimize the chance of a leak. It was elevated to allow the caribou to walk under it during their migration. The pipeline conflict turned out to be merely the first of many between the energy companies and the environmentalists.

The 1973 crisis in oil supply did not come as a total surprise to those in the industry. The National Petroleum Council, a DOI-sponsored group of one hundred and twenty-five industry advisers, forecast the looming shortages in its report, *US Energy Outlook,* dated December 1972. Consumer and environmental groups considered members of the council to be industry lackeys with a privileged inside track on information. The report recommended that companies be given easier access to leases on federal lands, along with access to offshore fields, and that the import quota in effect since 1959 be continued. Rejecting the advice on imports, President Nixon ended the quotas in April. With his broader understanding of the global economy, he recognized that domestic production could not increase enough to meet the demand.

Petroleum prices, which had been controlled under the president's New Economic Policy of 1971, climbed sharply once controls were relaxed. In June 1973, the president decreed a sixty-day freeze on prices, specifically singling out gasoline. Nixon seemed oblivious to the irony of a Republican president regulating prices. The National Petroleum Council, composed primarily of experts from domestic companies, could not bring itself to recognize the full implications of the trends, but Nixon recognized the cross-pressures of inflation and having oil supplies available.

The mild recommendations of the council report looked paltry in October, when, following the Yom Kippur War between Israel and the Arabs, the Arab oil producers announced a boycott of oil purchases by the United States and the

Netherlands. The result was a general price rise that immediately doubled the cost of oil. Although the Arabs had embargoed oil exports, American importers like Exxon and Chevron were able to reroute tankers from non-Arab countries like Venezuela, Iran, and Indonesia as replacements. Arab oil could go to Europe and Japan. The result was that American imports fell only one-third for a four-month period. Since imports then made up about one-third of American consumption, the net effect was a decline of about 11 percent for those months.

Price was a greater problem. After doubling the price in October, OPEC continued to increase the price until, within a year, a barrel of oil cost six times as much. Suddenly, domestic oil was more valuable than before. The remnants of Nixon's price control played havoc with production, rewarding many small producers. A well pumping only thirty barrels a day was once more profitable.

Even though Nixon had abandoned nearly all the price controls of the New Economic Policy, he maintained them on petroleum under the rationale that this fuel was too important to leave to the free market. The idea was that if a well was already in production, its owners did not need any more incentive. Permitting price raises for oil from existing wells would create a windfall profit. Congress validated this in the 1973 Emergency Petroleum Allocation Act. In order not to discourage new drilling, the law restricted prices only on existing wells; new wells could charge whatever the market would pay, which was approximately $12 per barrel. For a few months, the possibility of high profits stimulated a land rush.

Thus, energy policy was elevated to the national policy agenda thanks to a gradual downturn in U.S. oil reserves, coupled with the emergence of the OPEC cartel and efforts of member nations to restrict supply and raise prices. Recognizing the vulnerability of the United States in this scenario, President Nixon took the initiative to propose a larger role for the federal government in meeting domestic energy needs.

The Ford Administration: Absent-Minded Central Planning

When Nixon resigned in August 1974 because of the Watergate scandal, the country lost a sophisticated president who understood both the OPEC strategy and domestic inflation and whose pragmatism could combine free market forces with price controls. The new president, Gerald Ford, took a simpler view and depended more on his advisers. The temporary White House task force, now formalized as the Federal Energy Administration, preferred to abandon the hybrid of controlling old oil but not new oil. The Democrats, who controlled both houses of Congress, did not like the hybrid, either. The Ford administration and Congress agreed that the government should control the price of new oil so that the average would be $7.66, a level too low to stimulate drilling. The president did have a loophole; he could raise the price 10 percent a month to compensate for inflation.

Simultaneously, the Ford administration was pushing ahead with Project Independence and its institutional companion, the Energy Independence

Authority. This planning initiative, which was directed by Vice President Nelson Rockefeller and was reminiscent of Franklin Roosevelt's New Deal, proposed that the United States become independent of petroleum imports by 1985 and soon thereafter begin exporting oil to Japan.

Key components of Project Independence included manufacturing synthetic gasoline from coal and shale and secondary and tertiary recovery of abandoned oil and gas wells. The feedstock and crude oil were to come primarily from federal lands. This emphasis on national planning and a large federal role was unprecedented for a Republican administration. Many Republicans blamed the shift on Rockefeller, but in fact, this proposal was a logical extension of efforts to craft a pragmatic response to changing international conditions that originated with President Nixon.

While members of President Ford's White House and Federal Energy Administration were thinking the big thoughts about oil, Department of the Interior officials were thinking the little thoughts about coal on federal lands. The 1973 "energy crisis" demonstrated that demand for coal would increase, perhaps as feedstock for synthetics, but definitely as a fuel source for factories and the production of electricity. The largest source of coal reserves for additional mining was found on federal lands in the West. The Clean Air Act of 1970 provided a further impetus for the development of western coal, nearly all of which was low in sulfur (sulfur oxide is a pollutant that is regulated under the Clean Air Act). Thus, power plants and other large industrial users could burn western coal without producing as much air pollution as the high-sulfur Illinois Basin coal.

When the DOI began planning for leasing coal lands in 1973, western production amounted to one-tenth of the national output. Of that, federal coal amounted to 15 percent, for a total contribution of less than 2 percent. It was apparent to the DOI that additional production would come disproportionately from the west and that many of the new mines would be located on federal lands. In the period from 1945 to 1970, Bureau of Land Management leases of coal had been issued on an ad hoc basis. The bureau had no comprehensive strategy, merely responding to specific requests under the Mineral Leasing Act of 1920. Production from federal lands actually decreased from a high of 10 million tons to 7 million tons annually (GAO, 1983).

In 1970, in view of the low production and new environmental requirements, the DOI placed a temporary moratorium on leasing to develop a new plan. The Interior Department announced its new coal leasing program in 1973, issued the draft environmental impact statement in May 1974, and promulgated the final EIS in September 1975. The Natural Resources Defense Council sued to block the new program on the basis that the EIS was inadequate. The court agreed and enjoined the DOI from issuing leases other than to continue existing mining. Once more, a leasing moratorium was in effect.

In the meantime, Congress passed two laws in 1976 that affected energy from federal lands: the Federal Coal Leasing Amendments Act (FCLAA) and the

Federal Land Policy and Management Act. The FCLAA substantially amended the 1920 Mineral Leasing Act to provide for systematic study of reserves and the integration of resource use with comprehensive land use planning. Mining companies could no longer prospect and receive rights automatically; leasing was to be competitive.

Royalties switched from twenty cents per ton to a percentage of the value of the coal, the minimum being 12.5 percent. Previously, a lease had run indefinitely; now it was to run twenty years before adjustment, with further adjustments every ten years. The Department of the Interior was to determine a fair market price to guide competitive bidding. If the mining occurred through stripping or was located in a national forest, the governor of the state needed to approve the lease.

FLPMA was far more comprehensive, extending to all uses of federal land, that is, the law was not confined to the development of coal or energy resources. The DOI was required to prepare plans for 488 million acres, weighing future and present uses, long-term and short-term benefits, coordinating with other federal and state agencies, and protecting the environment. The law gave the states 50 percent of the revenues of the sales, bonuses, royalties, and rentals. In addition, the DOI was required to review all roadless areas to identify tracts possessing wilderness characteristics and to recommend which of these should be preserved permanently. Many of these areas contained coal, oil, and natural gas deposits.

Although much of energy policymaking under Ford was a continuation of decisions initiated during the Nixon years, other sources of political influence could be identified through actions taken within the DOI and by Congress. DOI officials demonstrated the importance of organizational routines as well as the absence of direct presidential involvement in planning for the development of coal, oil, and gas resources on the federal lands. And the enactment of FCLAA and FLPMA provides a good example of pluralistic politics, with statutory provisions containing benefits for both energy companies and environmentalists.

Carter Administration Reforms and Changes

In the 1976 presidential campaign, Jimmy Carter promised a comprehensive energy plan within ninety days of his inauguration. Upon taking office, he followed through by supporting the creation of the Department of Energy (DOE) under the Department of Energy Organization Act of 1977. Subsequent efforts by the Carter administration within the energy policy arena led to the enactment of the 1978 National Energy Act and the Synthetic Fuels Act of 1980.

Energy policy changes during the late 1970s reflected, in part, the continuing interplay between international events and the world price of oil, a relationship that influences production decisions on coal as well as oil and gas. President Carter communicated the urgency of the issue in a television speech in which he elevated the need for a reliable energy supply to the "moral equivalent of war."

How then can Carter's energy initiatives be understood within the context of the western public lands?

On occasion, Carter made decisions with Congress and others that resulted in policies that placed energy needs above ecological concerns. Perhaps the best example was his support of the Synthetic Fuels Act of 1980. This law, which folded in five synfuel projects originally authorized in 1978, offered sizable government subsidies to industry for the extraction and production of oil from geological sites that had been considered too risky for private sector initiatives. For the most part, these sites were located on federal lands and included projects such as shale oil development in Colorado, coal gasification in North Dakota, and coal liquefaction in West Virginia, among others. The stated policy objective was to encourage the development of domestic fuels, but these projects were eventually to flounder because of unacceptable economic and environmental costs.

In general, however, Carter was more sensitive to the environmental impact of energy development on public lands than either Nixon or Ford had been. Although he sought to increase the production of domestic energy resources such as coal, oil, and gas, he also placed emphasis on the need to maintain environmental quality. In his 1976 campaign, Carter promised to sign a mining reclamation bill that Ford had twice vetoed as being too costly to industry. Carter also wrote to Interior Secretary Cecil Andrus suggesting that he "manage the coal-leasing program to assure that it can respond to reasonable production goals by leasing only those areas where mining is environmentally acceptable and compatible with other land uses" (Durant, 1992).

There were two areas of decision directly affecting the development of coal resources on public lands—leasing agreements between the DOI and the private sector and the enactment and implementation of mine reclamation policies. Most of the federal coal lands in the West are placed within the jurisdiction of the Bureau of Land Management within the DOI. A smaller portion belongs to the Forest Service within the Department of Agriculture. Both agencies have a mission that requires multiple-use planning. Combined, their coal amounts to 60 percent of the coal reserves west of the Mississippi and one-third of the total for the nation. The BLM takes the lead in managing the Forest Service lands as well as its own.

Besides the coal on federal lands, including subsurface rights, the BLM controls another 20 percent because of the commingling of public and private land. Much land lies in a checkerboard pattern, so coal deposits on private land cannot be mined by energy firms alone; that is, coordination with federal land managers is required. When the demand for western coal picked up in the 1960s, DOI officials recognized that the old procedures under the Mineral Leasing Act were inadequate. The energy companies' demand for coal clashed with the emerging concern with protecting the environment of pristine mountains and arid prairies.

Inside the DOI, there was disagreement between those officials who were wedded to the old conservation movement tradition of government planning for the long term, which avoided resource exploitation, and the new force of economists who believed that employing the market was the best way to allocate resources. The newer market orientation began to influence leasing policy during the Johnson and Nixon administrations, resulting in a decisionmaking approach that was labeled "planned market" (Nelson, 1983).

The Carter team had economists in its planning office and countered their influence with political appointees and careerists devoted both to noneconomic environmental values and to the New Deal, big government tradition. The environmental opponents of leasing found many opportunities to play off the two forces. Courts often proved willing to intervene, a trend that was promoted by the growing tendency of Congress to incorporate citizen suit provisions within natural resource policies. On numerous occasions, the DOI thoroughly prepared for a lease, adhering to all the requirements of the various laws according to its interpretation, only to face a last-minute court injunction based on a pro-environmental legislative provision.

When leasing under the planned market approach, the first step for DOI officials was to estimate the amount of coal the whole nation would burn in a given period of years. Next, they calculated the amount that would come from each region. Finally, they determined how much acreage was needed to lease so that enough, but not too much, coal would be available. The Coal Leasing Act required that mining companies dig the coal diligently and not just leave it in the ground for speculative reasons.

The political stakes for diverse groups complicated the decisionmaking process. The DOI also attempted to get the highest royalty payments possible; thus, minimum bids for the leases were established. Mining companies wanted to avoid paying too much, while seeking assurances that an ample supply of coal would be available. Environmentalists wanted assurances that mining operations would not result in the neglect of ecological values. And state government officials had a clear economic incentive for involvement as well. Many western coal-producing states relied on a severance tax for revenue, a tax that was levied on energy production on federal land as well as on private land. Some states like Montana obtained nearly all their severance tax revenue from federal lands (Lagace, 1988).

The needs of affected parties proved to be incompatible. The DOI could not obtain the infinite information necessary to predict the demand for coal, and the companies did not have confidence that the demand would materialize. The result was that few companies bothered to bid, and the benefits of competition were lost. DOI officials prepared to lease large tracts, encountered objections from environmentalists, and ultimately imposed a moratorium while Interior Secretary Cecil Andrus ordered a full-scale review of federal coal policy. Following a period of consensus building that involved representatives of DOI, the states, tribal governments, energy companies, and environmental groups, a Coal Management Plan was released in 1979 (McFarland, 1993). The net result was a process that was designed to incorporate environmental criteria, current and projected market conditions, and impacts on alternative land uses in a complex computer-driven program administered by the DOI (Durant, 1992).

The conditions dictating whether or under what conditions leasing occurred clearly had environmental quality implications, but an equally important policy concern was associated with reclaiming the land after mining operations had ceased. This concern was addressed by the enactment of the Surface Mining Control and Reclamation Act in August 1977. SMCRA was welcomed by environmental groups such as the National Wildlife Federation that had lobbied hard for its passage. Under SMCRA, environmental protection was given greater priority than energy production. Coal mine operators were required to reclaim the land (public or private), and a trust fund was created to restore abandoned land damaged by mining operations.

The new law established uniform environmental standards to be administered by the newly created Office of Surface Mining and Reclamation (OSM) within the DOI rather than the EPA. The decision to establish a coal regulatory function within the DOI rather than within the chief pollution control agency derived from chance as much as logic. The campaign in the House of Representatives to pass a national law began in the mid-1960s, prior to the establishment of the EPA. Two early advocates, Ken Heckler of West Virginia and Wayne Hayes of Ohio, represented eastern states, so a western orientation was not inevitable.

With the departures from Congress of Heckler and Hayes, Morris Udall of Arizona took up the banner. The bills came under the jurisdiction of the House Committee on the Interior, later chaired by Udall. In anticipation of the eventual passage of a law, interior committee members sought to maintain oversight. The committee oversaw the DOI, not the EPA. The committee's desire to maintain control was compatible with an industry preference for the Interior Department (which was not yet infused with its Carter administration environmental leanings) rather than the EPA (which had an environmental mission from the start).

The western states had a function (and perhaps an incentive) not found in the East and the Midwest: authority to regulate mines on federal land. In the West, 80 percent of all coal is located on BLM or Forest Service lands. One of the great worries among OSM officials was that the agency would be forced by default to manage a big or medium-sized program. The law did not intend for this to occur, and the OSM lacked the personnel to undertake such tasks. For private land, the strategy contained within the legislation was to minimize the need for federal staff by having the states administer the program. In compensation, the states received grants that covered 50 percent of their operating costs.

OSM officials also wanted to shed the agency's responsibility for administering the program on federal lands. Viewed nationwide, these lands were a small fraction of the total acreage affected by SMCRA, and they were located in the western states that were more sympathetic to the program. Agency administrators wanted to save their efforts for the tough battles with eastern and midwestern states (Shover, Clelland, and Lynxwiler, 1986).

In every state with coal mining on federal lands, the OSM negotiated a cooperative agreement for the state agency to assume primary jurisdiction. The specific state law and regulations would apply (as they would even if OSM had run the federal lands program directly). The state agency would review permits, conduct inspections, levy penalties, consider permit modifications, and so on. Acting chiefly on a state agency recommendation, the secretary would approve the permits. In return, the OSM would compensate the state for 100 percent of its costs under the rationale that otherwise it would have to do the job alone.

During the second and third year of implementing SMCRA, the OSM's chief function was to delegate the fledgling regulatory program to state agencies, which were then to have "primary regulatory authority." To do this, SMCRA required the secretary of the interior to certify that the states complied with the federal law and regulations. The OSM and the solicitor's office found cooperation with several western states easier than with most eastern and midwestern states (Shover, Clelland, and Lynxwiler, 1986).

One contributing factor to regional differences in SMCRA compliance was Interior Secretary Cecil Andrus's good rapport with western governors, owing, in part, to his earlier tenure as governor of Idaho. Western states like North Dakota, Wyoming, and Montana cooperated with the OSM. In contrast, Pennsylvania and West Virginia had control programs that predated SMCRA. Public officials in these states maintained an attitude of superiority in their relations with OSM administrators, whereas other eastern and midwestern states like Virginia and Indiana were openly hostile to federal regulatory efforts (Shover, Clelland, and Lynxwiler, 1986).

This is not to say that western states were without enforcement problems of their own. In addition to a general ethos of cowboy independence, those states were accustomed to negotiating with DOI bureaus that had broad discretionary authority. But the OSM was tightly constrained by the law, so there was little room to accommodate state interests. Other region-specific problems affecting program implementation included special programs for Indian lands and the OSM's responsibility to review permit applications for mines located on BLM land (Shover, Clelland, and Lynxwiler, 1986).

One of the more politically volatile provisions in SMCRA was Section 522, which allowed the OSM to declare land unsuitable for mining. Action taken under this section frequently produced conflict between interest groups; moreover, it has more often been implemented on federal lands than private lands. In writing the law, Congress reasoned that certain locations are so fragile that mining can never take place without irreparable damage.

The first, and still largest, unsuitability petition was undertaken for a proposed mine near Alton, Utah, at the entrance to Bryce Canyon National Park. Because the mine was on federal land, the petition went directly to the DOI for a decision by Secretary Andrus. The environmentalists made three arguments, two of them aesthetic. First, the park was entitled to a buffer zone beyond its boundaries to protect visitors from having to see the mine with its draglines, trucks, and pit. Second, the park had "integral vistas." One of the great natural wonders of Bryce Canyon is the opportunity to see mountains fifty and one hundred miles away through the ultraclear air. Mining would create dust that would reduce this dramatic visibility. Third, prohibition of mining was considered necessary to protect the Navajo aquifer.

Secretary Andrus decided to craft a decision that offered something tangible for both the environmentalists and the energy companies. He ordered a ban on mining for 325,000 acres, while permitting it on other portions of the Alton coalfield. The boundary line was drawn in a way that spared visitors the sight of mining operations. As a large and important precedent for subsequent DOI actions on unsuitability section petitions, this case revealed divisions within the agency about the appropriate way to proceed.

Many of the Carter appointees who held pro-environmental beliefs favored the petition. However, the specific controls demanded were outside the boundary of the park and were not directly covered by the law. The Carter team wanted a successful petition process to go forward in the Alton case to vindicate the new law and to prepare the way for future petitions.

The DOI staff favored formal, even legalistic, procedures for several reasons. Lawsuits by the Natural Resources Defense Council, the National Wildlife Federation, and others had succeeded during the Nixon and Ford years, when federal decisions had not favored the environment over development. SMCRA and the new environmental laws provided for public intervention but required a few successful petitions to establish a precedent. Finally, the staff anticipated that the coal industry would appeal an unfavorable decision on the Alton coalfield. Consequently, it wanted to adhere to airtight procedures that could not be overturned by the courts. Zealous leaders (both political and career) within the DOI wanted to consolidate the environmental victory of SMCRA (Shover, Clelland, and Lynxwiler, 1986).

Fall 1980 became a desperate time for the Carter team working on the surface mining program. By August, many recognized that President Carter might not be reelected, a perception that grew until election day. This horrifying realization energized the staff. Many state applications for authorization to manage the SMCRA program had been progressing at a snail's pace and were being minutely scrutinized by the engineers, geologists, and lawyers so that they would be nearly perfect. The staff, with its strong commitment to environmental values, had been determined to write as many safeguards as possible into the state plans signed by the secretary. They described themselves as "strict constructionists" of SMCRA and had initially rejected the idea of approving plans conditionally.

As it became increasingly apparent that Carter's reelection was in jeopardy, OSM officials attempted to approve as many state programs as possible, even with conditions and perhaps imperfections. Of twenty-five applications, Secretary Andrus signed fifteen by January 19, 1981, his last day in office. The same desperate phenomenon occurred for the technical regulations such as hydrology and blasting. Hundreds of pages of proposed regulations were presented to the secretary for signature and were rushed by taxi to the *Federal Register* office for printing. At the same time, those outside the department who opposed the program had a strong incentive to stall. Several state agencies that were unenthusiastic withdrew their applications or just stopped cooperating, thereby sabotaging their applications, to await the new administration, which they anticipated would be more lenient.

While the DOI was wrestling with the Alton unsuitability petition, the EPA was drafting regulations to implement Section 169A of the 1977 Clean Air Act amendments. This law revealed the tension between the development of a plentiful energy resource—coal—found on public lands and the goal of protecting the environment. Congress had included the section in order to protect western parks from haze and particulates.

Witnesses before Congressman Paul Rogers's Subcommittee on the Environment had testified to the growing problem of smog that made it impossible to see across the Grand Canyon on some days. They showed photographs of the haze there and at Bryce Canyon National Park. Some haze came from mine-mouth electric power plants, often burning coal from federal lands. Some haze came from mining, such as the dust emissions from the proposed Alton mining operation, and some haze drifted in from as far away as Los Angeles. The EPA faced the question of how much authority it had to regulate scenic vistas outside the park. As DOI officials had concluded with the Alton petition, EPA officials interpreted the Clean Air Act to mean that the views were an integral part of the park experience for visitors, hence the term "integral vistas." Taking a pro-environmental stance, EPA officials promulgated regulations that put developmental restrictions into place (Freemuth, 1991).

A less prominent issue associated with energy and public lands was the problem of how to dispose of contaminated uranium mill tailings that lay scattered next to abandoned mills on BLM land near twenty-three Rocky Mountain towns. Grand Junction, Colorado, was a particularly notorious example of a community that was adversely affected by mining activities. During the 1940s and 1950s, the Climax Company, one of the nation's biggest uranium refiners, had piled its spoil from mining operations outside its mill and even sold the sand to construction companies to fill in under the slab and mix for concrete in new houses. The sand and concrete emitted radon that was especially dangerous to young children.

Congress responded to the problem in 1978 by passing the Uranium Mill Tailings Reclamation Act, which provided funds to identify and move or bury tailings that had been left near residences. The tailings were located on both private and federal land. When possible, the law required mining companies to pay for cleanup actions, but often the government had to pay when the parties responsible were either bankrupt or no longer in business. This legislation foreshadowed the growing awareness of Congress that the production of uranium for the generation of nuclear power resulted in significant environmental and health-related costs at the front end of the cycle, whereas legislation aimed at the disposal of spent nuclear wastes would be enacted several years later.

Thus, policy changes in the 1970s arose from the realization that energy development could harm environmental quality. In part, this stemmed from the physical properties of energy sources like synthetics, uranium, or coal that produced pollution during the process of extraction or use, thus ensuring that natural resource development would be constrained by the politics of pollution. Changes in organizational routines also contributed to decisional shifts because of the infusion of economists and policy analysts within the DOI to counter the preferences of technical staff. But the most significant contribution came from the actions taken by Carter administration officials, actions that reflected a stronger emphasis on environmental values than in preceding administrations.

The Reagan Revolution

The election of Ronald Reagan in 1980 produced a reversal of many Carter policies and accelerated others. Although the term "Reagan Revolution" soon took hold, in fact Carter (a bit of a chameleon) had already reversed some of his own policies. The main policy that was altered was regulation of the price of oil. In 1977 and 1978, Carter had urged elaborate regulation of the price of crude oil, but within months of signing the 1978 law, he began to increase the price to the market level. Reagan supported the removal of government price controls but saw no reason to do it gradually. Within days of his inauguration, he eliminated all controls using the authority granted under the 1978 law.

Meanwhile, Reagan's new Interior Secretary, James Watt, took steps to increase domestic production of oil and coal reserves located on public lands, a responsibility that has historically resided within the BLM. Perhaps the most controversial proposal made by Watt was a decision to open up wilderness areas for oil and gas leases. Energy companies had lobbied hard to gain access because departmental authority to open up these areas for development was scheduled to expire in 1983. Although leasing was a perfectly legal action that was permissible under the Wilderness Act of 1964, no previous interior secretary had allowed it.

However, political opposition from environmentalists and elected officials to this proposal was both immediate and forceful. The entire congressional delegation in California and the wholly Republican congressional delegation from Wyoming protested loudly when the DOI approved lease applications near the Big Sur coastline and the Washakie Wilderness, respectively. Representative Manuel Lujan (R-NM) introduced a bill to ban leases in wilderness areas, and Representative Sidney Yates (D-IL), the chair of the House Appropriations Committee, succeeded in attaching a rider to upcoming interior spending bills forbidding the expenditure of funds for these activities. In the face of this opposition, Secretary Watt agreed to withdraw his proposal (Culhane, 1984).

A different source of oil and gas found on western public lands also failed to be developed—but for different reasons. The abandonment of the synthetic fuels projects was a complete reversal of the Carter program. In early 1981, the new administration toyed with the idea of continuing the Synthetic Fuels Corporation, established in 1980. After all, it had businesslike features like letting private business take care of production while the government took care of loan guarantees and promised to buy the synthetic oil, gasoline, and coal gas manufactured by these companies. In summer 1980 President Carter had nominated directors and officers of the new Synthetic Fuels Corporation and had sent their names to the Senate for confirmation. Sensing victory in the election, Republican senators stalled.

Once inaugurated, Reagan sent a different list of nominees. But as their confirmation hearings proceeded, the White House and the Republican senators became disenchanted with the Synthetic Fuels Corporation as a concept and as a business. Beguiled by "supply-side economics," the new administration and the Senate, now controlled by Republicans for the first time in twenty-seven years, backed away from the corporation. Increasingly, it looked like a New Deal monstrosity, that is, an organization designed to allocate energy resources through central planning rather than markets. Their support for the corporation and its proposed directors and officers withered away.

The Reagan team at the DOI pushed forward with a new coal-leasing program begun by the Carter team. Reagan's BLM director was Robert Burford, a former state legislator and sagebrush rebel in the Colorado legislature. Burford wanted to accelerate coal development. One way to achieve this goal was to promulgate regulations formalizing the distinction between competitive and emergency leases. The 1976 Coal Leasing Act had directed the BLM to plan for competitive leasing, but this method did not fit many situations. For example, an operator might be running out of coal and still have several years to wait until the next date for the BLM to offer new deposits. Or a company might have extended a mine to the edge of its property; the adjoining federal coal was easy for this operator to mine but was too expensive for another company to mine. The Interior Department had granted leases like this on an emergency basis.

The new regulations explicitly provided for noncompetitive leasing through negotiations. In order for the BLM to lease competitively, it first identified the tracts, then sought the opinions of industry, state governments, the public, and Indian tribes. The bureau next ranked the tracts according to geological, economic, environmental, and social factors. The objective of the extensive planning, which took three to five years, was to offer tracts capable of supporting new, independent operators.

The provisions for emergency situations were far simpler. In areas with extensive federal reserves, the operator only had to demonstrate that it was mining at the time and needed the federal coal in the short term. In areas where federal deposits were limited and dispersed, this in itself was enough. The U.S. treasury benefited because otherwise the operator would bypass the coal and it would be lost forever. The BLM did not consider it worthwhile to prepare elaborate economic and environmental studies. Competition was not realistic because only one company would bid. When the GAO studied thirty-nine emergency leases, it found that only one company had bid in thirty-six of these cases (GAO, 1984).

One of the chief obstacles to the rapid development of energy resources as well as to the collection of revenue from industry leases was the need to comply with environmental laws and regulations. Reagan appointees came into the DOI gunning for the surface mining program. OSM environmentalism seemed to be evil incarnate to Interior Secretary James Watt, who had previously opposed SMCRA while directing the Rocky Mountain Legal Foundation, an organization financed by coal operators who had backed Reagan and conservative Republicans who had gained control of the Senate in 1980.

To direct the OSM, the president appointed James R. (Dick) Harris, a consulting geologist and Indiana legislator. During the 1970s, Harris had been at the forefront of those in the Hoosier state who tried to block a delegated SMCRA program. He came into an agency with weakened leadership and personnel who were dispirited in anticipation of having their programmatic accomplishments rolled back. All the remaining Carter political appointees were fired within days. A number of the career civil servants also resigned, transferred, or retired in spring 1981, either unwilling to see their efforts undone or fearing that they had no future in government. Of fifty-one top career officials, fifty were gone within a few months.

As soon as Harris took office, he suspended most of the technical regulations that the Carter team had promulgated. Environmental groups sued in court to block the suspension. The result was confusing to state officials since they didn't know whether the old rules should be applied to ongoing projects. On the one hand, the Carter administration regulations often remained in force from a strictly legal point of view, but on the other hand, state officials knew that the new OSM team would not enforce them. The Reagan team began to write and promulgate replacement regulations, eventually promulgating them by 1983.

The National Wildlife Federation challenged the new rules in court before Federal District Judge Thomas Flannery, who had presided over two earlier challenges to the surface mining regulations in 1979 and 1980. The federation succeeded in strengthening provisions for mining in national forests. The OSM accelerated the process of delegating primary authority to the states and, in the opinion of critics, of holding the states to less stringent standards. The Natural Resources Defense Council took the lead in suing to overturn the state approvals, with little success. Delay rather than reform was the consequence of these efforts (Culhane, 1984).

In the early years of the Reagan administration, the Interior Department took a negative stance toward unsuitability petitions. It denied petitions covering

200,000 acres along the Tongue River in Montana, in the Medicine Bow area of Wyoming, and in the Red Rim area of Wyoming. With respect to the Medicine Bow decision, the DOI maintained that an EIS already dealt with the issue. In 1983, the department denied a petition for Camp Swift Military Reservation in Texas, thus addressing an issue relating to Defense Department land. All of these denials were on procedural grounds (McElfish and Beier, 1990).

For the OSM, the first four years of the Reagan administration, 1981–1985, were marked by anti-environmental attitudes from the top leadership and turmoil for careerists within the agency. Harris felt his role was to turn around the agency on behalf of the industry. His deputy, Stephen Griles, was even more zealous. The pair did not wholly succeed in aiding industry because of the strength of the law, the survival of most of the Carter administration regulations, and lawsuits by the National Wildlife Federation and the Environmental Policy Institute. Yet the agency's political leaders did succeed in decimating and disheartening the career staff. Harris himself resigned in July 1983, and Griles was promoted to become an assistant secretary elsewhere within the department.

By this time, the OSM's problems of mismanagement were becoming an embarrassment to the Reagan administration. The chief deficiency was lack of enforcement. State agencies with delegated programs were not making the minimum number of inspections required, were not citing violations, and were not collecting the fines. Direct OSM enforcement was nearly as bad. Violators owed the OSM over $200 million, and several states were making little attempt to comply with the program (Shover, Clelland, and Lynxwiler, 1986).

After Harris resigned, Jed Christensen was nominated to become the new OSM director and was confirmed by the Senate, despite his lack of experience in natural resource development or policy. His previous career had been in municipal finance until he received a political appointment in the department with the Watt team. Nevertheless, Christensen's appointment became a turning point for the OSM. Having failed to win confidence with an extreme pro-industry stance, the new agency strategy was to try competence.

Although the OSM's performance still did not please the environmentalists, the era of hostility toward SMCRA ended, and the agency began to implement the law. During the third and fourth years of the Reagan administration, policy was reversed elsewhere in the DOI and in the EPA. The OSM collected fines, stabilized its technical regulations, and took over control of the renegade Oklahoma and Tennessee programs. The Tennessee legislature had repealed its surface mining law in an act of defiance, knowing that it would disqualify the state from exercising primary regulatory control. Thus, an assessment of the OSM's performance throughout the Reagan years reveals that agency's early tendency to ignore SMCRA, followed by a return to normalcy in program enforcement during the mid- to late 1980s (Hedge, Scicchitano, and Metz, 1989).

The Reagan administration also attempted to shape other, less visible, energy policy concerns affecting the public lands, but it was either unsuccessful in undertaking the initiative or was acting in response to congressional policy proposals. The former tendency is revealed in the efforts of Interior Secretary Donald Hodel (who was appointed in 1985) to change policy on the generation of hydroelectric power in the Pacific Northwest. Hodel was a career administrator in DOI, having headed the Bonneville Power Administration for five years. With his background in government hydroelectric power, Hodel could see the need to make both organizational and programmatic changes.

On the organizational front, Hodel announced a plan to downgrade the Bureau of Reclamation, moving its headquarters from Washington to Denver. The plan acknowledged that the bureau would engage in minimal new construction of reservoirs or power plants and that agency responsibilities would increasingly include environmental protection or the operation and maintenance of existing facilities. On the one hand, this move was consistent with President Reagan's desire to downsize many domestic agencies and programs. On the other hand, from a technical perspective, DOI officials believed that, after eighty years of building water projects, nearly all the good sites had been dammed (Wilkinson, 1992).

On the policy front, DOI operations were influenced by policy decisions rendered by the federal courts and by Congress that laid the groundwork for integrating ecological needs within the process of generating electrical power on public waters. Decisions to alter the timing and volume of water release from reservoirs were made to satisfy court edicts requiring federal agencies to develop power in ways that offered more protection to threatened or endangered species of salmon within the Columbia River Basin (Wilkinson, 1992). DOI officials did not make these decisions unilaterally but were involved in a complex decision-making process involving other institutions such as members of Congress from the Pacific Northwest, tribal and state governments, and organizations representing an array of stakeholders.

One example of the changing political climate was a DOI proposal to enhance riverine fish runs by tearing down existing dams, a surprising move that represented a stunning reversal of the American urge to build and to conquer nature. One target was the 210-foot high Glines Canyon Dam in the Olympic National Park in Washington state that blocked the spawning runs of the giant chinook salmon. In 1988, Secretary Hodel proposed tearing down the dam that had turned the beautiful Hetch Hetchy valley in Yosemite National Park into a large reservoir. However, none of these proposals were implemented.

Another policy arena that produced policy conflict among energy producers, environmentalists, and state officials on the federal lands was the need to find a permanent site for the storage of high-level radioactive waste, a highly toxic byproduct of both U.S. military weapons production and the generation of electricity from nuclear power plants. In 1982, Congress came up with what it hoped would be a solution to the problem of waste disposal by enacting the Nuclear Waste Policy Act. The main objective of this law was to find two permanent, underground repositories for the storage of spent wastes, one in the East and one in the West. Although the sites were not necessarily to be on federal land, there was an inexorable drift in that direction. When finding an eastern site proved impossible, the Department of Energy suspended the search, and Congress then amended the law in 1987 by restricting the search to a single site.

Even in the West, finding a site proved difficult because of the NIMBY syndrome. Efforts to consider sites in Texas and Utah were rejected. The Department of Energy tried its old standby at Hanford, Washington, a DOE facility that already stored a sizable volume of nuclear wastes, but this, too, was not feasible for technical reasons. DOE officials then identified a preferred site. Yucca Mountain lies in Nye County, Nevada, adjoining the nuclear testing site northwest of Las Vegas. The spot has no residents, is dry, stable, and remote, is too arid for ranching, and lacks any minerals worth mining. Nevada state officials have made staunch efforts to avoid the dubious distinction of becoming the main dumping ground for high-level wastes. However, the issue has not been resolved.

As Robert Durant (1992) indicates, most of the actions taken on energy policy by federal land management agencies was a product of administrative rather than legislative initiatives. Decisions were shaped by a strong probusiness ideology among political appointees at the DOI and the Forest Service and by a preference for the invisible hand of the market over government regulation as a means of allocating energy resources, particularly in the early 1980s. Nevertheless, a number of controversial proposals were stalled or reversed by the opposition of environmentalists and their supporters in Congress.

The Bush Administration Moves Back to the Middle

Many observers see the Bush administration as the third wave of the Reagan Revolution. The first wave involved the fiery attacks on bureaucracy during the 1981–1983 period, the second dealt with the process of regrouping from 1983 to 1989, and the third wave, the Bush years of 1989–1993, was a mellow return to normalcy. The DOI experienced the first two waves, but the Bush years were hardly mellow. The president appointed Manuel Lujan, a former Republican congressman from New Mexico, to be the new secretary of the interior.

The transition between the Reagan and Bush administrations was not entirely smooth. As a valediction, Hodel attempted to transfer 55,000 acres of oil shale in Colorado from federal to private control, revised the method of calculating royalties for coal, and suggested private owners might have the right to mine in national parks. The shale reserves in the northwestern portion of Colorado, which hold billions of barrels of oil locked into rock formations molecule by molecule, were now sought for potential deposits of natural gas and conventional oil. The proposed price was $2.50 an acre.

Hodel promulgated a change in royalties so that operators would deduct taxes and fees before calculating the amount to pay to the government. Previously, they had figured the royalty first. Although promulgated, the regulations did not go into effect for two years. Increasing the rights to mine coal in the parks did not get beyond the talking stage. The new Bush team objected to all three decisions, arguing that each was an unjustifiable giveaway to industry.

The new team did not object to a fourth farewell proposition made by Secretary Hodel. The DOI proposed to give native corporations 166,000 acres in the Arctic National Wildlife Refuge in exchange for 900,000 acres that the natives owned in other Alaskan wildlife refuges. Hodel contended that the other land was "pristine" and more than five times as extensive. Environmentalists rebutted this, saying that the North Slope refuge was the breeding ground for the largest caribou herd on the continent; the substitute tract would not help the caribou. Once sworn into office, Lujan vigorously defended giving developmental rights on the refuge to the native corporation, saying it "was a campaign promise" by Bush.

One complication arose because of George Bush's promise to be "an environmental president" during the campaign. A key aspect was his pledge to produce "no net loss of wetlands"—a promise that set off alarms within the energy industry as well as among farmers and real estate developers. By fall 1989, the EPA and the Army Corps of Engineers had agreed to procedures for issuing permits to assure this goal. The petroleum industry immediately objected that it would impede development of the North Slope of Alaska. The DOI Fish and Wildlife Service followed by issuing its own directive that would cover 4.2 million acres of wetlands out of the 91 million acres under its jurisdiction.

Carrying the canny title of *Wetlands: Meeting the President's Challenge* (1989), the pro-environmental directive was supposed to be implemented immediately. The plan bore the signature of Bush's FWS appointee, John Turner. But within weeks, the White House and top Interior Department appointees had suspended the EPA-Corps agreement and the Fish and Wildlife document amid pressure exerted by realtors and the energy industry. In spite of pro-industry sentiment at the White House and secretarial office, midlevel Interior Department appointees and career officials pushed on the environmental side. Turner again attempted to mold a wetlands policy for the Fish and Wildlife Service the following year.

But the North Slope energy question remained on the policy agenda, and both advocates and opponents of drilling in the National Wildlife Federation refuge received a boost from regional and international events. The importance of environmental concerns was highlighted only two months after Bush's inauguration when the giant tanker, the *Exxon Valdez,* loaded with 1.3 million barrels of crude oil from the North Slope of Alaska, hit a shoal in Prince William Sound, spilling 250,000 barrels. The oil seeped out and floated in a enormous slick that washed up on the shore of the sound. It blackened the beaches, fouled the feathers of the birds, contaminated the seals, and poisoned the fish. Eventually, the spill defiled 800 miles of shoreline. Even though the shipwreck occurred hundreds of miles away from the North Slope, the news on television and in magazines and newspapers mobilized popular opinion against drilling (Rosenbaum, 1993).

But in 1991, the Persian Gulf War broke out in the Middle East, largely because U.S. policymakers thought it strategically necessary to maintain access to oil reserves in Kuwait and other countries in that region. Advocates of "energy independence" within the United States seized the opportunity to emphasize the importance of becoming less dependent upon foreign oil sources by removing restrictions on exploration and drilling in Alaska.

This issue was confronted head on in 1991 in congressional deliberations over a national energy policy, a complex and massive set of policy proposals that included sections dealing with nuclear power licensing reforms, stronger gasoline conservation measures for automobiles and appliances, and requirements for the federal government to purchase vehicles powered by alternate fuels, as well as North Slope access issues. Environmentalists, led by policy entrepreneurs such as Senator Tim Wirth (D-CO), eventually succeeded in obtaining a ban on oil and gas drilling on the National Wildlife Federation refuge in exchange for concessions elsewhere, such as easing the restrictions on the licensing of nuclear power plants, and in 1992, the Energy Policy Act was enacted (Kraft, 1996).

Other efforts to drill for oil and gas on public lands met with similar fates. The National Parks and Conservation Association (NPCA) used its right under NEPA public participation requirements to oppose a BLM permit for exploratory drilling near the Hovenweep National Monument on the Utah-Colorado border. The park protects 745 acres of archeological sites of the ancient Anasazi Indians. Other ruins lie nearby on BLM land. Under a cooperative agreement with the National Park Service, the BLM is responsible for the protection of 5,000 acres. The NPCA complained to the DOI Board of Land Appeals, which ruled that under NEPA the bureau had to complete a formal environmental impact statement before drilling would be allowed. The decision extended beyond Hovenweep to affect 80 percent of the wells on 70 million acres.

The BLM response was to demand that Secretary Lujan overrule his own board. After two years of internal debate, the department promulgated regulations that allowed drilling to proceed during an appeal. Meanwhile, the Forest Service proposed to do the same thing for appeals in the U.S. Department of Agriculture (USDA). Since early in the century, USDA had not permitted mining or drilling during an appeal. On Capitol Hill, the House Appropriations Subcommittee for Agriculture blocked the pro-industry change by inserting a provision in the 1993 appropriation bill that banned developmental activities before appeals had been exhausted.

Greater sensitivity to energy industry priorities could also be observed in the approach taken by the Bush administration to the development of coal on public lands. The DOI promulgated draft regulations to strengthen the hand of coal operators whose deposits were subject to the Surface Mining Act restrictions on mining in national parks and forests. Departmental administrators dusted off the Reagan era proposal that solidified the owners' rights under Section 523, which protected "valid existing rights" without defining them. The DOI then offered to buy the rights in nineteen parks, forests, and refuges in Ohio, Alabama, Illinois, Indiana, Kentucky, Pennsylvania, Virginia, and West Virginia. The department estimated the value of the rights at $11 million; environmentalists rebutted that the government would end up paying hundreds of millions of dollars.

One such case involved the Belville Coal Company and its rights to mine 7,200 acres in the Wayne National Forest in Ohio, a tract estimated to hold 15 million tons of coal. Its owner, Thomas Belville, was a prominent Republican who used his party connections to have the OSM substantiate his rights in 1988. When the government reversed its ruling one year later, the flabbergasted operator sued in both district court and the court of claims. In 1994, the court of appeals reinstated his claim as it applied to 1,800 acres, holding that the Interior Department had taken his property in violation of the Fifth Amendment. Although coal owners had lost the "taking" case in Virginia in 1981 before the Supreme Court, based on general regulation under the Surface Mining Act, this decision was based on a more narrow aspect of the law.

Although Bush administration officials clearly favored a public lands policy that was more user-friendly for energy companies, they could occasionally take a pro-environmental stance if decisions were not wholly confined to DOI but were shared with agencies headed by individuals more sympathetic to ecological goals. Two appointees who were more inclined to recognize the environmental costs of energy-related actions included EPA Administrator William Reilly and DOE Secretary James Watkins.

The DOI confronted the issue of controlling air pollution in the national parks from sources outside their boundaries, which was a concern originally raised by Carter administration officials in 1978. The issue of visibility in Grand Canyon National Park, a major factor in the 1980 Alton unsuitability petition, was the center of an agreement in 1990 between the EPA, the National Park Service, energy companies, and four environmental groups. In keeping with a long-term trend, the government tipped the balance a bit more from energy toward environmental protection.

To reduce air pollution in the canyon, the electric companies agreed to reduce emissions from the Navajo Power Plant in northern Arizona. The plant's owners include the DOI Bureau of Reclamation as well as the Los Angeles Department of Water and Power, the Arizona Public Service Company, and the Nevada Power Company. This was the first time the Clean Air Act was applied solely to improve visibility in a national park.

Another source of tension between public lands energy development and environmental protection during the Bush administration was over the cleanup of nuclear waste from producing weapons and mining uranium. Bush's secretary of energy, James Watkins, made the administration's earliest and most dramatic splash by revealing that four government sites for manufacture of nuclear weapons suffered from serious radioactive contamination: Barnwell in South Carolina, Fernald near Cincinnati, Rocky Flats near Denver, and Hanford in Washington state. Over a period of four decades, the Atomic Energy Commission and its successor, the DOE, had been negligent in disposing of its wastes. At Rocky Flats, plutonium chips lay scattered about. At Barnwell and Hanford, radioactivity seeped into the Savannah and Columbia Rivers. Worse still, the government had kept the problem secret and had punished workers who complained.

The Atomic Energy Commission–DOE disposal method was not illegal because federal agencies were exempt from the Resource Conservation and Recovery Act and other laws. Congress remedied this loophole with the Federal Facilities Compliance Act of 1991, making the Departments of Energy and Defense subject to the same cleanup laws as the private sector. The EPA gained authority to enforce the laws, as did state environmental agencies. Plans called for state investigators to inspect army and navy bases and poke around Energy Department facilities. Federal agencies resisted the idea of state enforcement.

To summarize, the Bush administration exhibited a more mixed record in attempting to reconcile energy production with environmental protection than had the previous administration. DOI efforts to accelerate the development of coal, oil, and gas resources on public lands met with approval from key constituencies within the energy industry and the Republican Party. But the Bush administration attempted to show an environmental side as well, by enacting laws and making agreements to clean up pollution affecting national parks and DOE facilities.

The Clinton Administration Puts Energy on the Back Burner

The Reagan Revolution's impact on environmental quality became less pronounced after about 1983, but mining and development interests still remained powerful in the Bush years. Environmentalists backed the Clinton campaign enthusiastically and were delighted with his appointment of Bruce Babbitt as secretary of the interior. As a former governor of Arizona and, briefly, as a presidential candidate, Babbitt's beliefs and practical experience indicated that he would be a friend of the environment. New appointees within the DOI such as BLM director James Baca, OSM director Robert Uram, and Bureau of Reclamation commissioner Daniel Beard were strong supporters of the environment as well.

On the one hand, despite the renewed support of the environmental community, federal land policy dealing with petroleum was not altered significantly from that of the Bush administration. The DOI and DOE proposed stimulating domestic production by expanding offshore drilling, simplifying Clean Air Act regulations for refiners, and giving tax breaks. All things considered, the proposal resembled initiatives of the Bush or Nixon administrations. Indeed, the Clinton team proposed to lease 55,00 acres in Colorado for drilling for natural gas—the same 55,000 acres that Secretary Hodel had tried to lease in the last days of the Reagan administration.

On the other hand, the Clinton administration remained faithful to the environmentalists' strong belief that the Arctic National Wildlife Refuge should not be developed. Despite the imposition of a drilling ban under the recently enacted Energy Policy Act of 1992, energy industry officials wanted to explore further the North Slope of Alaska. Industry geologists had certified this area as the most promising location within the United States for the discovery of oil and gas. When congressional supporters of the environment introduced bills to permanently ban exploration on the Arctic coastal plain, the two Alaskan senators, both Republicans, vowed to block the legislation.

Thus, industry hopes of drilling for oil and gas in the National Wildlife Federation refuge have not died. Nor have the environmentalists given up on their quest to make the 1992 ban permanent. The DOI floated a plan to merge management of the refuge with two Canadian national parks that adjoin it across the border. The entire area could be designated a wilderness, making it the largest such area in the world. Industry cried foul, calling the proposal an end run designed to prevent future drilling under the guise of international coordination (*Oil and Gas Journal*, 1994). Since taking control of Congress in 1994, congressional Republicans have redoubled their efforts to open up the refuge for development, but they had not succeeded as of mid-1996.

Another example of a more environmentally friendly approach to energy development can be found within the management of federal hydroelectric projects. The Bureau of Reclamation moved forward with its new pro-environmental mission. After ninety years of building dams, Commissioner Beard finally announced that the agency would build no more. The bureau's new goal was to manage water to conserve it and protect endangered species. Two thousand engineers and planners in its Denver office stopped designing dams. Even its conference rooms were renamed for rivers rather than dams, as in the old system.

This new approach is manifest in recent efforts to manipulate water flows to achieve power production goals in a more environmentally benign fashion. In the Southwest, the construction of the Glen Canyon Dam on the Colorado River has altered the river's course through the Grand Canyon. During each afternoon, water swirls through the turbines to generate electricity to meet the peak demand in Los Angeles and Phoenix, but at night, little electricity is generated. The water volume can fluctuate from 3,000 to 30,000 cubic feet per second in a single day. The effect is an artificial tide up to ten feet high downstream that erodes beaches.

On the lower Colorado River, the bureau adopted new standards for the operation of Glen Canyon Dam that would reduce the fluctuation in the level of the river from ten feet to only three feet. The extreme daily fluctuations damaged the beaches, killed plants, and harmed Indian artifacts. Following up on a study begun during the Bush administration, bureau officials limited the peak flow to

20,000 cubic feet per second. This restriction has reduced the bureau's capability for generating electricity to meet the peak demands in Los Angeles and Phoenix, but it will probably aid in restoring the health of the fragile ecosystem along the banks of the Colorado River.

The Bureau of Reclamation controlled some of the biggest dams, but the mission of the Federal Energy Regulatory Commission (FERC) in the Department of Energy encompassed a wider range of activity. The 1986 Electric Consumers Act required FERC (for the first time) to relicense dams, weighing environmental and recreational factors equally with electric generation. The first wave under the new law began in 1993. Many private dams are on federal lands. American Rivers, an environmental group, has urged FERC to insist on requirements like fish ladders, efficient machinery, and antidevelopment promises.

Yet another example of efforts to minimize the impacts of energy production on environmental quality is found within the DOE. Although some controversies such as the decision to site a high level nuclear waste facility at Yucca Mountain continued to simmer,[1] DOE Secretary Hazel O'Leary has continued the nuclear waste cleanup begun under her predecessor, James Watkins. Several of these facilities are located on western federal lands, notably the Rocky Flats facility near Denver and the Hanford facility in Washington state. Like Watkins, O'Leary has attempted to change the DOE organizational culture that once emphasized building bombs. O'Leary has faced formidable hurdles, for example, that the department continues to rely on private contractors and, until recently, that few incentives were built into these contracts to reward contractors for good environmental management as well as attaining production goals (Kettl, 1993).

Interior Secretary Babbitt's early lovefest with environmentalists has cooled since 1993. Environmental leaders have been critical of his seeming preoccupation with process and consensus building at the expense of achieving programmatic results. Although energy and federal lands policies have remained low priority issues in the Clinton administration, actions taken thus far have produced greater emphasis on ecological health than policy decisions reached under the Reagan or Bush administrations did. However, the Republican victory in the 1994 congressional election pushed the greening of federal lands and energy issues even further down on the policy agenda.

Conclusions

For the past twenty-five years, industry and environmental groups have attempted to shape energy policy on federal lands, but in some ways, the environmentalists have gained the upper hand, politically speaking. The first reason appears to be the pattern of cooperation among environmental groups initiated during congressional debate on the Trans-Alaska Pipeline bill, a pattern that has continued ever since. The groups' national headquarters learned the benefits of teamwork when the Environmental Defense Fund led the lobbying. Since then, this elastic coalition has found common goals time after time. The groups rotate leadership according to the particular focus for each issue. By topic, their focus may be on forests, coal, nuclear energy, and so forth. By skills, their focus may be legal, scientific, grassroots organizing, Washington lobbying, or mobilizing the public through a media campaign.

A second reason for the differential effectiveness of the two sides can be attributed to the fragmentation among business interests. Whereas environmentalists tend to advocate general policy goals and usually want to preserve the status quo, businesses have specific goals such as drilling a particular oil well or building a specific electric generating station. Indeed, it is a simplification to describe the situation as bipolar. Many controversies pit a broad coalition of environmentalists against a specific company.

A further reason for the unity of the environmentalists appears to be the provisions for public participation in almost every national environmental law enacted since NEPA in 1970. This has given environmental groups access that they lacked previously. Some laws even provide payment for expert consultation and testing. Public intervention also opens up the opportunity for a local group to participate, resulting in NIMBY-related actions. Even though federal lands are often remote, the objections of neighbors may lead to political conflict.

Examining the actions of the national government shows that the role of political parties is more complex than the generalization that Republicans favor business and Democrats favor environmentalists. Although it is true that comparing the Carter and Reagan administrations offers the sharpest contrast, the Nixon administration was very favorably predisposed to environmental policy goals. Even if one acknowledges that intraparty differences exist among presidents and within Congress, it is clear that Republican presidents since 1960 have been more inclined than Democratic presidents to favor a greater emphasis on energy development over conservation and to prefer market-based solutions to regulatory approaches.

Obviously, agencies follow bureaucratic routines; it is their nature. What is not so obvious is that many of those routines are products of the Environmental Decade. NEPA, the Clean Air Act, the Clean Water Act, the Federal Land Policy Management Act, the Federal Coal Leasing Amendments Act, and their ilk set procedures. The first three laws established delegated programs implemented by the states, but with detailed controls from Washington. Other routines are considered by affected parties (such as states and regulated industries) to be dysfunctional, leading to complaints of federal arrogance, legalism, the persistence of "big government," price regulation, and central planning.

The fourth factor is not political but economic. The "energy crisis" of 1973 changed the equation for using energy resources. The price of oil is determined by the international marketplace and drives exploration and production decisions throughout the United States, including resources located on federal lands. Because coal and natural gas can be partially substituted for oil, world oil prices influence their prices also. Shale oil is a complete substitute. Nevertheless, the national and world economies have adjusted to more expensive oil. Efficient auto and jet engines, houses with more insulation and better furnaces, and supplies from new wells in places like the North Sea have decreased the high price and the power of the OPEC cartel. In the 1990s, the demand to drill and dig on federal lands has moderated.

Although the price of oil dominates all of energy policy, the pendulum has swung back toward the middle, permitting the Clinton administration to put it on the back burner. Two other factors not present in the 1960s have stabilized. Environmental values are now widely accepted and are guarded by federal and state agencies. The benefits of market prices rather than regulated prices are widely accepted as well. Perhaps ironically, the former may be seen as a victory for the Democrats and the latter, for the Republicans.

NOTES

1. In 1995, a nuclear scientist from the Los Alamos National Laboratory raised the alarm about the Yucca Mountain nuclear waste repository. Charles Bowman, a Department of Energy physicist, argued that the buried plutonium could explode in a chain reaction as the steel canisters rust away in future years. The rocks would slow down the neutrons, causing them to split other atoms rather than fly away harmlessly. Other Energy Department physicists directed to evaluate the danger concluded that the theory was probably wrong. They believed that the plutonium dispersal would take far longer, that as the spent fuel heated up it would automatically expand, causing the reaction to slow down, and in any case, the heat would be too slight to cause an explosion. Nevertheless, the possibility of danger could not be ruled out absolutely, leaving the future of Yucca Mountain in doubt.

REFERENCES

Berry, Mary. 1975. *The Alaska Pipeline*. Bloomington: Indiana University Press.

Culhane, Paul J. 1984. "Sagebrush Rebels in Office: Jim Watt's Land and Water Politics." In Norman Vig and Michael Kraft, eds., *Environmental Policy in the 1980s*. Washington, DC: CQ Press.

Durant, Robert F. 1992. *The Administrative Presidency Revisited: Public Lands, the BLM, and the Reagan Revolution*. Albany: State University of New York Press.

Freemuth, John. 1991. *Islands Under Siege: National Parks and the Politics of External Threats*. Lawrence: University Press of Kansas.

General Accounting Office (GAO). 1983. *Coal Leasing*. GAO/RCED 83.

General Accounting Office. 1984. *Legislative Changes Are Needed to Authorize Emergency Federal Coal Leasing*. GAO/RCED 84 17, August 2.

Hedge, David, Michael Scicchitano, and Patricia Metz. 1989. "The States and Deregulation: The Case of Surface Mining." *Policy Studies Review* 9 (Autumn):120–131.

Kettl, Donald. 1993. *Sharing Power*. Washington, DC: Brookings Institution Press.

Kraft, Michael. 1996. *Environmental Policy and Politics*. New York: HarperCollins.

Lagace, Gerard L. 1988. "State Energy Severance Taxes, 1972–1987." *Monthly Energy Review* (July):1–6.

McElfish, James M., and Ann E. Beier. 1990. *Environmental Regulation of Coal Mining: SMCRA's Second Decade.* Washington, DC: Environmental Law Institute.

McFarland, Andrew S. 1993. *Cooperative Pluralism: The National Coal Policy Experiment.* Lawrence: University Press of Kansas.

Nelson, Robert H. 1983. *The Making of Federal Coal Policy.* Durham, NC: Duke University Press.

Oil and Gas Journal. 1994. August 22 and August 29.

Rosenbaum, Walter. 1993. "Energy Policy in the West." In Zachary Smith, ed., *Environmental Politics and Policy in the West.* Dubuque, IA: Kendall/Hunt.

Shover, Neal, Donald Clelland, and John Lynxwiler. 1986. *Enforcement or Negotiation: Constructing a Regulatory Bureaucracy.* Albany: State University of New York Press.

Wilkinson, Charles F. 1992. *Crossing the Next Meridian.* Washington, DC: Island Press.

8

National Parks Policy

WILLIAM R. LOWRY

The recent history of Yosemite National Park is, in many ways, a microcosm of the recent history of national parks in the United States. The site of such marvels as El Capitan and Yosemite Falls, roughly 700,000 acres were set aside as protected ground more than a century ago. For decades, the National Park Service attempted to manage the park by setting a balance between preservation and use, striving to maintain natural conditions even while making it more accessible to cars and more accommodating to tourists. By the mid-1960s, Yosemite hosted nearly 2 million visitors per year, many of whom stayed in the hotels and ate at the restaurants in Yosemite Valley, enjoying such environmentally questionable activities as the famous firefall of burning wood pushed off Glacier Point every evening. Other issues stirred concern about NPS management of the park: traffic jams, automobile pollution, a riot in Stoneman Meadow, concessionaire plans for a tramway to Glacier Point, and even a short-lived television series. In 1974, partly as a result of these concerns, the park's master plan was rejected and a new planning process was begun. The 1980 plan reflected a more ecological orientation by calling for the removal of development in the valley and the elimination of automobile traffic. By 1990, however, the NPS director was calling that plan only "a concept, a good ideal."[1]

Policy toward the fifty parks and three hundred other units of the NPS has evolved through several stages comparable to those experienced at Yosemite. For decades, the policy was one of "balanced use," an application of traditional conservation values within the unique settings of national parks. Normally, the physical reduction of natural wonders through such means as mineral extraction was not to be allowed, and parks were to be made usable and enjoyable to visitors. By the late 1960s and early 1970s, the perceived excesses of too much use and the growing political importance of environmental concerns caused an apparent shift in parks policy. Planning became more open, management policies adopted a more ecological tone, and rhetorical priorities shifted to emphasize preservation over use. In reality, however, this apparent shift in parks policy was not completely realized. The failure to achieve consensus on park goals and the lack of political support for the NPS have prevented significant adoption of a more ecologically friendly approach to America's national parks. Ironically, perhaps, several of the changes made during the late 1960s and 1970s made attainment of preservation ideals even less likely.

This chapter describes shifts in the management policies of national parks over the last thirty years. The first section describes the state of national parks policy in the mid-1960s. The second section considers the changes of the late 1960s and 1970s, exploring what caused those changes and what resulted. The third section explains why the more ecologically oriented emphasis of the 1970s did not result in vast changes in real park management in the 1980s and thus far in the 1990s. Overall, this chapter attempts to answer two questions: Why did official policy change, and why have those changes not been matched by actions?

"Parks Are for People": The Mid-1960s

The National Geographic Society celebrated the fiftieth birthday of the NPS with a special issue of its magazine in July 1966. Society president Melvin Grosvenor wrote the lead article, in which he succinctly summarized agency policy: "I stress 'use and enjoy'; that, after all, is the fundamental purpose of our parks as Congress established them" (Grosvenor, 1966, 5). Although the accuracy of that statement is debatable, Grosvenor did summarize the prevailing policy attitude toward parks.

A Legacy of Balance

Grosvenor's accuracy is questionable because, in fact, when Congress initially established national parks, members did not explicitly state use as the primary purpose of parks. Rather, in legislation establishing Yellowstone National Park in 1872, Congress called for "the preservation, from injury and spoliation, of all timber, mineral deposits, natural curiosities, or wonders . . . and their retention in their natural condition." Each park is established in separate legislation, but the general theme is apparent in the mandate given the NPS in 1916: "[to] conserve the scenery and the natural and historic objects and the wild life therein and to provide for the enjoyment of the same in such manner and by such means as will leave them unimpaired for the enjoyment of future generations."[2] These statutes mandate use but also preservation, a dual mission that has posed a demanding challenge for the agency ever since.

Over its first fifty years, the NPS managed to pursue, to varying degrees, both use and preservation. The balancing act was rooted in the conservation philosophy so prevalent at the time of the agency's ceation but was modified to fit the special circumstances of the parks. The conservation philosophy was one of "controlled use" of publicly owned lands that achieved the greatest good for the greatest number.[3] Still, parks were not rangelands or national forests, but rather lands set aside to be preserved even while being used. The "father" of the NPS, Steve Mather, a strong advocate of increased visitation to the parks, argued against certain developments in parks by stating: "The nation has wisely set apart a few national parks where a state of nature is to be preserved. If the lakes and forests of these parks cannot be spared from the hand of commercialization, what hope can there be for the preservation of any scenic features."[4] This mission made the NPS unique among public land agencies.

Inevitable Contradictions

The dual attempt to keep parks natural and to make parks user-friendly created inevitable contradictions that became more apparent during the 1960s. Those contradictions created momentum for a reassessment in the latter part of the decade.

For the most part, park policies and programs reflected a traditional conservation assumption that use, development, and accessibility of parks could be increased without violating the principles of preservation. The agency was still in the process of completing a major project designed to make the parks more user-friendly. Mission 66 was a ten-year project begun in 1956, as then Director Conrad Wirth said, to "restore to the American people a national park system adequate for their needs" (Wirth, 1980, 237). The resource needs of the parks were secondary to those of the users. For example, Mission 66 built 1,197 new road miles, three times as many as trail miles, and reconstructed 1,570 more to make parks more accessible to automobiles. Over 1,500 new parking areas were constructed, with a capacity of 50,000 cars. Over 100 new, spacious visitor centers were created. Specific plans, such as the building of a transmountain road across the Smoky Mountains and the proposed installation of tramways in the Cascade Range displayed a continued emphasis on use (Frome 1992, 71–73). In contrast to these construction proposals, few NPS programs focused on increasing or retaining natural conditions.

In general, parks policy called for more parks but also for more people, thereby spawning the slogan "Parks are for people." Even when authorizing Fire Island and Assateague National Seashores as natural refuges for nearby city dwellers, President Johnson and DOI officials urged that the units be made more readily accessible (Everhart, 1983, 69; Porterfield, 1965). In a 1966 article, NPS director George Hartzog outlined five goals for the agency's future: expand, cooperate with related agencies, develop urban parks, publicize existing parks, and advise other countries on management (Hartzog, 1966, 50). Notably absent are themes concerning the restoration of natural conditions or the minimization of human impact.

Still, growing momentum for a changing policy emphasis was evident throughout the decade. President Kennedy made several speeches in which he touted the virtues of preserving relatively undeveloped conditions (Schlesinger, 1965, 659, 1016). Interior Secretary Udall proposed a "New Conservation" that would involve parks as "spacious areas of superior scenery to be preserved forever for the highest forms of outdoor recreation" (Udall, 1963, 124). Udall also called for doubling the acreage under the NPS by the end of the decade (Caulfield, 1989, 29). The government-sponsored Leopold Report of 1963 called for preserving or, if necessary, recreating parks "as nearly as possible in the condition that prevailed when the area was first visited by the white man" (Leopold, 1963, 101). The Wilderness Act of 1964 called for the designation of roadless areas throughout the country to be protected in their natural state. The Land and Water Conservation Fund (LWCF) was established in the same year to provide a source of finances for federal and state park projects. Also in 1964, Director Hartzog created a three-part classification system to designate parks as recreational, historic, or natural. Presumably, this system would facilitate greater protection of truly natural areas.

The voices for change were fueled by increasing concern over the costs of a traditional conservation approach encouraging human use of parks. One month after the special *National Geographic* issue hit the stands, the *Wall Street Journal* published a front-page article about Yosemite. The piece described the growing problems in the park with crime, traffic, and smog, concluding, "Indeed, this spectacularly beautiful park is wrestling with problems that would give any fair-sized city cause for alarm" (Mapes, 1966, 1). The contrast between this article and articles in the *National Geographic* issue espousing the beauty of Yosemite and other places is striking. Even the conservative *Wall Street Journal* had noticed that the emphasis on accessibility to and development in the parks had generated cause for concern.

Many of the problems resulted from increases in visitation for which park managers were not prepared. In the dozen years between 1954 and 1966, as Table 8.1 shows, total visits to NPS units nearly tripled, increasing from 48 million to over 133 million. More visitors translated to more of everything else—more congestion, crime, automobile pollution, deterioration of the infrastructure, and extraction of natural objects. But the increase in visitors did not necessarily translate to higher funds for the parks, since the NPS was completely dependent upon appropriations for its budget. Further, as parks became more popular, encroachment of commercial development and neighboring cities increased, bringing external threats such as air pollution.

Agency behavior also fueled the criticisms. The NPS leadership first opposed passage of the Wilderness Act and then displayed considerable reluctance in accepting it. By 1970, only two areas within national parks had received wilderness designation. The agency also encouraged the construction of restaurants, lodges, and shops to accommodate tourists. Without systematic planning or consistent central direction, many areas within individual parks such as Yosemite Valley and the South Rim of the Grand Canyon became heavily commercialized. The system for awarding concessions contracts encouraged building and commercialism

TABLE 8.1   Visits to National Park Service Units (1954–1988)

Year	No. of Visits
1954	54,210
1955	56,573
1956	61,602
1957	68,016
1958	65,461
1959	68,901
1960	79,229
1961	86,663
1962	97,045
1963	102,711
1964	111,386
1965	121,312
1966	133,081
1967	139,676
1968	150,836
1969	163,990
1970	172,005
1971	200,543
1972	211,621
1973	215,580
1974	217,438
1975	238,849
1976	267,762
1977	262,603
1978	283,090
1979	282,435
1980	294,582
1981	327,348
1982	331,455
1983	337,947
1984	328,392
1985	347,221
1986	352,156
1987	370,982
1988	371,489

SOURCES: National Park Service *Statistical Abstracts* and the U.S. Department of the Interior, 1990: NPS-12.

within the parks. The Concessions Policy Act of 1965 stipulated long-term, monopoly, renewable contracts for individual concessionaires within each park who would pay a fee back to the government. The NPS was quite decentralized, with field managers negotiating nearly all terms of the agreements (Abbey, 1968, foreword; Chase, 1987, 386; Nienaber and Wildavsky, 1973; Pyne, 1989, 114). Concessionaires could negotiate a lower fee in return for capital improvements to the park. Since the fee revenue did not necessarily return to the park but the "improvements" did, it is little wonder that field managers negotiated contracts that facilitated additional development.

An Apparent Shift Toward Preservation: 1968–1981

In a speech to Congress on March 8, 1968, President Johnson announced the beginning of a new era. "Man, who has lived so long in harmony with nature, is now struggling to preserve its bounty," Johnson said. "History will say that in the 1960s the Nation began to take action so long delayed." That and subsequent promises apparently signaled a shift in policy toward public lands, a shift that meant greater emphasis on the preservation aspect of the national parks mandate. Although such rhetoric had been heard before, the next twelve years were different in that employees within the NPS took it to heart. The shifting emphasis was also different this time because it was supported by a powerful new political player, environmental interest groups. Seemingly, parks management policy of conservation and controlled use had been replaced.

The Changing Policy Arena

Changes in national park policy during the late 1960s and 1970s resulted from several changes occurring in the broader political arena. These changes included shifts in public opinion, more aggressive political behavior by interest groups, the resurgence of Congress, and the opening up of planning processes. The following sections describe how these broad changes affected the policy arena of parks.

Increased Environmental Awareness. Prior to the mid-1960s, pollsters rarely even asked questions about the environment. In 1965, roughly one in three Americans said air or water pollution was a serious problem. By 1970, those numbers had jumped to 69 percent for air and 74 percent for water.[5] That change alone reflects the huge increase in environmental awareness among the American public in the late 1960s. This dramatic growth resulted from exposure to books like Rachel Carson's *Silent Spring,* media attention to events like the Torrey Canyon oil spill, and political events such as Earth Day in 1970. In one survey after another, Americans expressed broad concern for environmental problems.

This surge in sympathy for environmental causes affected parks policy. First, the issue became more national in scope. For decades, park policy had been dominated by policymakers and a few close supporters cultivated by Mather and other early pioneers. Only occasionally did the public at large get seriously involved in parks issues. Now, a large portion of the public was interested. This vast interest was also facilitated by the newly constructed network of roads and the ease of accessibility that now tempted visitors to the parks from all over the country. As Table 8.1 shows, visits increased each year by between 5 and 10 percent.

Second, parks policy became an increasingly salient agenda topic for elected officials, attracting the attention of Democrats and Republicans alike. Neither party had a monopoly on interest in the parks. Further, neither party had a monopoly on environmental support yet, competing instead on a variety of issues such as air pollution control. Thus, both Democrats and Republicans were eager to at least sound supportive of preservation rhetoric.

Not surprisingly, legislation to that end passed by overwhelming bipartisan margins. In 1968, for example, the initial bill to establish Redwoods National Park in northern California passed in the House by a 389–15 margin over the objections of logging and other interests. In this case, most of the dissent (13 no votes) was supplied by Democrats. The National Trails System legislation passed by a 378–18 vote, with unanimous Democratic support.

Aggressive Interest Group Behavior.   The late 1960s and early 1970s witnessed the growth of numerous interest groups with headquarters in the nation's capital. According to one study, approximately 70 percent of interest groups have opened their Washington offices since 1960 (Schlozman and Tierney, 1983, 356; Walker, 1983). These changes were reflected in interest groups involved in parks policy as well.

Table 8.2 displays the growth in membership of three interest groups that often focus on national parks policy. The National Parks and Conservation Association was established in 1919 at the urging of NPS director Mather to be largely a support group for the agency. The Sierra Club, founded in 1892, formed around John Muir's interest in Yosemite and the Sierra Nevada mountains. The Wilderness Society was founded in 1935 to pursue and protect undeveloped areas. As Table 8.2 shows, all three groups experienced dramatic growth in membership between the early 1960s and 1975.

Partly because of this growth, the groups were able to change their approach to the NPS. Although these groups had often deferred to the agency before or even offered consistent support, they now became much more independent and often critical of agency policies. The Wilderness Society was a major force in promoting the passage of the Wilderness Act in 1964, even though the NPS was not in favor. The Sierra Club attained national attention by leading the fight against proposed dams in Grand Canyon in 1966–1967. However, the NPCA has displayed the most dramatic shift among park-oriented groups. In its publication and its lobbying efforts, the NPCA has become increasingly willing to criticize actions affecting the parks, even when they have been endorsed by the NPS leadership.

TABLE 8.2 Membership in Relevant Interest Groups (1962–1990)

Year	National Parks and Conservation Association	Sierra Club	Wilderness Society
1962	25,000	22,000	21,000
1966	35,000	35,000	30,000
1968	41,000	80,000	50,000
1970	55,000	135,000	70,000
1971	55,000	135,000	77,000
1973	55,000	140,000	80,000
1974	55,000	140,000	73,000
1975	55,000	162,000	90,000
1976	45,000	174,000	70,000
1977	45,000	183,000	70,000
1978	45,000	183,000	70,000
1979	35,000	183,000	55,000
1980	30,000	199,000	50,000
1981	33,000	225,000	50,000
1982	45,000	310,000	60,000
1984	45,000	350,000	110,000
1985	60,000	350,000	140,000
1987	65,000	416,000	190,000
1988	100,000	416,000	225,000
1989	100,000	500,000	315,000
1990	200,000	565,000	390,000

SOURCE: *Encyclopedia of Associations* (Detroit: Gale Research, Inc., various editions). The year shown is two years before the date of the volume to allow for compilation and publication time.

All three groups have consistently demanded policies that contribute to preserving natural conditions in the parks. Further, their actions, lobbying, and publications have had an impact. As one scholar noted in 1984, "From the mid-1960s onward, the relationship of the NPS to the national preservation organizations was very different from that of any preceding era, and much of the difference was due to the increased strength of these organizations" (Foresta, 1984, 69).

The Resurgence of Congress. A third broad trend in American politics of the 1970s involved institutional changes in Congress.

Inspired largely by the perceived excesses of the "imperial" presidents, particularly those associated with the Nixon administration, members of Congress reasserted institutional power during the 1970s. At the same time, they "looked anxiously inward" to reform their own procedures by diffusing and decentralizing the power of individual members (Sundquist, 1981, 367; Smith, 1985). The new arrangements facilitated entrepreneurial behavior by members and enhanced their ability to intervene in the affairs of individual agencies.[6]

Parks policy was not immune to these changes. In fact, many members were particularly aggressive in their relations with the NPS. Many representatives resented the fact that the agency had been told by Nixon's White House not to cooperate with Congress. Increased congressional intervention was slowed for a while by the abilities and determination of NPS director Hartzog to resist political initiatives. But after he was fired by Nixon in 1972, the agency became even more vulnerable. Parks were also tempting targets for congressional interest for their potential pork barrel value, especially when other similar opportunities, such as those with the Army Corps of Engineers, were diminishing (Foresta, 1984, 75–78; Hartzog, 1988; Mazmanian and Nienaber, 1979).

Initially, this increased congressional intervention seemed to push parks policy toward preservation. First, individual members, now eager to cultivate their own support groups, were cognizant of the public opinion shifts and interest group behavior described earlier. Second, reinforcement for such a perspective came in 1972 with the primary defeat of House Interior Chairman Wayne Aspinall, largely as a result of environmental objections to his emphasis on land use by ranchers and grazers (Roberts, 1972, 42). Third, with the reassertion by House members and a growing preoccupation with energy issues by the Senate committee with jurisdiction over parks, the power of antipreservation, prodevelopment western Senators was somewhat diminished (Foresta, 1984, 80). Fourth, membership within the House Subcommittee on Parks increased from seventeen to twenty-six between 1963 and 1973, while the number of potentially antipreservation representatives from states closely associated with the Sagebrush Rebellion remained at seven.

Opening Up the Policy Process.   A fourth broad trend affecting American government in the late 1960s and early 1970s was the opening up of the policymaking process. The Freedom of Information Act was passed in 1966 to facilitate access to government documents and was strengthened in 1974. In 1970, Congress passed legislation requiring the recording of teller votes. Sunshine laws were commonly used after 1973 to open up hearings and mark-up sessions.

Many government agencies took steps to open up their own internal procedures to public participation. Indeed, the National Environmental Policy Act of 1969 mandated increased public involvement for many actions affecting parks (Mazmanian and Nienaber, 1979; Sundquist, 1981, 368).

In parks policy, the major impact of this trend was in the planning process. Planning for each park is based on two documents. The basic document is a General Management Plan (GMP) that sets forth the explicit objectives and strategies in management of the park. The GMP is to be reviewed and rewritten by a team of NPS officials roughly every fifteen years. Each park also uses a

TABLE 8.3   National Park Service Expansion (1964–1990)

Type of Unit	1964	1970	1982	1990
National Parks	31	35	48	50
National Recreation Areas	4	13	17	18
Total	201	281	334	357

SOURCE: U.S. National Park Service, *Statistical Abstracts*, various years.

Statement of Management, prepared every two years or so by the park superintendent and the regional director, that identifies major problems.

Public participation through workshops, meetings, review, and comment are to be used throughout the process. Such opportunities were used extensively by propreservation individuals and groups throughout the 1970s. For example, the 1980 Yosemite GMP was completed after years of public involvement, including forty open workshops involving over sixty thousand people, many of them environmentalists.

An Apparent Change in Policy Emphasis

Together, these changes stimulated an apparent change in emphasis for parks policy. As one noted expert (and later critic of park policy) wrote in a comparison of public lands agencies in 1971, "Give several agencies a single problem to solve and each will respond with its own solution . . . the NPS is apt to prescribe preservation" (Frome, 1971, 141). In that effort, the NPS seemingly received support from environmental groups, members of Congress, and executive branch officials. Many apparent changes were evident.

Expansion

The new ecologically friendly approach to parks stimulated a dramatic expansion of the system. Table 8.3 lists the number of different types of units for several different years. Between 1964 and 1982, the number of total units increased by 66 percent, the number of parks by 55 percent. Further, many of these units were added to fill previously unrepresented areas according to the 1972 National Park System Plan. This plan climaxed attempts to establish scientific criteria for new parklands based on ecosystems and geologic history rather than just pretty scenery. Expansion peaked in 1980 with the Alaska National Interest Lands Conservation Act, adding 44 million acres of new national parks and 54 million acres of new wildlife refuges.

Diversification

Expansion also entailed diversification in the stated purposes of park units. As Table 8.3 shows, the number of National Recreation Areas increased between

1964 and 1982 by over 400 percent. In addition, the NPS gained a number of urban units. Sites had existed in Washington and Philadelphia for decades, but policymakers, under pressure from environmental organizations, made a concerted effort to establish urban areas in the 1970s that could provide a relatively natural experience for urban dwellers. These included Gateway (New York City) and Golden Gate (San Francisco) in 1972, Cuyahoga (Cleveland) in 1974, Chattahoochie (Atlanta) in 1978, and Santa Monica (Los Angeles) and Jean Lafitte (New Orleans) in 1978. By 1982, over 16 percent of the units and nearly 33 percent of the recreation visits to the NPS were at urban locations (U.S. National Park Service, *Statistical Abstract,* 1982, 8).

Specific Policies

Many management policies of the NPS changed to reflect a more environmental orientation. Between 1972 and 1976, fire control policy shifted from "one of total suppression" to the let-burn approach, allowing naturally occurring "fire to play its natural role in the park and thus perpetuate natural ecosystems" (U.S. National Park Service, 1991, 33). Wildlife policies encouraged replacement of artificial with natural conditions. For example, between 1968 and 1970, the garbage dumps at Yellowstone where grizzly bears had fed for decades were closed in order to return the bears to "natural" feeding habits. Parks adopted a system of zoning whereby different areas could receive greater protection. Agency officials called for reduction of roads and accommodations within parks, with Director Hartzog displaying his own changing priorities in a 1971 interview: "We've simply got to do something besides build roads in these parks if we're going to have any parks left."[7] The agency also established an Office of Science and Technology to provide ecological research with which to guide management principles. The NPS even conducted a fairly systematic assessment of threats to the parks that culminated in the 1980 *State of the Parks* document.

Specific Park Plans

NPS employees made a conscientious effort to renew plans for specific units by involving the public in their deliberations. The plans for individual parks showed the results. For example, consider three "crown jewels" of the system. The 1974 Yellowstone GMP reflected a preservation orientation in calling for the removal of a campground, store, and trailer park at Fishing Bridge. Removal of this settlement was a trade-off for the continued construction of a commercial center at Grant Village. Both settlements were located in prime grizzly bear habitat.

At Grand Canyon, the 1979 Colorado River Management Plan called for a phased removal of motorized watercraft from the river. The NPS used scientific research showing that oar-powered trips were quieter, safer, and more satisfying to the consumer and were nearly as profitable to the operator as motorized rafts. The 1980 GMP for Yosemite stated that "the intent of the NPS is to remove all automobiles from Yosemite Valley and Mariposa Grove and to redirect development to the periphery of the park and beyond." Although the plan did not provide an exact timetable, it did use ten years as a framework (U.S. National Park Service, 1974, 1979, 1980).

An Apparent Shift

Park policymakers talked a significant preservation game in the 1970s, and many believed them. Upon assuming office at the NPS in 1973, Director Ron Walker said, "Our first duty above all others, is preservation."[8] Many in the agency took that seriously. A 1980 survey of NPS personnel showed that 84 percent felt preservation was "the major purpose" of the agency, whereas only 9 percent emphasized use.[9] In his research, Ronald Foresta discovered "a widespread acceptance of environmentalism by the agency's rank and file" and cited several of the plans described earlier as evidence of the subsequent shift in policy emphasis (Foresta, 1984, 89, 109). Another outside expert concurred in 1978, writing that "the Park Service . . . has gradually come to favor park preservation emphases as more important than facilitating recreational uses" (Culhane, 1978, 238). Finally, the agency's own historian agreed, promising that "the Park Service will continue to move in the direction of preservation, but only slowly" (Everhart, 1983, 180).

Deemphasizing Preservation

The progress on implementation of a preservation-oriented policy toward the parks that had begun in the 1970s was slowed and often even reversed in the 1980s and early 1990s. Attempts by agency personnel to realize the changes promised in the preceding decade were often undercut, overruled, or simply not funded. The reasons for this failure to institutionalize the policy shift are ironically related to the reasons it occurred in the first place.

Why the Shift Toward Preservation Stalled

Even though NPS employees tried to adopt a more ecological approach to parks by emphasizing preservation, their efforts were largely unsuccessful for two reasons. First, rather than clarifying the agency's goals, political events of the 1980s obscured them. Second, political support for the agency decreased rather than increased during the period. Ironically, both the lack of consensus and the diminution of support were fueled by the trends of the 1970s described earlier.

Lack of Consensus on Policy Goals

Many political scientists have described the importance of clear, consensual goals for agency behavior and the corresponding ineptitude that results from vague or contradictory criteria (Kaufman, 1960; Lowi, 1979, 93; Pressman and Wildavsky, 1984, 70, 90; Rosenbaum, 1989, 123). During the 1980s, the NPS was subject to severe demands on both extremes of the perceived dichotomy between preservation and use. The resulting confusion was exacerbated by conflicting messages from political superiors, unfocused public opinion, ambiguous interest group impact, and contradictory responsibilities for the agency.

The fate of a preservation-based parks policy became quickly apparent with the arrival of the Reagan administration in 1981. Shortly after taking office, Interior Secretary James Watt announced, "If I err, I'm going to be erring on the people side."[10] Watt also guaranteed free rein to park concessioners in a speech to their conference: "If a personality is giving you a problem, we're going to get rid of the problem or the personality, whichever is faster."[11] Watt and other Reagan appointees attempted to make parks more accessible and usable for tourists and commercial operators throughout the 1980s. Those attempts included leasing coal mining in Chaco Canyon, allowing strip mining near Bryce National Park, opening up Lassen Volcanic National Park to snowmobile use, and censoring personnel for opposing development and commercial interests. Nor did such efforts cease with the Bush administration in 1989.[12] Even while this was going on, NPS Director William Penn Mott promised, "We must err on the side of preservation."[13] Such comments only heightened confusion among agency employees.

The public support for preservation that had seemed evident in the 1970s did little to sustain the momentum for that shift. One reason is that public support for environmental causes is broad but not salient. Public opinion was neither intense enough nor focused enough on parks to provide steady pressure. Rather, public concern bounced from one environmental "crisis" to another. Also, relevant interest groups lost some strength during the early 1980s. As Table 8.2 shows, membership actually decreased in the NPCA and the Wilderness Society until 1984, when backlash against the Reagan actions inspired dramatic growth.

Participation declined in part because of the plethora of interest groups competing for new members. This resulted in a more crowded decisional arena that made consistent objectives difficult to achieve. Propreservation interest group activities were also countered by the growth of pro-use movements, exemplified by the Sagebrush Rebellion and the Wise Use Movement. Members of the latter, in particular, advocate private uses in parks such as development, logging, grazing, and mining. As other scholars have described, the ultimate impact of interest groups in such a contentious political sphere is more often stability than significant policy change (Heinz et al., 1993, 413).

The lack of consensus over policy goals was also enhanced by the growth of responsibilities for the agency. The rapid expansion of recreation areas and the creation of urban parks in the 1970s created quite different challenges for the NPS to handle than management issues associated with remote, natural-based parks (Shanks, 1984, 217–223). Further, the increased awareness of the presence and impact of external threats meant that park managers could no longer simply concentrate on managing their resource like an island. According to State of the Parks, "More than 50 percent of the reported threats were attributed to sources and activities located *external* to the parks" (U.S. National Park Service, 1980a;

TABLE 8.4   Total Appropriations to the National Park Service (1987$)

Year	Total Appropriation
1981	1,100,788
1982	955,586
1983	1,219,518
1984	1,036,076
1985	1,010,959
1986	871,019
1987	878,980
1988	922,429
1989	993,480
1990	1,054,047

SOURCES: Raw data from U.S. Department of the Interior, 1990, *Budget:* NPS-12; price deflator from *Economic Report of the President,* 1993:352.

Freemuth, 1991). As many NPS field personnel have told me, the job of park managers became increasingly complex.

To summarize the absence of goal consensus, the momentum that had existed to establish preservation as the primary policy goal had disappeared by 1992. In an internal assessment of that year, NPS employees begged for "leadership that is capable of enunciating and implementing clear and compelling goals for parks policy and Park Service management" (U.S. National Park Service, 1992, 14).

Diminution of Political Support

Political support is evident in the supply of material resources, the relative autonomy given an agency, and the degree of institutional deference to bureaucratic expertise. Effective bureaucratic behavior is dependent on consistent levels of resources and the necessary discretion to implement policy mandates (Clarke and McCool, 1985, 7; Halperin, 1974, 51; Ripley and Franklin, 1976, 48; Wilson, 1989, 181). During the 1980s, the political support given the NPS by elected officials diminished. Resources did not keep pace with demands, and political intervention into agency affairs, in part due to the trends of the 1970s, increased.

Financial support for parks policy suffered in the 1980s. Table 8.4 shows the total appropriations to the NPS during the decade in constant 1987 dollars.[14] As the table indicates, resources actually declined for a few years before rising to a level below where they had been at the start of the period. This progression occurred even while the parks were experiencing increased demands, such as those deriving from the increased visitor totals shown in Table 8.1. Nor did financial resources increase dramatically as the result of higher entrance fees in 1986 because the revenue was funneled into the General Treasury Fund rather than being returned to the parks (Lowry, 1993).

TABLE 8.5   Congressional Hearings on the National Park Service[a]

Congress	Years	House	Senate	Total
84th	1955–1956	4	5	9
85th	1957–1958	4	4	8
86th	1959–1960	3	2	5
87th	1961–1962	5	4	9
88th	1963–1964	3	4	7
89th	1965–1966	4	3	7
90th	1967–1968	7	2	9
91st	1969–1970	6	3	9
92d	1971–1972	2	4	6
93d	1973–1974	7	2	9
94th	1975–1976	7	10	17
95th	1977–1978	10	5	15
96th	1979–1980	5	4	9
97th	1981–1982	9	13	22
98th	1983–1984	13	10	23
99th	1985–1986	10	14	24
100th	1987–1988	11	11	22
101st	1989–1990	11	21	32

[a]These totals do not include appropriations hearings.

SOURCES: *Congressional Information Service Annual Index* for each year; *Congressional Information Service Annual Abstracts* for each year; *U.S. Serial Set Index* for 1959–1969; *U.S. Serial Set Index* for 1947–1958.

The financial situation was even less supportive, given the pork barrel potential of parks. Members of Congress had always found opportunities to use the parks to provide benefits to their constituents, such as those in the 1978 "Park Barrel Bill" that affected over two hundred members in forty-four states with expansions and projects (Everhart, 1983, 147; Foresta, 1984, 77–80). With the congressional resurgence of the 1970s and the entrepreneurial behavior of individual members described earlier, financial manipulation of parks dramatically increased. Such maneuvering made the limited dollars that were available even more scarce for meaningful NPS projects.

Financial manipulation was just one means of congressional micromanagement of the NPS in the 1980s. More freedom for individual members, increased staff, and greater incentives for legislators to alter park policies for personal political gain stimulated increased usage of such tools as oversight and casework. Table 8.5 displays the increased number of nonappropriations hearings on NPS behavior in Congress over the last several decades. Only in 1976, largely due to Bicentennial activities, did the totals approximate those of the 1980s. As corroborating evidence, a summary analysis of General Accounting Office (the investigative arm of Congress) reports shows similar results. The GAO prepared five reports on the NPS during the 1970s and twenty-six in the 1980s. Congressional members could use these tools to respond to political demands and not necessarily to the natural needs of the parks.

Institutional changes within the executive branch also stymied the NPS shift toward preservation. The Reagan administration centralized and politicized the executive bureaucracy more than any other modern presidency (Durant, 1992; Moe, 1985, 235; Pfiffner, 1987, 58; Rourke, 1991). For the NPS, this translated into active, determined leadership from the secretary of the interior and his assistants. Secretary Watt and his successors showed a great willingness to censor NPS officials who advocated preservation, such as Howard Chapman, Director of the Western Region, to alter antidevelopment documents prepared by field employees such as Lorraine Mintzmayer's *Vision for the Greater Yellowstone Area,* and to micromanage career paths by giving political appointees the power to transfer NPS employees at Government Service level 14 or above (most regional officials and superintendents) (Cahn and Cahn, 1987, 32–33; Frome, 1992, 12; Hartzog, 1988, 272; Mintzmayer, 1992, 25).

Together with the absence of consensus over agency goals, diminished political support for the NPS meant an inability to sustain the new policy direction. Again referring to the agency's 1992 assessment, employees admit that the NPS has "lost the credibility and capability it must possess in order to play a more proactive role in charting its own course, in defining and defending its core mission" (U.S. National Park Service, 1992, 12).

A Policy of Political Utility

The parks policy that emerged in the 1980s and early 1990s did not consistently emphasize the preservation focus of the 1970s, but rather focused on political utility. Far more often than NPS employees wished, the parks were managed to capitalize on a political opportunity or to satisfy the demands of specific constituents. Such decisions usually meant more development, more commercialism, and less wilderness. As a result, the natural conditions in the parks often suffered. As Yosemite superintendent Mike Finley told me in 1992, "Today, decisions are made for politics instead of for the resource." The following section discusses what became of the apparent changes in the 1970s.

Expenditures for Political Purposes

The Reagan budget cuts of the early 1980s and congressional manipulations precluded systematic expansion of the park system. The administration refused to spend the money from the Land and Water Conservation Fund that was already designated for the purchase of new lands and private inholdings. Appropriations for the study program identifying new areas were terminated in 1981, and the Office of New Area Studies was subsequently phased out. Even using NPS calculations, more than 40 percent of the designated regions were not even potentially represented by the end of the decade (National Parks and Conservation

Association, 1988, 34). Rather, units were often added to achieve political ends. Congressional intervention into NPS expansion reached new depths with questionable projects such as Steamtown, a $63 million attempt to convert an abandoned railroad yard into a historic theme park in the district of Joe McDade, ranking Republican member of the House Appropriations Committee. Nor is Steamtown the only case. By 1990, NPS employees complained in an internal memo that the system was becoming a "repository for what are in essence economic development type projects."[15] Expenditures of limited agency funds on political projects came at the expense of NPS preservation efforts in other units.

Restoring and maintaining natural conditions in parks requires substantial expenditures on research, planning, the redeployment of commercial operations, and the development of alternative means of making parks accessible (such as fleets of buses). The agency budget for research remains abysmal. A National Academy of Sciences study in late 1992 was quite critical, pointing out that only 2 percent of the NPS budget goes for actual research (National Parks and Conservation Association, 1992, 16).

Planned projects continue to await funding. For example, estimates for the 1980 Yosemite plan called for at least $22 million for construction of parking areas outside the park and $33 million for new buses. None of this was forthcoming. Given the severe fiscal deficits of the 1980s and the fact that Yosemite's annual budget is only $15 million, the failure to secure these funds seems understandable until one recalls that the total is actually less than what has been spent on Steamtown. That circumstance alone reflects the priorities present in national parks policy.

Failure to Continue Policies

Several of the policy changes of the 1970s were either reversed or not implemented in the 1980s in response to demands from political constituents. Changes in fire control policy are illustrative. The massive 1988 Yellowstone fires left the let-burn fire control policy in ashes. Even though preservationists argue that the fires resulted largely from not going far enough with let-burn to include prescribed burning of dry-fuel buildup, threatened economic and commercial interests damned NPS management of the Yellowstone situation. They were supported by many western legislators. Senators Alan Simpson and Malcolm Wallop from Wyoming, for example, denounced NPS policies as a "disaster" (U.S. Congress. Senate, 1988, 16). Following a review by officials from several public lands agencies, the policy was rewritten to let fires burn only when superintendents sign documents stating that property is not at risk. Wallop boasted, "All the words about natural fires are in there, but the fact is they're now going to have to suppress the fires."[16] As one ranger told me, "Superintendents now say, 'By God, I just can't take a chance.'"

Attention to other policies has not been as dramatic. Still, most have not changed as much as had been promised in the 1970s. Wildlife assistance programs remain unscientific, grazing continues in certain parks despite the objections of field employees, questionable new recreational activities like snowmobiling have actually increased, and commercial development of projects such as golf courses still proceeds in many parks (Chase, 1987; Frome, 1992; Lowry, 1994).

Attempts to address external threats have been tragically unsuccessful. In its investigation several years after publication of the 1980 *State of the Parks*, the GAO concluded that 80 percent of the threats remained unresolved and 43 percent undocumented (U.S. General Accounting Office, 1987, 4). One example shows why: Air pollution from coal-burning power plants has damaged the ecosystem in Shenandoah National Park and cut average annual visibility from eighty to fifteen miles. The number of offending plants actually increased during the 1980s, despite the objections of park officials. NPS opposition was undercut by higher officials in the Interior Department and was overruled by Vice President Dan Quayle's Council on Competitiveness (Lowry, 1994, 186–187). As one NPS manager commented to me about external threats in 1992, "Isn't it interesting that nobody's updated that document [*State of the Parks*]? Have these threats gone away in the last twelve years?"

Failure to Implement Plans

The plans for specific parks cited earlier have also not been implemented. As mentioned before, Yosemite's plan was never funded. The Yellowstone compromise was never enforced, leaving a full settlement at Grant Village and a store and a 350-unit recreation vehicle park at Fishing Bridge. Internal NPS documents admit that their plans were countermanded by "policy considerations beyond Yellowstone" (U.S. National Park Service, 1988b, 342; Chase, 1987, 228). The plan to remove motorized boats from the Colorado River in the Grand Canyon was stopped by an amendment from Senator Orrin Hatch (R-UT), acting to protect the investments of local motorized raft companies.

The failure to sustain a preservation emphasis in parks policy has not been limited to these major parks. Instead, parks policy in general can be characterized as short-term, opportunistic, and useful for political purposes. As one review of a variety of recent books on park policy concludes, "While the declared mission of the NPS has not changed, the de facto policies of the NPS have been responsive to politics, and so also have agency-developed natural resource and visitor management policies" (Soden, 1991, 571).

Speculation and Conclusions

Will parks policy shift back toward preservation with a Democratic administration supported by many environmental groups? Shortly after President Clinton took office, new Interior Secretary Babbitt delivered a preservation-based speech emphasizing research and ecosystem management. Other administration statements have also promised a renewal of the preservation focus. Further, legislation is pending in Congress to revise concessions contracting and to raise agency revenue through fee increases. As yet, however, administration promises and legislative proposals remain largely unfulfilled.

Many other factors discussed in this chapter affect parks policy—like congressional micromanagement from members of both parties—factors that are not immediately responsive to the stated desires of the Clinton presidency. Further, the actions of the Clinton administration in specific cases, such as the new plan for the Everglades, show a willingness to compromise that does not suggest a radical change of course for the NPS. Finally, although it has not yet offered specific revisions to national park policy, the new Republican majority in Congress is not likely to be sympathetic or supportive of preservation emphases.

To summarize, the history of national parks policy in the United States over the last thirty years reflects some of the broader factors that contribute to change in American politics. Stated policies have shifted in response to changing public opinion and the efforts of interest groups. The policymaking process for the parks was altered by a resurgent, proactive Congress and by greater public involvement in specific plans and decisions. Finally, ultimate agency performance was determined by a short-term and politically opportunistic focus.

In conclusion, American parks policy has changed mainly in rhetorical terms and in the growth of greater awareness of problems facing these national treasures. Those changes are not insignificant, representing at least a start toward developing a consistent policy that will match the task ahead. Still, they are only a start. A real policy shift awaits political consensus on the goals to be achieved in parks policy and support for the implementing agency.

NOTES

1. James Ridenour, quoted by Nolte in the *San Francisco Chronicle* (September 29, 1990): A1.
2. NPS Organic Act, U.S. Code Annotated, title 16, sec. 1:66.
3. For a review, see Caulfield, 1989, 20–26.
4. Mather's 1919 report in Shankland, 1951, 213.
5. Opinion Research Corporation survey results reported in Dunlap, 1989, 97.
6. For an example, see Ferejohn and Shipan, 1989.
7. Quoted in McPhee, 1971, 62.
8. Quoted in Frome, 1992, 81.
9. Survey by Daniel McCool, cited in Foresta, 1984, 104.
10. Reported by Omang in the *Washington Post*, March 9, 1981, A9.
11. Reported in Frome, 1992, 175.
12. For more on these, see Lowry, 1994.
13. Reported by McCombs in the *Washington Post*, June 28, 1985, D1.
14. Comparisons of appropriation figures from years before 1981 are problematic since the NPS totals beginning in that year include some LWCF and Heritage Conservation funds.
15. Reported by Lancaster in the *Washington Post*, December 1, 1990, A1.
16. Reported by Reid in the *Washington Post*, June 2, 1989, A3.

REFERENCES

Abbey, Edward. 1968. *Desert Solitaire*. New York: Ballantine Books.

Cahn, Robert, and Patricia Cahn. 1987. "Disputed Territory." *National Parks* (May/June):28–33.

Caulfield, Henry P. 1989. "The Conservation and Environmental Movements: An Historical Analysis." In James P. Lester, ed., *Environmental Politics and Policy*. Durham, NC: Duke University Press.

Chase, Alston. 1987. *Playing God in Yellowstone*. San Diego: Harcourt Brace Jovanovich.

Clarke, Jeanne Nienaber, and Daniel McCool. 1985. *Staking Out the Terrain*. New York: State University of New York Press.

Culhane, Paul J. 1978. "Natural Resources Policy: Procedural Change and Substantive Environmentalism." In T. J. Lowi and A. Stone, eds., *Nationalizing Government*. Beverly Hills, CA: Sage Publications.

Dunlap, Riley E. 1989. "Public Opinion and Environmental Policy." In James P. Lester, ed., *Environmental Politics and Policy*. Durham, NC: Duke University Press.

Durant, Robert F. 1992. *The Administrative Presidency Revisited*. Albany: State University of New York Press.

Everhart, William C. 1983. *The National Park Service*. Boulder: Westview Press.

Ferejohn, John A., and Charles R. Shipan. 1989. "Congressional Influence on Administrative Agencies." In L. C. Dodd and B. I. Oppenheimer, eds. *Congress Reconsidered*. 4th ed. Washington, DC: CQ Press.

Foresta, Ronald A. 1984. *America's National Parks and Their Keepers*. Washington, DC: Resources for the Future.

Freemuth, John. 1991. *Islands Under Siege: National Parks and the Politics of External Threats*. Lawrence: University Press of Kansas.

Frome, Michael. 1971. *The Forest Service*. New York: Praeger.

———. 1992. *Regreening the National Parks*. Tucson: University of Arizona Press.

Grosvenor, Melvin Bell. 1966. "Today and Tomorrow in Our National Parks." *National Geographic* 130:1–15.

Halperin, Morton H. 1974. *Bureaucratic Politics and Foreign Policy*. Washington, DC: Brookings Institution.

Hartzog, George B., Jr. 1966. "Parkscape USA." *National Geographic* 130:48–93.

———. 1988. *Battling for the National Parks*. Mt. Kisco, NY: Moyer Bell Limited.

Heinz, J. P., E. O. Laumann, R. D. Nelson, and R. H. Salisbury. 1993. *The Hollow Core*. Cambridge: Harvard University Press.

Kaufman, Herbert. 1960. *The Forest Ranger*. Baltimore: Johns Hopkins University Press.

Leopold, A. S. 1963. "Wildlife Management in the National Parks." Report of the Advisory Board on Wildlife Management to Secretary of the Interior Udall, March 4, 1963.

Lowi, Theodore J. 1979. *The End of Liberalism*. 2d ed. New York: Norton.

Lowry, William R. 1993. "Land of the Fee: Entrance Fees and the NPS." *Political Research Quarterly* 46:823–845.

———. 1994. *The Capacity for Wonder: Preserving National Parks*. Washington, DC: Brookings Institution.

Mapes, Glynn. 1966. "Severe Overcrowding Brings Ills of the City to Scenic Yosemite." *Wall Street Journal* (June 24):1.

Mazmanian, Daniel A., and Jeanne Nienaber. 1979. *Can Organizations Change?* Washington, DC: Brookings Institution.

McPhee, John. 1971. "Profiles—George Hartzog." *New Yorker* (47):45–89.

Mintzmayer, Lorraine. 1992. "Disservice to the Parks." *National Parks* 66:24–25.

Moe, Terry M. 1985. "The Politicized Presidency." In John Chubb and Paul E. Peterson, eds., *The New Direction in American Politics.* Washington, DC: Brookings Institution.

National Parks and Conservation Association. 1988. *Investing in Park Futures.* Washington, DC: National Parks and Conservation Association.

———. 1992. "Study Finds Overhaul of Park Science Needed." *National Parks* 66:16.

Nienaber, Jeanne, and Aaron Wildavsky. 1973. *The Budgeting and Evaluation of Federal Recreation Programs.* New York: Basic Books.

Pfiffner, James P. 1987. "Political Appointees and Career Executives: The Democracy-Bureaucracy Nexus." *Public Administration Review* 47 (1):57–65.

Porterfield, Byron. 1965. "Fire Island Park Gets Ten-Year Plan." *New York Times* (October 28):36.

Pressman, Jeffrey L., and Aaron Wildavsky. 1984. *Implementation.* 3d ed. Berkeley: University of California Press.

Pyne, Stephen J. 1989. *Fire on the Rim.* New York: Ballantine Books.

Ripley, Randall B., and Grace A. Franklin. 1976. *Congress, the Bureaucracy, and Public Policy.* Homewood, IL: Dorsey Press.

Roberts, Steven V. 1972. "Colorado Vote Reflects New Mood of West." *New York Times* (September 14):42.

Rosenbaum, Walter A. 1989. "The Bureaucracy and Environmental Policy." In J. P. Lester, ed., *Environmental Politics and Policy.* Durham, NC: Duke University Press.

Rourke, Francis. 1991. "Presidentializing the Bureaucracy: From Kennedy to Reagan." In James P. Pfiffner, ed., *The Managerial Presidency.* Pacific Grove, CA: Brooks/Cole.

Schlesinger, Arthur M., Jr. 1965. *A Thousand Days.* Boston: Houghton Mifflin.

Schlozman, Kay L., and John T. Tierney. 1983. "More of the Same: Washington Pressure Group Activity in a Decade of Change." *Journal of Politics* 45:351–377.

Shankland, Robert. 1951. *Steve Mather of the National Parks.* 3d ed. New York: Alfred A. Knopf.

Shanks, Bernard. 1984. *This Land Is Your Land.* San Francisco: Sierra Club Books.

Smith, Steven S. 1985. "New Patterns of Decisionmaking in Congress." In J. E. Chubb and P. E. Peterson, eds., *The New Direction in American Politics.* Washington, DC: Brookings Institution.

Soden, Dennis L. 1991. "National Parks Literature of the 1980s." *Policy Studies Journal* 19 (3):570–576.

Sundquist, James L. 1981. *The Decline and Resurgence of Congress.* Washington, DC: Brookings Institution.

Udall, Stewart L. 1963. *The Quiet Crisis.* New York: Holt, Rinehart and Winston.

U.S. Congress. Senate. Subcommittee on Public Lands, National Parks, and Forest Hearings. 1988. *Current Fire Management Policies.* 100th Cong., 2d Sess. Washington, DC: Government Printing Office.

U.S. Department of the Interior. 1990. *Budget Justifications FY 1991.* Washington, DC: Government Printing Office.

U.S. General Accounting Office. 1987. *Limited Progress Made in Documenting and Mitigating Threats to the Parks.* Washington, DC: General Accounting Office.

U.S. National Park Service. 1974. *Yellowstone Master Plan.* Washington, DC: Department of the Interior.

———. 1979. *Colorado River Management Plan.* Washington, DC: National Park Service.

———. 1980a. *State of the Parks 1980.* Washington, DC: National Park Service.

———. 1980b. *Yosemite General Management Plan.* Washington, DC: Department of the Interior.

———. 1988a. *Management Policies.* Washington, DC: National Park Service.

———. 1988b. *Yellowstone Fishing Bridge Environmental Impact Statement.* Washington, DC: Department of the Interior.

———. 1991. *Yellowstone Statement for Management.* Washington, DC: National Park Service.

———. 1992. *National Parks for the 21st Century.* Washington, DC: National Park Service.

———. Various years. *Statistical Abstract.* Washington, DC: Department of the Interior.

Walker, Jack L. 1983. "The Origins and Maintenance of Interest Groups in America." *American Political Science Review* 77:390–406.

Wilson, James Q. 1989. *Bureaucracy.* New York: Basic Books.

Wirth, Conrad L. 1980. *Parks, Politics, and the People.* Norman: University of Oklahoma Press.

9

Wilderness Policy

CRAIG W. ALLIN

This chapter examines the evolution of wilderness policy on western public lands over a period of approximately thirty years. Our national commitment to statutory wilderness preservation began with the 1964 Wilderness Act (PL 88-577), reached its climax with the Alaska National Interest Lands Conservation Act of 1980 (PL 96-487), and continues today. The area protected by law as wilderness has increased from none in mid-1964 to approximately 100 million acres at the end of 1994. Issues of wilderness management that were given very little attention thirty years ago are now regarded with increasing seriousness. Wilderness policy, once mostly distributive in nature, is now largely regulatory. With that shift has come more conflict, involving more actors. The process has spawned new organizations on both sides of the wilderness issue. Increasingly, the major decisions concerning wilderness policy have been removed from the hands of agency bureaucrats and delivered over to Congress and the courts.

If what has happened is relatively clear, why it has happened is not. Political change is rarely simple. The forces that have shaped wilderness politics are many, and they interact in ways that are complex and only partly understood. Among the forces at work in wilderness politics over the past thirty years are the increasing scarcity of the wilderness resource itself, the changing demography of the American nation, the effects of electoral politics, the varying strength of private coalitions with conflicting views on wilderness policy, the political culture of the executive agencies and the competition among them for scarce resources, the competition between Congress and the executive branch over control of public policy, and chance.

The interaction of these political forces has created different political environments and different policy outcomes in different periods. Where wilderness policy is concerned, the past thirty years subdivide rather evenly into an era begun by the Wilderness Act of 1964 and into another era begun by the Alaska National Interest Lands Conservation Act of 1980. Understanding what makes these two periods different helps explain why wilderness policy has evolved as it has and may even provide some limited insight into the politics of the near future.

The Origins of American Wilderness Policy

Any reasonably sophisticated understanding of recent wilderness policy requires some knowledge of the history from which it grew. The public lands of the American West have been a subject of political contention for more than one hundred and fifty years. Following the secession of southern states in 1861, Congress embarked on a western lands policy designed to encourage emigration, settlement, nation building, and economic development by exploiting the region's abundant natural resources. The Homestead Act of 1862 (PL 37-75) promised free land for settlers, and the Pacific Railway Act (PL 37-120), passed later the same year, promised massive land grants in return for railroad construction.

These were followed by a multitude of land laws designed to vanquish a wilderness and establish a civilization (Gates, 1968). Economic development was assumed to depend upon a balance among the classic factors of production: land (natural resources), labor, and capital. Labor and capital were scarce in the West; land was abundant. Under those circumstances, wilderness was a condition to be overcome. With so much available, giving away natural resources to attract labor and capital made good sense. As a nation, we indulged that instinct throughout the West for a generation. By 1890, however, the frontier had come to an end, and the balance of economic factors had been fundamentally altered.

The seeds of the modern wilderness preservation system were sown in the latter half of the nineteenth century. Economic and technological changes in this era transformed the American landscape and the American mind. Much of what had recently been wilderness was cut, mined, cleared, plowed, or roaded. Resources that had once appeared limitless were now seen as finite. As wilderness gave way to development, its increasing scarcity bestowed a cultural value previously unrecognized, and its ruthless exploitation was no longer a self-evident good.

At the same time, Americans were becoming more affluent and more urban, and they were beginning to appreciate that industrial capitalism created social costs as well as the obvious social benefits. The mood of the country was hospitable to preservation to a degree unimaginable only a few decades earlier. Voices were raised for conservation of forests, scenery, and wildlife, and those voices were heard (Allin, 1982; Nash, 1982). The preservationist mood found its early expression in the creation of Yellowstone (1872, PL 42-24), Sequoia (1890, PL 51-926), Yosemite, and General Grant (1890, PL 51-1263) National Parks, and in the establishment of the first national forest reserves (1891, PL 51-561).

By 1920 the national parks had grown to 7 million acres and the national forests to 156 million (U.S. Bureau of the Census, 1975). The National Park Service was charged with preservation, the Forest Service with wise use. Each had a cozy relationship with business interests, and neither was much interested in wilderness preservation. The Park Service was allied with transportation interests, especially railroads, eager to develop the parks for the convenience of tourists. The Forest Service was allied with loggers, miners, and grazers, each accommodated by the service's commitment to multiple-use management of forest resources. Despite these limitations, each agency controlled millions of acres of de facto wilderness. These areas and the Alaska Territory constituted the resource base from which most of the modern wilderness system would eventually be created.

In fact, the earliest important efforts at formal wilderness preservation were facilitated by competition between the two agencies. In the 1920s the Park Service was eager to increase the number of national parks. Not surprisingly, most of the areas coveted by the Park Service were already managed by the Forest Service. The Park Service argued that transfer of scenically superlative areas to its control would leave them better protected. The Forest Service countered, creating a number of national forest wilderness areas, protected from roads, hotels, and other tourist developments popular in the parks. The Forest Service strategy appears not only to have blunted expansion of the parks but to have elicited a prowilderness shift in park policy as well (Allin, 1987, 132–134). By 1938 the Park Service was promising to maintain wilderness conditions in its new parks (Cammerer, 1938).

By the early 1960s the Forest Service had established eighty wilderness and wilderness-like areas in eleven western states with a total area of about 13 million acres. There were forty eight units of the national park system containing de facto wilderness of about 22 million acres, most of it in the West. Another 22 million acres of de facto wilderness was distributed over about a score of national wildlife refuges, mostly in Alaska (U.S. Congress. House, 1961; U.S. Congress. Senate, 1963). To wilderness advocates, it appeared as if a wilderness system might be created that would eventually protect 50 million acres, but only if they took affirmative action to protect what remained.

The extant wilderness had no statutory protection and was continuously at risk. National forest wilderness had been created administratively, largely to blunt the growth of the national park system and by an agency that remained committed to scientific forestry and multiple use. Without statutory protection, national forest wilderness units might be returned to multiple-use management by a stroke of the agriculture secretary's pen.

The prospects were not so different for national park wilderness. The Park Service had initiated recreational development in wilderness areas of the parks. It had built roads and campgrounds, encouraged railroads, and contracted with concessionaires for the construction of hotels, stores, and the infrastructure of automobile tourism generally (Albright, 1985; Foresta, 1984; Ise, 1961). As park visitation grew, the Park Service felt pressured further to develop park wilderness. Wilderness in the wildlife refuges of Alaska was protected only by its remoteness, surely a transient condition.

If the agencies did not abandon their wilderness estates to development, the Congress might. Mining, irrigation, and hydroelectric interests regularly proposed development projects that threatened public wilderness. In the postwar boom of the 1950s, the Army Corps of Engineers and the Bureau of Reclamation had designs on wilderness areas in Glacier, Kings Canyon, Big Bend, and Grand Canyon National Parks and Bighorn National Forest (Ise, 1961, 471–472). The most immediate threat was a Bureau of Reclamation proposal to dam the canyon in Dinosaur National Monument. It stirred a national debate and motivated the preservation community to work for statutory wilderness protection.

The Rise and Fall of a Distributive Wilderness Policy, 1964–1980

A period beginning sometime in the 1960s and spanning the 1970s has been called the Environmental Decade.[1] During this time, the United States fashioned a legal and organizational infrastructure to wrestle with the increasingly complex issues of environmental degradation. It would be difficult to find better mileposts for the beginning and end of the Environmental Decade than the Wilderness Act of 1964 and the Alaska National Interest Lands Conservation Act of 1980. The former created the National Wilderness Preservation System, and the latter expanded the system by 56 million acres.

The Wilderness Act was introduced in the Eisenhower era but could not be passed until the Kennedy and Johnson administrations endorsed preservation by statute and prevailed on the land management agencies to support it.[2] The Alaska lands law was passed in the final days of the Carter presidency by a lame-duck Democratic Congress. This section examines the Wilderness Act and its aftermath. The next section takes up the significantly different policy regime introduced by the Alaska lands legislation.

In the effort to pass a wilderness bill, the prowilderness agenda was determined primarily by Howard Zahniser, executive director of the Wilderness Society. He proposed combining administrative designation with statutory protection. The agencies managing conservation lands—the Forest Service in the Agriculture Department and the Park Service and the Fish and Wildlife Service in the Interior Department—would inventory their lands and designate those appropriate for preservation as wilderness. Lands already so designated by the Forest Service would be protected under the Wilderness Act, and areas subsequently designated by the administrative agencies would automatically fall under the act's protection. In short, administrative agencies would establish wilderness areas, but only Congress could abolish them (Zahniser, 1955). The environmental community believed this approach offered the best chance for a wilderness system that was both large and well protected.

The antiwilderness agenda was effectively articulated by Wayne Aspinall, chairman of the House Interior Committee from 1959 to 1972. Aspinall had two great passions where the public lands were concerned. The first was a preference for development over preservation. Aspinall represented Colorado's western slope, a district that had a frontier ethos and was heavily dependent on extractive industries. Consistent with his preference for development, Aspinall generally advocated a best-use strategy in public lands management. Lands best suited to timber production ought to be managed intensively for timber production; those best suited to grazing ought to be intensively managed for grazing; and so forth. This approach favored mining, and Aspinall was particularly fierce in his defense of mining. Mineral deposits tend to be valuable and localized. Aspinall shared the miners' view that prospecting should be encouraged and commercially viable deposits developed without arbitrary restraint. He opposed wilderness designations because they logically preclude prospecting and subsequent mineral development.

Aspinall's second passion was a commitment to congressional power over executive power. He believed Congress had allowed its constitutional prerogatives to be usurped by the departments and agencies of the executive branch, and he meant to reclaim the rights of Congress if he could (Allin, 1982, 118–135).

The Wilderness Act signed by President Lyndon Johnson on September 3, 1964, represented a compromise between the Zahniser and Aspinall agendas. In keeping with Zahniser's agenda, it created a National Wilderness Preservation System and bestowed congressional protection on 9.1 million acres of "wilderness," "wild," and "canoe" areas previously created by the Forest Service. It directed the secretary of agriculture to review every national forest "primitive area"[3] for possible inclusion in the wilderness system and to make recommendations through the president to the Congress. The secretary of the interior was given a similar charge regarding roadless areas in the national park system and the national wildlife refuge system (78 Stat. 891–893).

The Wilderness Act also reflected Aspinall's interests. First, agencies were denied the power to create wilderness areas; they were limited to forwarding recommendations to Congress. Congress retained for itself the sole and exclusive right to add new areas to the National Wilderness Preservation System. Although Aspinall's preference for congressional control was principled, it also appeared to encourage the results he preferred. Both proponents and opponents of wilderness preservation assumed that requiring an act of Congress for every addition to the system would result in less wilderness than Zahniser's plan for administrative designation.

Second, agencies were required, before submitting recommendations, to give public notice "in the vicinity of the affected land" (78 Stat. 892), to hold public hearings in the localities of proposed wilderness areas, and to solicit the views of state and local officials and other federal agencies. This procedure also disfavored wilderness. The constituency for wilderness preservation was national and was organized nationally in associations like the Wilderness Society and the Sierra

Club. The opposition was localized in the extractive industries that might be threatened by wilderness designation and in the communities that depended upon those industries. Thus, the requirement that a public hearing record be developed locally was also tailored to benefit wilderness opponents.

Third, special provisions of the Wilderness Act, applicable to national forest wilderness, diminished the scope of the preservation victory and provided concessions to extractive industries, especially to mining. The law allowed minerals prospecting and required recurrent mineral surveys by federal agencies. National forest wilderness areas were to remain available for mining, drilling, producing, and processing until December 31, 1983, "to the same extent as prior to [the Wilderness Act]" (78 Stat. 894), and minerals development that had begun before the deadline could continue indefinitely. Aircraft and motorboats were to be allowed where they were already in use, and grazing could be continued where established. Timber harvesting was to continue in the Boundary Waters Canoe Area of Minnesota. Proponents had achieved legislative protection for wilderness, but they had conceded a lot in the process.

The era begun by the Wilderness Act was one of distributive policy[4] revolving around the issue of wilderness allocation. As is typical of distributive policy, there was a clear beneficiary—the wilderness lobby—and it could receive benefits without any other constituency incurring a loss. This result was possible because the first allocation decisions were the direct result of reviews mandated by the act—reviews of roadless areas in the national park and wildlife refuge systems and of primitive areas in the national forests.

Whether by law or by administrative regulation, each of these areas had already been withdrawn from most forms of economic or commercial use. A decision to allocate a particular parcel to wilderness had little or no effect on its management. To be sure, every decision to designate an area as wilderness had its detractors, but most of the criticism came from commodity groups that opposed wilderness designation on principle rather than because of any immediate or tangible loss to them.

Politicians and bureaucrats love distributive policy. Congressional committees and executive agencies typically work in harmony to produce a benefit for some favored interest. Controversy is limited. There is little agency supervision from administrative superiors, and Congress tends to defer to its committees and subcommittees. These characteristics of a distributive policy regime suggested that allocation might go forward with limited attention and little controversy. As it happened, allocation politics affected the three major conservation agencies differently (Allin, 1982, 143–169). The Fish and Wildlife Service and the National Park Service received relatively little attention. The Forest Service received a great deal more because, in the end, its decisions departed from the distributive model.

Outside of Alaska, the national wildlife refuges were often too small or too intensively managed to qualify for serious consideration as wilderness. The large wilderness acreage in Alaska was simply too remote to receive much attention.

Although the Fish and Wildlife Service showed initial interest in wilderness designations, neither the agency nor wilderness advocacy groups viewed wildlife refuge wilderness as a national priority.

There were millions of acres of prime wilderness in the national parks, but the parks, too, received relatively little attention. The National Park Service completed the required reviews of roadless areas and forwarded its recommendations. After an initial period, in which it appeared that the Park Service would use the review process to reserve huge areas for future roads and other forms of intensive recreational development, the agency adopted a prowilderness posture.

Early recommendations were redone, generally with increases in the acreage proposed for wilderness. In the major western parks, the area proposed to be included in the national wilderness preservation system often exceeded 90 percent of the total. In 1984, 85 percent of Sequoia–Kings Canyon and 89 percent of Yosemite were designated as wilderness (PL 98-425). Four years later, 92 percent of Mount Rainier, 96 percent of Olympic, and 93 percent of the North Cascades complex were protected (PL 100-668).[5] Through 1995, there was no designated wilderness at all in Yellowstone, Glacier, Grand Teton, or Grand Canyon, but a high percentage of each park had been recommended.

Whether Park Service recommendations were approved by Congress or set aside for another day, there has been little fanfare. As a practical matter, any area within a national park that has been recommended for wilderness status is managed as wilderness. Wilderness advocates have been willing to leave well enough alone, concentrating their attention elsewhere.

Wilderness allocation in the national forests might have elicited equally small attention if the lands in question had remained limited to primitive areas already withdrawn from most forms of development. When the issue of national forest wilderness escaped the boundaries of the primitive areas, as it eventually did, the central feature of distributive policy—no losers—became inoperative. Unlike the wildlife refuges, where the primacy of wildlife management was established by law, and the national parks, where conservation of nature was paramount, the national forests were managed for multiple use. Multiple use has been the credo of the Forest Service since the earliest days under Gifford Pinchot, and Forest Service practice had been written into federal law (PL 86-517). Of course, multiple-use management was an invitation to conflict, and where wilderness was proposed on national forest lands not already withdrawn from development, the stakes were high.

Wilderness designation precluded active silviculture leading to eventual timber harvest, which many foresters saw as the agency's primary mission. Wilderness status also effectively barred new mining, grazing, road building, and water resource development. The multiple-use management possibilities foreclosed by wilderness status were central to the agency's ethos and to the interests of the agency's core constituency of resource users (Robinson, 1975).

Ironically, the wilderness issue in the national forests ultimately escaped the boundaries of distributive policy in part because the very mechanisms Wayne

Aspinall had put in place to limit growth of the wilderness system backfired. Aspinall had set a precedent for the Environmental Decade by his insistence on public notice and public hearing in the locality of the proposed wilderness. Historically, local influence in the mountain West had been exercised by those with consumptive interests in the public lands. Mining, grazing, timber harvest, and agriculture had been the pillars upon which western economies rested.

By the late 1960s, however, public attitudes were changing on a national scale, and even the West was greening. New immigrants arrived—some of them urban refugees. They brought with them environmental values developed in the places from which they came, making the West less homogeneous. Native westerners were changing as well. As economies grew and diversified, fewer residents were directly dependent on extractive industries for their livelihoods, and more people—such as those employed in recreation and tourism—had a stake in maintaining the area's natural beauty.

These trends benefited the wilderness movement, and wilderness advocates quickly overcame their initial organizational disadvantage in local arenas. Grassroots organizations sprang up, meeting the demands of public participation and pressing for inclusion of favored areas. National conservation organizations assisted through local chapters and by publishing information about successful tactics. Wilderness advocacy organizations appropriated information collected by the Forest Service to develop their own wilderness proposals. In some instances, local environmental groups were able to develop field data superior to that developed by the agency, which was often understaffed or gave higher priority to other tasks. For its part, the Forest Service seemed eager to please everybody. Often it managed to excise areas with high commodity values while increasing the total acreage recommended for wilderness.

Aspinall had also insisted that Congress, not the executive agencies, establish new wilderness areas. Aspinall's commitment to congressional prerogatives probably worked against his interest in limiting wilderness expansion. Although the additional step of congressional approval undoubtedly made the process of wilderness allocation more complex, the constituency for wilderness preservation in the United States was national. It was well represented by national organizations, most of which had a strong presence in Washington and were well served by a process that brought the ultimate decision into their preferred arena.

At the same time, other provisions of the Wilderness Act prevented the inevitable delays from unduly undermining preservation. Although the law gave the Forest Service only ten years to complete its "primitive area" reviews and submit its recommendations, it required wilderness management of the primitive areas "until Congress has determined otherwise" (78 Stat. 892).

The law also allowed for the recommendation of national forest lands contiguous to the primitive areas being reviewed. Unlike the primitive areas, contiguous areas were subject to multiple-use management. Any wilderness allocated from this source would produce losers as well as winners. Predictably, the Forest Service was reluctant to recommend contiguous areas for protection, but the wilderness lobby, buoyed by newly created grassroots groups, took up the cause. When the Forest Service refused to recommend the Magruder Corridor, an area connecting Idaho's Selway-Bitterroot Wilderness with the Salmon River Breaks and Idaho Primitive Areas, local advocates appealed to Congress. By the time they had finished, the Magruder Corridor had been added to the Selway-Bitterroot Wilderness and the Idaho and Salmon River Breaks Primitive Areas had been incorporated into a new River of No Return Wilderness,[6] just south of the Selway-Bitterroot (PL 96-312).

Wilderness advocates found success in the courts as well. In Colorado, wilderness activists sued the Forest Service to prevent the logging of land contiguous to the Gore Range–Eagle's Nest Primitive Area near the town of Vail (Kain, 1969). To the dismay of the Forest Service, the Tenth Circuit Court of Appeals concluded that the Wilderness Act required the agency to study the area, to recommend for or against its inclusion in the wilderness system, and to preserve its wilderness character until Congress and the president had made a final determination of its status (*Parker v. United States,* 1971). Congress eventually exercised its option, designating an Eagle's Nest Wilderness including the litigated lands (PL 94-352).

Decisions like these by Congress and the courts seriously undermined agency prerogatives. Management decisions once made quietly and generally to the benefit of the agency's core constituency of resource users had been thrown open to public scrutiny by the notice and participation requirements of the Wilderness Act and subsequent statutes like the National Environmental Policy Act (PL 91-184). Local wilderness groups, spawned by the notice and hearing requirements, refused to limit their advocacy to the primitive areas and adjacent lands. Congress had reserved final authority to itself, and wilderness advocates resolved to conduct studies and make recommendations. If the Forest Service could not be brought around, perhaps the Congress could be. The procedures required by Wayne Aspinall, as the price of his approving the Wilderness Act, had backfired. From an agency perspective, the national forests were out of control.

Badly needing to reassert its authority over the national forests, the Forest Service adopted a two-pronged strategy. The first prong involved a somewhat convoluted interpretation of the Wilderness Act. Section 4 of the Wilderness Act set strict standards for the management of wilderness areas; Section 2(c) set more flexible admissions standards. In an effort to minimize the law's impact on its management discretion, the Forest Service increasingly argued that the strict standards of Section 4 must be present as a minimum condition for the consideration of an area as possible wilderness (Costley, 1972; Foote, 1973; Roth, 1988).

Most of the wilderness areas Congress had created could not have passed this test of wilderness "purity," and if the Forest Service prevailed in its interpretation, few new areas would qualify. The Forest Service's purity doctrine was widely criticized and effectively repudiated by Congress in 1975, with the passage of an eastern wilderness law (PL 93-622) designating new national forest wilderness areas that were manifestly impure. The policy was formally abandoned by the Forest Service early in the Carter administration (U.S. Congress. House, 1977b).

The second prong of the Forest Service counteroffensive involved a national review. The Forest Service would undertake to study all the roadless areas of the national forests and classify them as either unsuited for wilderness or requiring further study. Lands unsuited for wilderness would be released to multiple-use management.

The Forest Service conducted its Roadless Area Review and Evaluation (RARE I) in 1971 and 1972, and after much criticism repeated it (RARE II) in 1977 and 1978. This strategy had mixed results. When RARE I failed to protect areas of de facto wilderness in which the preservation community had significant interest, an increasingly green Congress rejected the initial inventory results and enacted the Endangered American Wilderness Act of 1978 (PL 95-237) creating or enlarging seventeen national forest wilderness areas in eight western states.

Eventually, however, the inventory approach proved at least partly successful. Agency decisions concerning wilderness allocation were pushed out ahead of other national forest planning. Congressional statutes began to deal comprehensively with national forest wilderness allocation issues in one or more states, and beginning with the Alaska National Interest Lands Conservation Act of 1980, Congress often included language declaring wilderness studies sufficient and releasing lands to multiple-use management that were not designated wilderness or explicitly reserved for further wilderness study. By the end of 1995, sufficiency-release language had been enacted for national forest lands in Alaska, Arizona (PL 98-406), California (PL 98-425), Colorado (PL 96-560), New Mexico (PL 96-550), Nevada (PL 101-195), Oregon (PL 98-328), Utah (PL 98-428), Washington (PL 98-339), and Wyoming (PL 98-550).

The Wilderness Act made no provision for wilderness areas on the public lands managed by the Bureau of Land Management. Public ownership of these lands had historically been viewed as temporary, and little thought had been given to their management. All that changed with the Federal Lands Policy and Management Act of 1976 (FLPMA, PL 94-579). Congress declared its intention to retain most of the public lands in public ownership and charged the BLM to manage them under multiple-use principles. Section 603 called for a wilderness review of roadless lands comparable to what the Wilderness Act had required of the Park Service and the Fish and Wildlife Service and to what pressures from the environmental movement had eventually exacted from the Forest Service. Although the reviews are behind schedule, the BLM seems to be taking the task seriously. Congress may eventually follow the national forest model in dealing with BLM wilderness, taking up comprehensive state bills containing sufficiency-release language.

ANILCA and the Era of Regulatory Wilderness Policy

The Alaska National Interest Lands Conservation Act has straddled the great divide in western wilderness policy over the past thirty years.[7] First, passed by a lame-duck Democratic Senate and signed by a lame-duck Democratic president, ANILCA marked the end of the Environmental Decade. Second, it was the climax of the wilderness allocation process. It created 56 million acres of new wilderness areas, more than six times the acreage designated in the Wilderness Act. It was the greatest wilderness allocation statute ever, and nothing of its magnitude will ever be seen again.

Third, it provided a model for bringing the era of allocation to an end. Efforts by the Forest Service to use the RARE II process to free up forest lands for multiple use had been resisted by wilderness advocates. In a major victory for critics of the Forest Service, federal courts found the environmental impact statement for RARE II in California inadequate and blocked development on RARE II lands statewide (*California v. Block*, 1982). In ANILCA's sufficiency-release language, Congress declared the RARE II process sufficient for the State of Alaska, withdrew jurisdiction of the courts to review that conclusion, and released to multiple-use management those lands not designated for wilderness, wilderness study, or further review (94 Stat. 2421–2422). Comparable sufficiency-release language has since been enacted for every western state with significant wilderness except Idaho and Montana.

Fourth, the Alaska lands legislation ushered in the era of regulatory wilderness policy, an era that continues to the present. Regulatory policy is characterized by patterns of influence less stable than those associated with distributive policy. It produces losers as well as winners and greater levels of controversy. Agency decisions are more frequently reviewed by administrative superiors. Decisions once made in the executive branch are removed to a Congress less likely to defer to its committees and subcommittees. Regulatory policy is no picnic for bureaucrats and politicians; pleasing one set of constituents will inevitably displease another.

The shift from distributive to regulatory politics has been reflected in the recent arrival of a well-organized wilderness opposition. The champions of the wilderness lobby—the Wilderness Society, the Sierra Club, the National Audubon Society, the Izaak Walton League, and so on—all predate the Wilderness Act. They now find themselves joined in battle with a new Wise Use Movement represented by organizations, such as the Blue Ribbon Coalition and the Wilderness Impact Research Foundation, and supported by a broad coalition of public land users with interests in mining, grazing, timber harvest, and motorized recreation.

Finally, ANILCA demonstrated the increasing importance of management issues in wilderness policy. ANILCA included special management provisions for rehabilitating fisheries, building and maintaining cabins, salvaging logs from coastlines, using snowmobiles and motorboats in subsistence hunting and fishing, and constructing facilities related to mineral development. These special management provisions were typical of the new regulatory era.

In the early distributive policy era, wilderness management had not been a major issue outside the national forests. Neither the Park Service nor the Fish and Wildlife Service found it necessary to change administrative practices significantly. The dominant view within the Park Service was that if parks were well managed, wilderness would take care of itself. Engineering and law enforcement were emphasized in wilderness management because they were emphasized in park management generally. Officials in Fish and Wildlife saw wilderness designation not as an impediment to management discretion but as a tool to strengthen agency control over the refuge system. Only in the Forest Service was wilderness regarded as a significant constraint on agency prerogative. Its policy of purity in administration and admissions simultaneously communicated commitment to wilderness and reluctance to extend it (Allin, 1982; Allin, 1990a; Roth, 1988).

With the arrival of the regulatory era, interest in wilderness management increased. Three Forest Service recreation research scientists wrote the first textbook on wilderness management, and the interior and agriculture secretaries contributed a foreword (Hendee, Stankey, and Lucas, 1978); it is now in its second edition (Hendee, Stankey, and Lucas, 1990). The agencies have sponsored wilderness management schools for their personnel and a number of national conferences bringing agency personnel together with members of the academic community. There was increased interagency coordination in wilderness management planning, and the Forest Service instituted a program called "limits of acceptable change," which involved increased citizen participation in management planning.[8] In the private sector, an organization called Wilderness Watch has been established to lobby and litigate issues of wilderness management exclusively.

One impact of the changing nature of wilderness politics has been to reduce the management discretion of executive agencies. The Wilderness Act itself constituted a major reduction in agency discretion. Under its provisions only Congress could create or abolish a wilderness area. Still, the management direction imposed by the Wilderness Act was general, and agencies retained significant latitude in the implementation of its provisions. A major development of the past thirty years has been the increasing micromanagement of wilderness by Congress and the courts.

Congressional micromanagement has taken a multitude of forms. Prior to 1980, fewer than one-third of the wilderness laws passed by Congress specified any departure from the principles of wilderness management set forth in the Wilderness Act. Since then, nearly two-thirds of wilderness-related statutes have contained one or more special management provisions (Allin, 1990b). Decisions regarding grazing management and the Forest Service's "sights and sounds" policy constitute the most general and most significant intrusions to date on agency discretion.

The Wilderness Act specified that within national forest wilderness areas "the grazing of livestock . . . shall be permitted to continue subject to such reasonable regulations as are deemed necessary by the Secretary of Agriculture" (78 Stat. 895). This special provision was an exception to general provisions of the

Wilderness Act requiring wilderness areas to be managed "to preserve [their] wilderness character" (78 Stat. 893) and prohibiting commercial enterprises, motor vehicles, structures, and installations. During the Carter administration, the Forest Service imposed unwelcome restrictions on some wilderness grazing permittees. The permittees carried their complaints to Congress and were successful in overturning the agency's interpretation of the Wilderness Act. The Colorado Wilderness Act of 1980 (PL 96-560) required the Forest Service to manage grazing in national forest wilderness areas according to an interpretation of the Wilderness Act published in a House committee report, which stated, in part, that "there shall be no curtailments of grazing in wilderness areas simply because an area is . . . designated as wilderness" (U.S. Congress. House, 1979).

The Forest Service had also exercised management discretion in instituting a policy to protect wilderness from the sights and sounds of civilization. Like the purity policy, of which it was a part, the sights and sounds doctrine inhibited the creation of new wilderness areas at the same time that it protected those areas already established. Citing this doctrine, the Forest Service refused even wilderness-study status to some popular wilderness-like areas because they were within sight or sound of western cities. Under the same doctrine, the Forest Service created wilderness buffer zones, limiting some land use outside wilderness because of the impact it would have inside wilderness.

The House Interior Committee repudiated the wilderness-limiting function of the sights and sounds doctrine in its final report on the Endangered American Wilderness Act (U.S. Congress. House, 1977a), and the act itself gave wilderness protection to a number of areas the Forest Service had refused to consider. Later, Congress repudiated the doctrine's wilderness-protective function, prohibiting buffer zones in the New Mexico Wilderness Act of 1980 (PL 96-550) and in subsequent legislation.

Although congressional initiatives involving grazing policy and the sights and sounds doctrine have had the broadest impact, congressionally mandated management provisions affecting specific wilderness areas have also proliferated in the current era. Among the concerns regulated by Congress have been aircraft use, dams and reservoirs, facilities and structures, fish and wildlife, fire, grazing, insect and disease control, military use, mining, motor vehicles, and water rights. In addition, congressional hearings, General Accounting Office reports, and appropriations measures have been used to influence or direct agency wilderness management (Allin, 1990b).

Court decisions have also limited agency discretion. The issue of wilderness water rights provides a case in point. The framers of the Wilderness Act had sidestepped the issue, declaring, "Nothing in this Act shall constitute an express or implied claim or denial on the part of the Federal Government to an exemption from State water laws." This assertion of legal neutrality appears to leave unmolested the Winters Doctrine,[9] which states that "[w]hen the Federal Government withdraws its land from the public domain and reserves it for a federal purpose, the Government, by implication, reserves appurtenant water then unappropriated to the extent needed to accomplish the purpose of the reservation" (*Cappaert v. United States,* 1976).

Despite the apparent possibilities, management agencies have generally chosen not to assert the reserved water rights that might be claimed for wilderness areas. The mixed messages contained in federal court decisions have probably contributed to the agencies' reluctance to take up the issue of reserved water rights for wilderness. Without addressing wilderness directly, the Supreme Court's 1978 decision in *United States v. New Mexico* created serious doubt about whether reserved water rights exist in wilderness areas.

More recently, however, a federal district court in Colorado concluded that "without access to requisite water, the very purposes for which the Wilderness Act was established would be entirely defeated" (*Sierra Club v. Block,* 1985). The court chastised federal officials for failure to assert reserved rights. Since 1987, Congress has often included more explicit statutory provisions regarding water rights, sometimes reserving rights and sometimes disclaiming them. The consequences of increased activism by Congress and the courts vary with the case, but the result for managers is nearly always diminished discretion.

The Future of Wilderness Policy

Discussion of the future is always somewhat speculative, but certain predictions appear warranted. First, wilderness policy is likely to remain regulatory for the foreseeable future. It will be characterized by controversy, unstable patterns of power, and frequent challenges to agency discretion in Congress and the courts. Well-organized and well-funded interest groups will continue to compete for favor with government decisionmakers in a multiplicity of arenas.

Second, electoral outcomes will continue to determine the relative success of the preservation and development coalitions. A long view suggests that American interest in wilderness preservation has been on the increase for more than a century, and recent polls suggest that Americans remain interested in and concerned about environmental preservation. Nevertheless, environmental issues rarely determine electoral outcomes. The relative hospitality of elected officials to wilderness preservation is likely to be the accidental by-product of an electoral process that is driven by other concerns.

The 1994 congressional election provided a recent example. Environmental issues were tangential to the central issues of the campaign, and wilderness issues were nearly invisible. Still, the result was to wrest control of Congress from an entrenched Democratic majority that had been relatively friendly to wilderness preservation and to deliver it to a Republican majority that is relatively hostile. In 1995, that hostility was clearly manifest in efforts to deny the effect of the California Desert Protection Act by cutting off appropriations for its implementation.

Provisions of the proposed Utah Public Lands Management Act suggest that the new majority will use wilderness bills riddled with loopholes as vehicles for permanently releasing de facto wilderness to nonwilderness use. These strategies foster polarization between wilderness and antiwilderness interests. The likely outcome is gridlock, which may or may not be broken by succeeding elections. If gridlock persists, wilderness policy antagonists may devote increasing energy to the administrative arena and the courts.

Third, in the longer run, allocation will continue to engage the attention of activists, agencies, and lawmakers. Important wilderness laws remain to be written for national forest lands in Idaho and Montana. The process of review, recommendation, and legislation for BLM lands is far from complete. These decisions will stir controversy because they involve choices between wilderness and multiple-use management. Large areas of wilderness also remain to be designated in national parks, but here the stakes are low. Formal designation will likely await some future consensus.

Fourth, management issues will continue to grow in importance. In the past thirty years, much of the energy that might have gone into debating wilderness management has been absorbed by allocation politics. The strategy of the preservation lobby has been to concentrate on allocation now and worry about management later. When the allocation battles are over, sometime in the next century, wilderness policy will be management policy, and the inevitable conflicts will divide wilderness supporters from each other as well as from their traditional adversaries.

Indeed, we have already had a glimpse of that future. In summer 1988, much of the lodgepole pine forest in and around Yellowstone National Park burned. The conflagration served to attract public attention, albeit briefly, to wilderness fire management (Wuerthner, 1988). The issues surrounding wilderness fire are both numerous and profound (Keiter and Boyce, 1991). Should "natural" fires be allowed to burn? What constitutes a "natural" fire? Should the fires set by aboriginal human inhabitants of an area be considered a part of the "natural" fire regime? Can any fire be regarded as "natural," given the ecological changes produced by a half-century of aggressive fire suppression? Should fires be set by managers in an attempt to replicate a "natural" fire regime? Should fires caused by careless campers or smokers be suppressed? Should fires be suppressed when they threaten private property inside or outside the wilderness? How should the presence of historic structures, archeological sites, or endangered species affect fire policy? What level of risk to other values is acceptable?

Fire is but one of many issues that pits the ecological integrity of wilderness against some other social value (Hendee, Stankey, and Lucas, 1990). Demanding the pristine air quality associated with one-hundred-mile vistas in the West may exact a high price in terms of economic development. Any attempt to preserve natural flows in wilderness rivers and streams would seriously constrain upstream water users and constitute a taking of vested water rights.

Wilderness can provide a valuable setting for a variety of scientific studies, but the effects of scientific experimentation can compromise naturalness. Wildlife, weather, and fire traverse wilderness boundaries; management efforts on one side of a wilderness boundary inevitably affect the other side. The 1995 reintroduction of wolves into Idaho and Montana wilderness threatened the culture of nearby ranchers, who in turn threatened civil disobedience. Livestock grazing is a major perturbation of natural ecosystems in many western wildernesses, but to eliminate it would compromise the viability of some nearby ranching operations. Even recreational users bring needs and desires that must somehow be managed or conciliated. Some wilderness users love horses; others abhor them. Some prefer to travel in large groups; other seek solitude. Some rely on the equipment and expertise of commercial outfitters; others prefer independence and self-sufficiency.

Policymakers of the future will be hard-pressed to manage the inevitable conflicts as use increases in a wilderness system that is no longer growing.

NOTES

1. President Richard Nixon declared that the 1970s would be the "environmental decade" as he signed the National Environmental Policy Act of 1970, but this was an attempt to associate himself with a movement that had already established political momentum.

2. The Wilderness Act and the Land and Water Conservation Fund Act were both signed on September 4, 1964. Henry P. Caulfield uses this date to mark the beginning of the modern era in environmental policy (Caulfield, 1989, 31).

3. Primitive areas were wilderness-like areas established by the Forest Service beginning in 1929. They were established without great study, managed under flexible rules, and regarded by some to be withdrawn from development only temporarily. One decade later, new regulations required reevaluation of the primitive areas. If wilderness appeared to be the best use, they were to be reclassified as wilderness, wild, or canoe and managed permanently as wilderness. Areas not meeting this test were to be declassified. Despite the regulations, many primitive areas were never reevaluated. Congress recognized that wilderness, wild, and canoe areas had received careful study by the Forest Service and granted immediate wilderness status. Further study was prescribed for the primitive areas.

4. Theodore Lowi has distinguished "distributive," "regulatory," and "redistributive" policy types and has argued that each had its own distinctive political structures, processes, elites, and group relations (Lowi, 1964). Distributive policies are characterized by concentrated benefits and dispersed costs; there are winners but no losers. Regulatory policies are characterized by concentrated benefits and concentrated costs; there are both winners and losers. Redistributive policies are characterized by clear winners and losers, but the winners and losers are broad social classes.

5. The North Cascades complex includes North Cascades National Park, Lake Chelan National Recreation Area, and Ross Lake National Recreation Area. The three areas are managed as a unit by the Park Service.

6. Since its creation, the area has been renamed the Frank Church–River of No Return Wilderness in honor of the Idaho senator, who was floor manager for the Wilderness Act (PL 98-231).

7. In the real world of politics, paradigmatic shifts—such as the one from distributive to regulatory policy—are likely to be gradual rather than sudden. No bright line divides one era from the next. Still, the heuristic value of distinguishing eras is obvious, and the

Central Idaho, Alaska, New Mexico, and Colorado wilderness acts all suggest that a new era began in 1980. As the most important of the group, I have chosen ANILCA as the obvious marker.

8. The path to progress in citizen involvement is rarely direct. As a part of the "limits of acceptable change" process, wilderness-specific citizen work groups had been established, representing the full range of wilderness management interests. These groups had succeeded in increasing dialogue and reducing strife on some wilderness management issues, but they were recently disbanded because they appear to violate the Federal Advisory Committee Act.

9. Established by the Supreme Court in *Winters v. United States*, 207 U.S. 564 (1908), the doctrine of a federal reserved water right attaching to the purposes of a federal reservation of land has been called the Winters Doctrine ever since.

REFERENCES

Albright, Horace M. 1985. *The Birth of the National Park Service: The Founding Years, 1913–33*. Salt Lake City, UT: Howe Brothers.

Allin, Craig W. 1982. *Politics of Wilderness Preservation*. Westport, CT: Greenwood Press.

———. 1987. "Wilderness Preservation as a Bureaucratic Tool." In Phillip O. Foss, ed., *Federal Lands Policy*. New York: Greenwood Press.

———. 1990a. "Agency Values and Wilderness Management." In John D. Hutcheson, Jr., Francis P. Noe, and Robert E. Snow, eds., *Outdoor Recreation Policy: Pleasure and Preservation*. New York: Greenwood Press.

———. 1990b. "Congress or the Agencies: Who'll Rule Wilderness in the S Century?" In Patrick C. Reed, ed., *Preparing to Manage Wilderness in the S Century, Proceedings of the Conference, Athens, Georgia, April 4–6*. Asheville, NC: Southeastern Forest Experiment Station, U.S. Department of Agriculture.

California v. Block. 1982. F. 2d 690 (22 October): 753. U.S. Court of Appeals, Ninth Circuit.

Cammerer, Arno B. 1938. "Maintenance of the Primeval in National Parks." *Appalachia* 22 (December):207–213.

Cappaert v. United States. 1976. 426 U.S. 128 at 138. U.S. Supreme Court.

Caulfield, Henry P. 1989. "The Conservation and Environmental Movements: An Historical Analysis." In James P. Lester, ed., *Environmental Politics and Policy*. Durham, NC: Duke University Press.

Costley, Richard J. 1972. "Wilderness: An Enduring Resource." *American Forests* 78 (June):8–11, 54–56.

Foote, Jeffrey P. 1973. "Wilderness—A Question of Purity." *Environmental Law* 3 (Summer):255–266.

Foresta, Ronald A. 1984. *America's National Parks and Their Keepers*. Washington, DC: Resources for the Future, Inc.

Gates, Paul W. 1968. *History of Public Land Law Development*. Washington, DC: Government Printing Office.

Hendee, John C., George H. Stankey, and Robert C. Lucas. 1978. *Wilderness Management*. Miscellaneous Publication No. 1365. Washington, DC: U.S. Department of Agriculture, Forest Service.

———. 1990. *Wilderness Management*. 2d ed., rev. Golden, CO: North American Press.

Ise, John. 1961. *Our National Park Policy: A Critical History.* Baltimore: Johns Hopkins University Press.

Kain, Peter I. 1969. "The Battle for East Meadow Creek." *American Forests* 75 (October): 39.

Keiter, Robert B, and Mark S. Boyce, eds. 1991. *The Greater Yellowstone Ecosystem: Redefining America's Wilderness Heritage.* Part 2—Fire Policy and Management. New Haven: Yale University Press.

Lowi, Theodore J. 1964. "American Business, Public Policy, Case Studies, and Political Theory." *World Politics* 16 (July/August):298–310.

Nash, Roderick. 1982. *Wilderness and the American Mind.* 3d ed. New Haven: Yale University Press.

Parker v. United States. 1971. F.2d 448:793. U.S. Court of Appeals, Tenth Circuit.

Robinson, Glen O. 1975. *The Forest Service: A Study in Public Land Management.* Baltimore: Johns Hopkins University Press.

Roth, Dennis M. 1988. *The Wilderness Movement and the National Forests.* College Station, TX: Intaglio Press.

Sierra Club v. Block. 1985. F. Supp. 622:842 at 862. U.S. District Court, Colorado.

U.S. Bureau of the Census. 1975. *Historical Statistics of the United States: Colonial Times to 1970.* Washington, DC: Government Printing Office.

U.S. Congress. House. Committee on Interior and Insular Affairs. 1961. *Establishing a National Wilderness Preservation System for the Permanent Good of the Whole People, and for Other Purposes.* Report No. 635, 87th Cong., 1st sess. 27 July.

_____. 1977a. *Designating Certain Endangered Public Lands for Preservation as Wilderness.* Report No. 540, 95th Cong., 1st sess. 27 July.

_____. 1977b. *The Endangered American Wilderness Act.* Hearings on H.R. 3454, May 2 and 6, 1977. Washington, DC: Government Printing Office.

_____. 1979. *Designating Certain National Forest System Lands in the National Wilderness Preservation System, and for Other Purposes.* Report No. 617, 96th Cong., 1st sess. 11 and 14 November.

U.S. Congress. Senate. Committee on Interior and Insular Affairs. 1963. *Establishing a National Wilderness Preservation System for the Permanent Good of the Whole People, and for Other Purposes.* Report No. 109, 88th Cong., 1st sess. 6 and 3 April.

Wuerthner, George. 1988. *Yellowstone and the Fires of Change.* Salt Lake City: Haggis House Publications, Inc.

Zahniser, Howard. 1955. "The Need for Wilderness Areas." Speech before the National Citizen's Planning Conference on Parks and Open Spaces for the American People, May 24. *Congressional Record* 101:A3809–12.

PART THREE

POLICY CHANGE

10

Conclusion: Public Lands and Policy Change

CHARLES DAVIS

The U.S. public lands policy arena was once characterized by easy access to the development of natural resources with little or no thought given to environmental impacts. Policymaking was restricted to a small number of western legislators, administrators, and clientele groups with common programmatic interests. The result of this relatively closed system of governance was the enactment of programs from the late 1800s through the 1950s that encouraged resource use by subsidizing the developmental activities of miners, loggers, ranchers, and energy companies.

Although federal land management decisions were made within a value context that was sympathetic to policy goals such as economic growth and the settlement of the West, traditional user groups have never maintained a cordial working relationship with federal land management agencies. No fewer than five sagebrush rebellions have taken place over the past century, owing, in large part, to resistance from ranchers and other groups to the promulgation of fees and land use regulations (see Chapter 2). Over the past thirty years, public land use conflicts have intensified, resulting in a policymaking process that is simultaneously more open and unpredictable.

Nevertheless, it is possible to discern a number of patterns in the development of land use policies over the past three decades. Policy fluctuations both across and within issue areas are affected by a host of factors that have been discussed in the preceding chapters, including the rise of environmental groups, presidential influence, increasing involvement by Congress, federal courts, and state public officials, economic conditions, and political support.

Explaining Public Land Policy Change

Competing Interest Groups

Much of the credit for the greening of public land use goes to the increase in the number of environmental groups active within the public lands policy arena. Studies by Christopher Bosso (1994) and by John Hendee and Randall Pitstick (1992) have documented the rapid growth in the membership and resources of national environmental organizations between 1970 and 1990. Group leaders have also become more politically sophisticated. Public participation, greater use of media contacts, policy analysis, testimony at administrative and congressional hearings, lobbying, and litigation are often employed by groups' leaders to advance their policy goals.

Environmental leaders have become acutely aware of the need to "nationalize" issues long dominated by regional interests, and this is reflected in the increased use of venue shopping across political institutions and levels of government. In Chapter 4, George Hoberg describes the decision by groups opposed to the scale of timber harvests in the national forests of the Pacific Northwest to use the courts as a means of protecting the habitat of the northern spotted owl, since legislative leaders and administrators had shown no inclination to enforce the Endangered Species Act.

The importance of environmental action is affirmed in each of the policies discussed here. Lobbying by the Natural Resources Defense Council and the National Wildlife Federation contributed significantly to the inclusion of environmental criteria in land use policies such as FLPMA, NFMA, and the Energy Resources Act of 1992. Groups with a particular issue-focus like the Wilderness Society or the National Parks and Conservation Association have been effective in pushing for program-specific legislation.

Environmental organizations have also made frequent use of the courts over the past two decades. A major catalyst for the enactment of FLPMA in 1976 was a federal court case decided two years earlier, *NRDC v. Morton,* which required BLM officials to prepare site-specific environmental impact statements prior to the issuance of grazing permits instead of preparing a single massive EIS covering all affected rangelands under their jurisdiction. Although procedural flaws in the preparation of EISs have provided a useful legal toehold for challenging land use decisions, environmental lawyers have also taken advantage of citizen lawsuit provisions contained within other laws such as the Endangered Species Act, the Clean Water Act, or the Superfund.

However, efforts to alter long-standing political and institutional arrangements inevitably generate strong defensive actions. Traditional economic groups have not taken kindly to management changes that increasingly restrict or limit resource use. Both the Sagebrush Rebellion of the late 1970s and the more recent legal controversy over "takings issues" illustrate the depth of concern about preserving a way of life as well as an increasingly sophisticated awareness of political tactics.

Not only are user groups demonstrating an ability to funnel PAC (political action committee) monies to like-minded legislators (particularly associations representing energy, mineral, and timber interests) but they have finally overcome the tendency to operate independently on political issues such as hardrock mining or livestock grazing on public lands. Organizational leaders have recognized the importance of building coalitions that transcend specific issues and have created multi-issue umbrella groups such as the Public Lands Council and the Wise Use Movement.

Associational leaders have also capitalized politically on some of the issues ignored by environmental leaders, such as the social costs of change accompanying resource-dependent communities as they make the transition to recreation or amenity-based economies (Wilkinson, 1992). Protecting jobs has become a useful wedge issue for industries seeking to avoid or delay the implementation of resource management decisions. In other cases, political alliances are formed with local governmental officials who have become dependent upon the revenues generated by extractive land use activities such as energy royalties, grazing fees, or timber receipts (Fairfax, 1987).

Like environmental groups, resource user organizations and their allies (e.g., the Mountain States Legal Foundation) have turned to the courts to secure tactical advantages. With the support of high-level officials such as President Reagan's attorney general, Edwin Meese, industry groups succeeded in obtaining a favorable ruling from the U.S. Supreme Court that narrowed the criteria used to determine whether environmental or noneconomic interest groups could gain standing to sue (*Lujan v. National Wildlife Federation,* 110 S.Ct. 3177). More recently, efforts have been made to identify legal strategies (such as the "takings" clause of the Fifth Amendment to the U.S. Constitution) that may invalidate decisions made by federal land management agencies (Wenner, 1994).

Presidential Influence

Although the rise of the environmental movement is certainly a pivotal factor in helping us account for change within the public lands policy arena, an equally important factor is the amount of political influence wielded by presidents. Over the past thirty years, the perceived need to develop energy, range, timber, and mineral resources with greater sensitivity to ecological values has been more evident during the terms of Democratic presidents than Republicans. But this has been exhibited less in terms of personal involvement in policy development than in setting a generally pro-environmental policy direction and leaving it up to others to fill in the details.

To be sure, there are occasional examples of more visible presidential action on public land decisionmaking, such as Bush's appearance at the Grand Canyon to sign an agreement requiring the nearby Navajo Power Plant to cut back on emissions of air pollutants and Clinton's timber summit in the Pacific Northwest, which was designed to create a policy dialogue on land use between industry and environmental officials. But Democratic presidents have been more inclined to support environmental actions through capacity-building decisions such as the appointment of interior secretaries with a strong environmental record, the pursuit of new policy initiatives, and the use of federal budgetary processes to set priorities on preferred resource allocation decisions (Vig, 1994).

Congress

In like fashion, congressional Democrats have favored a stronger role for environmental concerns in public land management. From the mid-1980s until the midterm congressional elections of 1994, Democratic leaders within the House of Representatives pushed a series of policy reforms aimed at reducing environmental problems associated with grazing, mining, energy, and timber programs, along with the program subsidies given to resource user groups. These efforts bore fruit in the form of House bills, only to wither away under the watchful eye of a more prodevelopment Senate.

However, it is important to add a couple of caveats here. The pro-environmental stance adopted by congressional Democrats is decidedly national when restricted land use issues are considered. Here, federal lawmakers are more apt to echo Gifford Pinchot's phrase suggesting that the public lands belong to *all* Americans rather than to western residents, writ small.

This perspective is demonstrated by legislative actions undertaken to expand the geographical scope of wilderness areas and the parks. The Wilderness Act was amended in 1986 to include eastern lands within the National Wilderness Preservation System as well as western sites (Allin, Chapter 9). And members of Congress also saw the political benefits of park expansion during the 1970s and 1980s and added a larger number of historical sites and urban parks within the NPS (Lowry, Chapter 8).

These examples suggest that congressional attention to public land policy issues of this sort may be driven by the promise of distributive political benefits as much—or more—than by an abiding interest in the environment. Even so, the interaction between partisanship, regional influences, and legislative behavior is more likely to occur on policy decisions affecting programs administered by agencies with a multiple-use mandate. Some writers are convinced that federal elected officials will become increasingly sensitive to environmentalists and outdoor recreationists residing in western cities and become less beholden to traditional land use constituencies (Hays, 1991), but a cursory examination of recent voting on public land issues suggests that the long-standing link between commodity production and legislative support is still valid. U.S. lawmakers within this region, particularly those located in the interior West, tend to support developmental activities on public lands over environmental concerns—regardless of party affiliation (Davis, 1995).

Economic Influences

Economic factors have historically played a key and enduring role in the development of energy, range, timber, and mining subsystems (McConnell, 1966). Christopher Klyza (Chapter 6) suggests that the venerable Mining Law of 1872 epitomizes the idea of "economic liberalism," the idea that policy ought to be developed by affected private sector interests. Not only were miners in need of greater legal certainty in the establishment of property claims on federal land but there was a clear lack of governmental expertise and regulatory capacity as well. Other public land programs dealing with timber, grazing, and energy production also exhibit structural characteristics designed to promote or enhance the financial health of user groups.

Although it is difficult to find public land use controversies without a financial angle affecting stakeholders in some fashion, a glance at policy reform efforts indicates that economic factors are often used by opponents and supporters of change. Traditional land use constituencies often defend the need for existing programs by sensitizing lawmakers to the unpredictable market conditions for minerals, meat, wool, lumber, oil, or coal, coupled with the argument that beneficiaries are often operating at the margins of profitability.

A related argument is aimed at community survival goals that would be jeopardized if programs' benefits were slashed or eliminated. Often, these arguments are cloaked in exaggerated language (e.g., the war on the West) designed to invoke sympathy for individuals or firms that would be directly affected by the alteration of program requirements or objectives. Thus, testimony in support of affected programs is offered not only by permittees or license holders but by others with a financial stake as well, such as bankers, local government officials, and sawmill operators.

Those favoring policy change typically offer two forms of economic argumentation. One lies in the need to make the transition from an extractive and environmentally destructive form of land use to a recreation- or amenity-based economy that is both healthy and sustainable. The needs of affected energy workers, loggers, ranchers, and miners would be dealt with by phasing in program changes gradually (thereby allowing time for short-timers to seek out alternative work opportunities) and by implementing training programs to enhance the marketable skills of displaced workers. In some cases, environmental restoration would offer a source of employment. This approach was advanced by Clinton administration officials in the Pacific Northwest as a means of helping timber-dependent communities cope with an increasingly scarce resource.

A second justification used by policy reform advocates lies in the gradual elimination of subsidies for the development or use of natural resources within the public lands and the distribution of permits or licenses to individuals or firms for the extraction or production of these resources on the basis of fair market principles (Loomis, 1993). Bringing the cost of public land use into closer alignment with what the market will bear would yield the positive consequence of avoiding "giveaways" or disposing of public resources at subsidized rates (Krutilla et al., 1983). In addition, higher prices could also lead to a decline in developmental activities associated with negative environmental impacts.

Political Support

Consistently high levels of public support for the environment have contributed to the development or alteration of environmental policies over the past twenty-five years (Dunlap, 1993). However, political support for environmental policies can be measured not only in evaluative terms by the general public but also by the subsequent reaction to these programs by administrators, constituency groups, and elected officials. From a policy change perspective, political support (or heat) generated by policy elites is more important than public support since public land policy issues are clearly more salient for user groups and rural communities than for the larger (and mostly urban) set of state residents.

It is instructive to recall that commodity-based programs have traditionally benefited from a tightly knit coterie of supporters consisting of legislators serving on the interior committees of Congress, clientele groups, and land management agencies (BLM and the Forest Service). Policy change is more likely to occur if one or more of the relationships between subsystem participants has been altered or eliminated. Under these conditions, a window of opportunity for change occurs, and policy entrepreneurs attempt to cash in policywise through environmental group action or other previously mentioned factors.

The recognition of subgovernmental vulnerability by advocates of change may lead to the subsequent enactment of policy reforms. This is illustrated by the discussion of distributive natural resource policies in the preceding chapters. A relatively stable set of institutional relationships has been maintained to serve the hardrock mining and livestock grazing programs. No significant changes have taken place in either the organizational base of support or in congressional committee jurisdiction over affected policies. Consequently, in the late 1980s and early 1990s, program supporters were able to stave off a series of reform efforts designed to obtain both environmental improvements and reduced subsidies.

Environmentalists have had more success in scaling back timber harvests and in placing restrictions on oil drilling in coastal waters or in wildlife refuges. How can we account for these differences? First, reform advocates with the aid of media sources were able to promote greater public awareness of their policy preferences by projecting images of clearcut forests or of wildlife dying on oil-soaked beaches. Issues were thus elevated from regional to national significance.

Second, the timber and energy policy communities have been disrupted to a greater degree by external policies or events. The enactment of the National Forest Management Act of 1976 not only added a number of environmental objectives to the list of criteria used by Forest Service officials in making use allocation choices but it shifted decisionmaking authority from the appropriations committees where the influence of the timber industry was solidly entrenched to the authorizing committees where the environmentalists were more likely to be heard (Hoberg, Chapter 4).

Structural changes are even more evident within the energy policy subsystems (Jones and Strahan, 1985). Because of the energy crises of the 1970s and the variety of resources contributing to the overall mix of energy supplies, members of Congress began clamoring for part of the action in a policy sense. The result was fragmentation; that is, program jurisdiction for energy issues was divided up among a large number of committees and subcommittees. In short, the lack of committee jurisdictional autonomy, coupled with the greater degree of visibility associated with these issues, contributed to a more open form of policymaking where program changes became possible because of catalytic or focusing events, electoral swings, or actions taken by committed policy leaders.

The development of political support for noncommodity policies affecting wilderness, parks, and wildlife varies considerably. Support for the wilderness policy is relatively strong despite legal challenges from traditional groups over water rights and the increasing number of regulations affecting existing sites, thanks to staunch backing from several groups such as the Wilderness Society and the Sierra Club. However, some of the newer wilderness study areas under review by the BLM have engendered greater controversy since they are located in lower altitude sites with greater potential for competing resource uses.

Parks and wildlife refuges have not received the same degree of support for environmental protection as have wilderness areas. This can be attributed, in part, to the inability of weak agencies like the Park Service and the Fish and Wildlife Service to withstand continual intervention by members of Congress into policy and administrative concerns (Lowry, Chapter 8; Tobin, 1990). In addition, the primary clientele groups for these agencies (e.g., the National Wildlife Federation and the National Parks and Conservation Association) are less concerned with preservation or ecological objectives than with promoting increased visitation and the expansion of new parks and hunting opportunities.

Decisional Structures

Thus far, policy change has been examined within the context of fluctuations in legislation over the past thirty years and in regard to a number of factors that account for these changes. But it is also important to remember that much public land policy is administratively determined. This is particularly true for policies within the jurisdiction of land management agencies that are entrusted with a multiple-use mandate, namely the BLM and the Forest Service.

The term "multiple-use" management implies an ideal type of decisional balancing act where natural resource professionals administer a variety of land uses, including "outdoor recreation, timber or mineral production, livestock grazing, fish and wildlife habitat and watershed protection" in ways that minimize the likelihood that a particular land use will become dominant and crowd out or devalue other land use options (Culhane, 1981). However, land use conflicts do occur on a regular basis and as both Richard Miller (1987) and Gregg Cawley and John Freemuth (Chapter 3) indicate, the process is tailor-made for policy outcomes that reflect some combination of professional judgment and interest group politics.

From a political perspective, to what extent does this decisionmaking structure serve to accommodate environmental as well as commodity development interests? Although there are occasional studies of BLM and Forest Service administrators that suggest pro-industry attitudes (Twight, Lyden, and Tuchmann, 1990) or behavior (Booth, 1991), the weight of the empirical evidence conducted over the past fifteen years tilts in the direction of decisionmaking that is more balanced among resource uses.

A study of the BLM's organizational evolution from the beginning of the Kennedy administration through the early years of the Reagan administration concludes that the agency began implementing a multiple-use management philosophy closely patterned after the Forest Service approach in the 1960s, a decade before it received permanent authorization to do so under FLPMA. Despite budgetary and staff constraints, the agency began to undertake a number of initiatives aimed at rangeland improvement or recreation that would have been politically impossible to achieve a decade earlier. Notable actions included the development of more intensive range management practices based on the rest-rotation approach and the designation of both primitive areas and wildlife preservation areas (Fairfax, 1984).

Other researchers have attempted to link the attitudes of BLM or Forest Service officials to subsequent decisions or output indicators for the production of commodity or recreational resources. A study by Paul Culhane (1981) based on field research in the Rocky Mountain states in the early 1970s concluded that administrators were trying to accommodate the interests of differing stakeholders within use allocation decisions. A later study of BLM administrators in Wyoming produced similar results (Davis and Davis, 1988).

More recently, a comprehensive analysis of Forest Service decisions over the past twenty years found that particular forest outputs could be explained by the preferences of the forest supervisors on management plans, incrementalism (only slight adjustments from preceding years), and increasing representation of environmental and wildlife interests (Sabatier, Loomis, and McCarthy, 1995). In a collective sense, this suggests that public land managers are not captives of the commodity organizations but, in fact, tend to make decisions that take both amenity and production values into account.

Conclusions

An overall examination of public lands policymaking over the past thirty years reveals a shift in land use preferences from a largely commodity-production orientation to a more balanced perspective between development and amenity values. Change is more evident within some program areas (timber production, energy) than others (mining, livestock grazing). Key explanatory variables that were found to be important regardless of substantive policy focus included the increasing presence and influence wielded by environmental groups and the partisan orientation of presidential administrations. Under some circumstances, other factors such as constituency support or economic conditions also account, in part, for programmatic shifts.

What about the near future of public lands policy? Some argue that the Republican-controlled Congress of 1994 foreshadows a move in the direction of fewer environmental controls and a greater emphasis on both the preservation of property rights and commodity production values. This may well prove to be the case in the short run, although a more likely scenario is that a more modest shift in policies concerning such issues as the Endangered Species Act will occur, offering greater administrative flexibility as well as a more explicit consideration of costs and benefits.

However, public support for environmental policy goals remains strong, and it is conceivable that the threat of more radical policy shifts will be precluded by procedural tactics (such as a Senate filibuster) or a presidential veto. And it is also conceivable that core provisions of public land laws with an environmental emphasis will survive intact, thanks to procedural innovations (citizen participation, litigation) that have been built into existing laws.

REFERENCES

Booth, Douglas. 1991. "Timber Dependency and Wilderness Selection: The U.S. Forest Service, Congress, and the RARE II Decisions." *Natural Resources Journal* 31 (Fall):715–739.

Bosso, Christopher. 1994. "After the Movement: Environmental Activism in the 1990s." In Norman Vig and Michael Kraft, eds., *Environmental Policy in the 1990s.* 2d ed. Washington, DC: CQ Press.

Culhane, Paul. 1981. *Public Land Politics.* Baltimore: Johns Hopkins University Press.

Davis, Charles. 1995. "Public Lands Policy Change: How Congress Votes." *Journal of Forestry* 93 (June):8–12.

Davis, Charles, and Sandra Davis. 1988. "Analyzing Change in Public Land Politics: From Subsystems to Advocacy Coalitions." *Policy Studies Journal* 17 (Fall):3–24.

Dunlap, Riley. 1993. "Public Opinion: Does Public Concern for the Environment Differ in the West?" In Zachary Smith, ed., *Environmental Politics and Policy in the West.* Dubuque, IA: Kendall/Hunt.

Fairfax, Sally. 1984. "Beyond the Sagebrush Rebellion: The BLM as Neighbor and Manager in the Western States." In John G. Francis and Richard Ganzel, eds., *Western Public Lands.* Totowa, NJ: Rowman and Allanheld.

_____. 1987. "Interstate Bargaining over Revenue Sharing and Payments in Lieu of Taxes." In Phillip O. Foss, ed., *Federal Lands Policy.* Westport, CT: Greenwood Press.

Hays, Samuel P. 1991. "The New Environmental West." *Journal of Policy History* 3 (3):223–248.

Hendee, John C., and Randall C. Pitstick. 1992. "The Growth of Environmental and Conservation-Related Organizations: 1980–1991," *Renewable Resources Journal* 10 (Summer):6–11.

Jones, Charles O., and Randall Strahan. 1985. "The Effect of Energy Politics on Congressional and Executive Organization in the 1970s." *Legislative Studies Quarterly* 10 (May):151–178.

Krutilla, John V., Anthony C. Fisher, William F. Hyde, and V. Kerry Smith. 1983. "Public Versus Private Ownership: The Federal Lands Case." *Journal of Policy Analysis and Management* 2 (Summer):548–558.

Loomis, John B. 1993. *Integrated Public Lands Management*. New York: Columbia University Press.

McConnell, Grant. 1966. *Private Power and American Democracy*. New York: Alfred A. Knopf.

Miller, Richard O. 1987. "Multiple Use in the Bureau of Land Management: The Biases of Pluralism Revisited." In Phillip O. Foss, ed., *Federal Lands Policy*. Westport, CT: Greenwood Press.

Sabatier, Paul, John Loomis, and Catherine McCarthy. 1995. "Hierarchical Controls, Professional Norms, Local Constituencies, and Budget Maximization: An Analysis of U.S. Forest Service Planning Decisions." *American Journal of Political Science* 39 (February):204–242.

Tobin, Richard. 1990. *The Expendable Future: U.S. Politics and the Protection of Biological Diversity*. Durham, NC: Duke University Press.

Twight, Ben, Fremont Lyden, and E. Thomas Tuchmann. 1990. "Constituency Bias in a Federal Career System: A Study of District Rangers in the U.S. Forest Service." *Administration and Society* 22 (May):358–389.

Vig, Norman. 1994. "Presidential Leadership and the Environment." In Norman Vig and Michael Kraft, eds., *Environmental Policy in the 1990s*. 2d ed. Washington, DC: CQ Press.

Wenner, Lettie M. 1994. "Environmental Policy in the Courts." In Norman Vig and Michael Kraft, eds., *Environmental Policy in the 1990s*. 2d. ed. Washington, DC: CQ Press.

Wilkinson, Charles. 1992. *Crossing the Next Meridian: Land, Water, and the American West*. Washington, DC: Island Press.

About the Book

The "War over the West" being waged between environmentalists and the wise use movement that represents traditional user groups is becoming an increasingly bitter struggle to influence public land use decisions. Beset by these competing interests, federal agencies, Congress, and the courts have made efforts to balance ecological and economic values in the development of federal land policies that have produced a wide range of outcomes over the past three decades.

The contributors examine the interplay among political organizations, interest groups, economic conditions, and demographic shifts, offering an explanation of changes in policies that affect the management of rangeland, timber, energy, mineral, and wilderness resources. Their systematic rendering of historical context brings into focus the cyclical nature of policymaking and the fact that programmatic changes can rarely be attributed to the actions of a single group or institution. This accessibly written volume will be of interest to students and scholars of environmental politics and policy, natural resource management, public policy, and environmental history as well as to the general reader.

About the Editor and Contributors

Charles Davis is professor of political science at Colorado State University. His teaching and research interests lie in the areas of environmental policy and public administration. Professor Davis is the author of *The Politics of Hazardous Waste* (Prentice-Hall, 1993) and book chapters and articles dealing with environmental and public lands policy.

Craig W. Allin is professor of politics at Cornell College. His teaching and research interests include public land policy. Professor Allin is the author of *The Politics of Wilderness Preservation* (Greenwood Press, 1982) and the editor of *International Handbook of National Parks and Nature Preserves* (Greenwood Press, 1990) and has written book chapters and articles concerning wilderness policy.

R. McGreggor Cawley is associate professor of political science at the University of Wyoming. His teaching and research interests are in public lands and environmental politics. Professor Cawley is the coeditor of *The Wolf in the Garden: The Land Rights Movement and Renewing American Environmentalism* (Rowman and Littlefield, 1996) and is the author of *Federal Land, Western Anger: The Sagebrush Rebellion and Environmental Politics* (University Press of Kansas, 1993) and several book chapters and articles on public lands policy.

David Howard Davis is professor of political science at the University of Toledo. His teaching and research interests lie in the areas of energy policy and public administration, and he served as a special assistant for energy programs at the U.S. Department of the Interior during the Carter administration. Professor Davis is the author of *Energy Politics,* 4th ed. (St. Martin's Press, 1993) and has also written a number of articles and book chapters dealing with energy policy.

Sandra K. Davis is associate professor of political science at Colorado State University. Her teaching and research interests concern natural resource and environmental politics. Professor Davis has authored several articles and book chapters on public lands, water, and pesticides policies.

John Freemuth is associate professor of political science at Boise State University. His teaching and research interests are in public lands and environmental politics. Professor Freemuth is the author of *Islands Under Siege: National Parks and the Politics of External Threats* (University Press of Kansas, 1991) and other works dealing with parks and public land policy. He has also served on a number of advisory panels for the U.S. Park Service.

George Hoberg is associate professor and the graduate adviser in the Department of Political Science at the University of British Columbia. His teaching and research interests are in U.S. and comparative environmental policy. Professor Hoberg is the author of *Pluralism by Design: Environmental Policy and the American Regulatory State* (Praeger, 1992), the coauthor (with Kathryn Harrison) of *Risk, Science, and Politics: Regulating Toxic*

Substances in Canada and the United States (McGill-Queens, 1994), and a coeditor (with Keith Banting and Richard Simeon) of *Canada and the United States in a Changing World* (McGill-Queens, 1996). He has also written articles dealing with pesticides policymaking, comparative environmental politics, and timber harvesting controversies in national forests.

Christopher McGrory Klyza is associate professor of political science and director of the environmental studies program at Middlebury College. His teaching and research interests are in public lands and environmental politics. Professor Klyza is the author of *Who Controls Public Lands: Mining, Forestry, and Grazing Policies, 1879–1990* (University of North Carolina Press, 1996) and the coeditor (with Stephen Trombulak) of *The Future of the Northern Forest* (University Press of New England, 1994). He has also written several articles and book chapters dealing with public land politics. In 1991, he received the American Political Science Association's Harold Lasswell Award for the best doctoral dissertation in the field of policy studies for his "Patterns of Public Lands Politics: The Consequences of Ideas and the State."

William R. Lowry is associate professor of political science at Washington University. His teaching and research interests are in environmental policy and public administration. Professor Lowry's books include *The Dimensions of Federalism: State Governments and Pollution Control Policies* (Duke University Press, 1992) and *The Capacity for Wonder: Preserving National Parks* (Brookings Institution, 1994), and he has also written articles on state and national parks policy.

Index

Abandoned Locatable Minerals Mine
    Reclamation Fund, 95
Abbey, Edward, 2
Advisory boards, 75, 76, 81, 84, 85, 92
Agriculture, Department of (USDA), 77(table),
    78(table), 79–80, 90, 109, 142, 174
Aircraft, 177, 184
Alabama, 143
Alaska, 17, 66, 103, 109, 122, 142, 174, 177, 181
    Arctic National Wildlife Refuge, 22, 26, 141,
    145
    North Slope, 141, 142, 145
    Tongass National Forest, 26, 51, 60–63
    Trans-Alaska Pipeline, 124, 146
Alaska Forestry Association, 63
Alaska National Interest Lands Conservation
    Act (ANILCA), 61, 110, 159, 172, 175,
    181, 182–185
Alaska Pulp Corporation, 63
AMC. See American Mining Congress
American Mining Congress (AMC), 107–108
American Petroleum Institute, 124
American Rivers, 146
Anasazi Indians, 142
Anderson, Michael, 50
Andrus, Cecil, 17, 82, 130, 132, 133, 134
ANILCA. See Alaska National Interest Lands
    Conservation Act
Arctic National Wildlife Refuge. See under
    Alaska
Arizona, 11–12, 25, 28(n5), 103, 143, 181
Army Corps of Engineers, 141, 175
Aspinall, Wayne, 79, 101, 158, 176, 179, 180
Assateague National Seashores, 152
Association of Forest Service Employees for
    Environmental Ethics, 54
Atomic Energy Commission, 144
Audubon Society, 125, 182
Automobiles. See under National parks

Babbitt, Bruce, 22, 33, 58, 65, 66, 78(table), 84,
    92, 95, 144, 146, 167
Baca, James, 84, 144
Barber, Benjamin, 41

Barnwell nuclear plant, 144
Barrick Goldstrike Mine, 95, 112
Baumgartner, Frank, 85
Beard, Daniel, 144, 145
Behan, Richard, 35, 37
Belville Coal Company, 143
Biology, 53, 62, 83
    conservation biology, 54, 55, 63, 68
BLM. See Bureau of Land Management
Blue Ribbon Coalition, 182
Bosso, Christopher, 194
Bowman, Charles, 148(n)
Brower, David, 2, 18
Bryce Canyon National Park. See under Utah
Budget issues, 67, 88, 116
Bumpers, Dale, 66, 108
Bureaucracies, 122, 123
Bureau of Budget, 77(table), 79, 86, 89
Bureau of Land Management (BLM), 2–3, 12,
    15, 16–17, 29(nn 12, 14), 32, 36, 56, 74,
    75, 77(table), 79, 80–81, 82, 99, 109, 111,
    114, 119(n8), 127, 142, 181, 186, 199
    budget, 83
    creation of, 76, 99
    directors, 84, 136, 144
    funding cuts for, 22
    as multiple use agency, 18–19, 34–35, 37–38,
    77(table), 81, 89, 199, 200
Bureau of Mines, 97, 99–100
Bureau of Reclamation, 139, 144, 145, 146, 175
Burford, Robert, 78(table), 82, 136
Bush administration, 5, 21–22, 33, 57, 83, 89,
    140–144, 195
Byrd, Robert, 66

California, 12, 25, 28(n5), 96, 97, 103, 104, 109,
    156, 181, 185
    Big Sur, 135
    Coastal Commission (CCC), 13, 28(n4)
    Mohave National Park, 26
California Desert Protection Act, 33, 185
Campbell, Ben, 84
Canada, 145
Caribou, 125, 141

Carter administration, 17, 20, 89, 110, 115,
     128–135, 137, 175, 181, 184
Cascade Range, 152. *See also* North Cascades
     complex
Caulfield, Henry P., 187(n2)
Cawley, Gregg, 11
CCC. *See* California, Coastal Commission
Chaco Canyon, 162
Changes, 128. *See also under* Public land policy
Chapman, Howard, 165
Chemicals, 98
Christensen, Jed, 138
Church, Frank, 187(n6)
Clark, William, 83, 89
Classification and Multiple Use Act (CMU), 37,
     77(table), 79, 89
Clean Air Act, 4, 112, 123, 127, 134, 143, 144,
     147
Clean Water Act, 4, 112, 123, 147, 194
Clear-cutting, 51, 52
Clearwater National Forest, 26
Climax Molybdenum Company, 105–106, 134
Clinton administration, 5, 22, 33, 54, 58–59, 63,
     65, 66, 84, 89, 92, 116, 144–146, 167, 168,
     197
     forest plan of, 59, 60, 67, 196
CMU. *See* Classification and Multiple Use Act
Coal, 13, 98, 100, 122, 124, 127, 128, 129–134,
     135, 136, 140, 141, 142–143, 144, 162, 167
Coalitions, 5, 17–18, 61, 74, 80, 83, 84, 85–87,
     88, 89, 90, 91, 92, 147, 172, 182, 185, 195
Coal Leasing Act, 130, 136
Coal Management Plan, 130
Colorado, 28(n5), 29(nn 12, 13), 84–85, 92, 101,
     124, 129, 140, 144, 176, 181, 185
     Crested Butte, 107
     Gore Range-Eagle's Nest Primitive Area, 180
     Grand Junction, 134
     Leadville, 105–106
     San Juan Mountains, 112
     See also Rocky Flats
Colorado River, 145–146, 160, 167
Colorado Wilderness Act of 1980, 184
Columbia River Basin, 36, 63–64, 139
Common Varieties Act of 1955, 98
Community interest, 38–39
Comprehensive Environmental Response,
     Compensation, and Liability Act. *See*
     Superfund
Concessions Policy Act of 1965, 155
Congress, 6, 13, 14, 15–16, 17, 21, 27, 39–40, 41,
     49, 51–52, 55, 62, 64, 65, 68, 76, 86–87,
     100–102, 126, 140, 142, 151, 155,
     157–158, 164(table), 164–165, 166, 168,
     172, 179, 180, 181, 183, 185, 196
     appropriation/authorizing committees, 52,
     58, 67, 198–199

committee leadership in, 66, 86
Congressional Research Service (CRS), 35
elections of 1994. *See* Congress, 104th
     Congress
vs. executive branch, 176
filibusters in, 102
fragmentation in, 118(n2), 199
House Appropriations Subcommittee on
     Agriculture, 142
House Interior Committee, 58, 80, 83, 86,
     100–101, 110, 115, 131, 176, 184
House Resources Committee, 2, 66, 76,
     78(table), 86, 91, 99, 100–101, 102
House/Senate, 87, 88(table), 95, 115, 116
House Subcommittee on Mines and Mining,
     19
House Subcommittee on Parks, 158
Northwest delegation in, 56, 57, 58, 62
102nd Congress, 58
104th Congress, 25–27, 66, 67, 78(table), 91,
     92, 108, 146, 185
regulated areas by, 184
riders, 56, 57, 66, 67, 69(n15), 135
Senate Appropriations Committee, 66
Senate Energy and Natural Resources
     Committee, 2, 66, 76, 78(table), 86, 90,
     91, 102, 110, 116
Senate Interior Committee, 80, 86,
     101(table), 102
Subcommittee on Forests and Public Land
     Management, 66
Subcommittee on Mines and Mining, 110
Consensus, 42, 84, 130, 146, 161, 168
Conservation, 1, 16, 75, 98, 167–168, 173, 176,
     178, 179
     definitions, 17–18, 20, 22
     and national parks, 150, 151–152, 153,
     155–159, 160, 161–163
     New Conservation, 153
     See also Biology, conservation biology
Constitution, 13, 39, 56, 57
     Fifth Amendment, 143, 195
Contract with America, 66. *See also* Congress,
     104th Congress
Copper, 113
Corruption, 15
Council on Competitiveness, 167
Council on Environmental Quality, 106
County movements, 23, 24, 25
Courts. *See* Judiciary; Litigation; Supreme
     Court
Craig, Larry, 66
Crime, 153
CRS. *See* Congress, Congressional Research
     Service
Culhane, Paul, 3, 200
Cyanide, 113, 117

Darden, Buddy, 83, 86
Data, 99, 110, 179
Decisionmaking, 1, 11, 15, 33, 34, 39, 42, 47, 54,
    74, 75, 77(table), 91, 92, 122, 124, 128,
    130, 139, 140, 172, 177, 180, 182, 195,
    198–200
Defense Department, 40
Delaware, 25
Democratic Party, 87, 88(table), 123, 126, 147,
    156, 195, 196
Demographics, 4, 103, 104, 172
DeVoto, Bernard, 2, 15
Dietrich, William, 54
Dinosaur National Monument, 2, 175
DOE. *See* Energy, Department of
DOI. *See* Interior, Department of
Domenici, Pete, 84
Dukakis, Michael, 33
Durant, Robert, 140
Dwyer, William, 53, 56, 57–58, 60, 62

*Earth in the Balance: Ecology and the Human
    Spirit* (Gore), 33
Eastside and Upper Columbia River Basin
    projects, 36
Economic assistance, 59
Economic development, 13, 14, 22, 104, 166,
    173, 186
Economic liberalism, 97, 98, 116–117
Ecosystem management, 36, 41–42, 54, 55, 60,
    63, 68, 167
EIS. *See* Environmental issues, environment
    impact statements
Eisenhower administration, 34, 123, 175
Elected officials, 5
Electric Consumers Act of 1986, 146
Emergency Petroleum Allocation Act, 126
Employment, 4, 22, 23, 49, 64, 104, 105(table
    6.3), 105–106, 116, 118(n4), 195, 197. *See
    also* Unemployment
Endangered American Wilderness Act of 1978,
    181, 184
Endangered Species Act, 4, 56, 64, 66, 114, 194,
    201
Energy, 122–148, 196, 197, 201
    booms, 104
    changes in policy, 128, 199
    crises, 13, 122, 124–126, 147, 199
    See also Coal; Natural gas; Nuclear power;
        Oil
Energy, Department of (DOE), 128, 140, 144,
    146
Energy Independence Authority, 126–127
Energy Policy Act of 1992, 142, 145
Energy Resources Act of 1992, 194
Environmental Defense Fund, 125, 146
Environmental issues, 2, 17–18, 32, 47–48,
    50–51, 55, 61, 68, 101, 104, 106–107, 108,

    115, 118, 118(n6), 122, 123, 124–125,
    132, 142, 143, 155–156, 175, 195, 196,
    198–199
environmental groups, 18, 51, 76, 86,
    146–147, 157(table), 179, 194
environmental impact statements, (EIS), 3,
    4, 17, 56, 63, 77(table), 81, 114, 127, 142,
    182, 194
environmentalists' strategies, 52, 55, 56–57,
    59, 60, 67
environmental names of industry fronts, 23
extremists, 33
humans living within ecosystems, 41–42
organizations opposed to environmental
    regulations, 23
political support for, 198–199
and range policy reform, 80–82, 83
See also Conservation; Ecosystem
    management; Pollution; Regulatory
    issues; Sagebrush rebellions, and
    environmentalists; Superfund
Environmental Policy Institute, 138
Environmental Protection Agency (EPA), 4, 6,
    113, 131, 138, 141, 143, 144
EPA. *See* Environmental Protection Agency
Epstein, Richard, 23
Equity, 37
Everglades, 168
Executive branch, 27, 39, 88, 110, 111, 165, 172,
    176, 182, 195–196
    Executive Order No. 12548, 78(table)
    Executive Order No. 12630, 22
    fragmentation in, 98, 99–100
Experimental Stewardship Program, 82
Exxon Valdez, 141

Factions, 38
Fairfax, Sally, 11
FCLAA. *See* Federal Coal Leasing Amendments
    Act
Federal Advisory Committee Act, 60
Federal Coal Leasing Amendments Act
    (FCLAA), 127–128
Federal Energy Administration, 126
Federal Energy Regulatory Commission
    (FERC), 146
Federal Facilities Compliance Act of 1991, 144
Federal government, 97
Federal Land Policy and Management Act
    (FLPMA), 3, 17, 18, 35, 38, 39, 40,
    77(table), 81, 82, 89, 90–91, 99, 109, 113,
    128, 147, 181, 194, 200
Federal Land Right-of-Way Act, 125
Federal Power Act, 12
FERC. *See* Federal Energy Regulatory
    Commission
Finley, Mike, 165
Fire control, 160, 166, 186

Fire Island, 152
Fish, 1, 52, 53, 139, 182
    habitats, 59, 61, 64, 70(nn 24, 27)
Fish and Wildlife Service (FWS), 1, 26, 40, 56,
    59, 141, 177, 178, 183, 199
Flannery, Thomas, 81, 137
FLPMA. *See* Federal Land Policy and
    Management Act
Foley, Thomas, 58
Ford administration, 126–128
Foresta, Ronald, 161
Forest health, 64
Forests, area of, 48. *See also* Logging; Timber
    harvesting/sales
Forsling, Clarence, 75
Freedom of Information Act, 62, 158
Friends of the Earth, 18, 125
FWS. *See* Fish and Wildlife Service

Galactic Resources, 112
GAO. *See* General Accounting Office
Gas. *See* Natural gas
Gasoline, 127, 142
Gates, Paul, 79
General Accounting Office (GAO), 89, 90, 137,
    164, 167, 184
General Grant National Park, 173
General Land Office, 76, 97
General Land Ordinances of 1785/1787, 11, 14
General Revision Act of 1891, 15
Glacier Peak Wilderness, 109
Glen Canyon Dam, 145–146
Glines Canyon Dam, 139
Global economy, 125
GMP. *See* National parks, General Management
    Plan
Gold, 96, 104, 113, 117
Gore, Al, 33
Gore Range-Eagle's Nest Primitive Area, 180
Gorton, Slade, 66
Grand Canyon, 134, 145, 160, 167, 178
Gray wolf, 62
Grazing, 4, 15, 17, 19, 22, 32, 65, 74, 75, 167,
    177, 178, 179, 183, 187, 194, 195, 196,
    197, 198, 201
    fees, 75, 76, 77(table), 78(table), 79–80, 81,
    82, 83, 84, 86, 87–88, 88(table), 89, 91, 92,
    116, 195
Grazing Service, 75–76. *See also* Bureau of Land
    Management
Gridlock, 32, 33, 35, 36, 37, 38, 40, 42, 186
Griles, Stephen, 138
Grizzly bears, 160
Grosvenor, Melvin, 151

Hansen, James, 66
Harris, James R. (Dick), 137, 138
Hartzog, George, 152, 153, 158, 160

Hatch, Orrin, 167
Hatfield, Mark, 66
Hawaii, 103
Hayes, Wayne, 131
Hays, Samuel, 38–39
Hazardous waste, 106, 112. *See also* Nuclear
    waste
Health issues, 112, 135
Heckler, Ken, 131
Hendee, John, 194
High-grading, 61
Hodel, Donald, 83, 89, 139, 140
Homestead Act of 1862, 173
Hoover, Herbert, 15, 16
Hovenweep National Monument, 142
Hydroelectric power, 122, 139, 145–146, 175

Idaho, 25, 26, 28(n5), 29(n11), 63, 64, 65, 104,
    180, 186, 187
Illinois, 143
Incentive-Based Grazing Fee System (USDI), 90
Indiana, 132, 143
Indonesia, 126
Inflation, 126
Information, 89–90, 179. *See also* Data
Inner Voice, 54
Integral vistas, 133, 134. *See also* National parks,
    visibility in
Interest groups, 1, 5, 42, 49, 55, 57, 74, 122, 132,
    155, 156–157, 157(table), 158, 162, 168,
    185, 194–195
Interests, 38–39, 48
Intergovernmental relations, 11, 24, 27, 28. *See
    also* States
Interior, Department of (DOI/USDI), 1, 2, 5,
    75, 77(table), 78(table), 79–80, 86, 90,
    100, 109, 110, 124, 127, 128, 129, 130,
    131, 133, 136, 137–138, 139, 141, 145, 167
    agencies for mining, 99
    secretaries, 89, 140
Interior Columbia Basin Ecosystem
    Management Project, 63–64
International events, 124, 128. *See also* Energy,
    crises
Iowa, 12
Iran, 126
Iron triangle, 1, 49, 50
Irrigation, 14, 175
Izaak Walton League, 182

Jackson, Henry, 102, 115
Jamieson, Cy, 83
Janik, Phil, 62
Japan, 126, 127
Jenkins-Smith, Hank, 85
Jobs. *See* Employment
Johnson administration, 76, 86, 130, 152, 155,
    175

Johnston, J. Bennett, 66, 102
Jones, Bryan, 85
Judiciary, 50, 51, 55, 56, 60, 61, 102–103, 130,
    172, 182, 185
    Ninth Circuit Court of Appeals, 57, 69(n4)
    Tenth Circuit Court of Appeals, 180
    See also Litigation; Supreme Court
Julian, George, 118

Kennecott Copper, 109, 113
Kennedy administration, 76, 86, 89, 152–153,
    175
Kentucky, 102, 143
Kerr, Andy, 56

Land and Water Conservation Fund (LWCF),
    153, 165, 187(n2)
LASER. *See* League for the Advancement of
    States' Equal Rights
Lassen Volcanic National Park, 162
League for the Advancement of States' Equal
    Rights (LASER), 19, 20
League of Conservation Voter scores, 66
Leasing programs, 98, 115, 127, 128, 129, 130,
    135
    competitive vs. emergency, 136–137
Leopold Report of 1963
Leshy, John, 102
Libertarianism, 21, 23
Litigation, 3–4, 12, 24, 51, 52, 55, 59, 63, 67,
    133, 137, 138
    number of cases, 53
    and Section 318, 56, 57
    See also Judiciary
Lobbying, 23, 55, 59, 124, 125, 146, 157, 194
Local governments, 28. *See also* County
    movements
Localism, 49, 55, 64, 65
Logging, 4–5, 26, 32, 34, 55. *See also* Timber
    harvesting/sales
Los Angeles, 145, 146
Louisiana, 102
Loveladies Harbor Inc. v. United States, 28(n7)
Lowi, Theodore, 34, 39, 187(n4)
Lujan, Manuel, 33, 83, 89, 135, 140, 141, 142
LWCF. *See* Land and Water Conservation Fund
Lyons, Jim, 65

McArdle, Richard, 34, 35, 39
McCarren, Pat, 75
McClure, James, 82, 102, 110, 111
McDade, Joe, 166
McKay, Douglas, 123
Magagna, James, 35, 37
Magruder Corridor, 180
Management issues. *See* Ecosystem
    management; Multiple use; National

parks, General Management Plan; *under*
    Wilderness areas
Marine Preservation Association, 23
Mather, Steve, 152, 156
Media, 17, 19, 20, 57, 74, 108, 141, 155, 198
Meese, Edwin, 195
Mexican spotted owl, 25. *See also* Spotted owls
Mexico, 96
Military, 97, 184
Miller, George, 58, 61, 66, 86, 101
Miller, Richard, 200
Mineral Leasing Act of 1920, 13, 98, 124, 127,
    129
Mineral Policy Center, 108, 112
Minerals Management Service, 99, 100
Mining, 32, 65, 95–118, 104, 105(tables), 118,
    122, 175, 176, 177, 178, 179, 184, 1951,
    196, 198, 201
    employment, 105(table 6.3)
    free access denied for, 109–110
    land declared unsuitable for, 132–133,
        137–138
    and land reclamation, 131
    placer/quartz, 96–97
    strategic minerals, 100, 109–110, 111, 115,
        119(n7)
    in wilderness areas, 108–109, 111, 162
    See also Coal; Gold
Mining and Minerals Policy Act of 1970, 115
Mining Law of 1872, 96, 97, 98, 100, 102–103,
    106, 108, 110–111, 113–114. *See also*
    under Reforms
Minnesota, 28(n6), 177
Mintzmayer, Lorraine, 165
Mohave National Park, 26
Mondale, Walter, 18
Monongahela National Forest, 51
Montana, 13, 25, 28(n5), 63, 65, 104, 130, 132,
    138, 186, 187
Motor boats. *See* Watercraft
Mott, William Penn, 162
Mountain States Legal Foundation, 29(n10)
Muir, John, 18
Multiple Mineral Development Act of 1954, 98
Multiple use, 18–19, 20, 21, 22, 24, 50, 51, 52,
    60, 79, 84, 85, 92, 129, 174, 178, 179, 181,
    182, 196, 199–200
    critique of, 32–42
    definitions, 69(n4)
    and dominant use approach, 40, 75
    logic of, 36–38, 39
    See also Bureau of Land Management, as
        multiple-use agency; Classification and
        Multiple Use Act; Multiple Use and
        Sustained Yield Act
Multiple Use and Sustained Yield Act (MUSY),
    2, 34–35, 37, 39, 40, 50, 53

Multiple Use Classification Act. *See* Classification and Multiple Use Act
Mumma, John, 65
Murkowski, Frank, 26, 66, 102
MUSY. *See* Multiple Use and Sustained Yield Act

National Academy of Sciences, 166
National Cattlemen's Association, 74
National Critical Materials Act of 1984, 115
National Critical Materials Council, 111
National Energy Act of 1978, 128
National Environmental Policy Act (NEPA), 3, 53, 56, 66, 80, 114, 125, 142, 147, 180
National Forest Management Act (NFMA) of 1976, 3, 4, 52–55, 56, 58, 60, 67, 68, 194, 198
   minimum viable populations provisions, 62
National Geographic, 151, 153
Nationalization of issues, 55, 57, 59, 60, 63, 67, 68, 155–156, 179, 194, 198
National Marine Fisheries Service, 64
National Materials and Minerals Policy, Research and Development Act of 1980, 110, 111, 115
National parks, 109, 117, 122, 132–133, 134, 140, 141, 143, 144
   and automobiles, 150, 152, 153, 160, 174
   external threats to, 162, 167
   General Management Plan (GMP), 158, 159, 160
   policy for, 150–168
   urban units, 160, 196
   use of, 150, 151–152, 153, 154(table), 156, 160, 162, 174, 199
   visibility in, 143, 153, 167. *See also* Integral vistas
   See also National Park Service; Wilderness areas
National Parks and Conservation Association (NPCA), 142, 156, 157(table), 162, 199
National Park Service (NPS), 1, 26, 36, 40, 143, 150, 155, 156, 157, 173–174, 177, 178, 183, 199
   appropriations, 163(table), 164, 165, 166
   Congressional hearings on, 164(table)
   expansion of, 159(table), 159–160, 166, 196
   vs. Forest Service, 174
   Mission 66, 152
   personnel views, 161, 162, 163, 165
   political support for, 161, 163–165
   research in, 166
National Petroleum Council, 125
National Security Minerals Act, 111
National Trails System, 156
National Wilderness Preservation System, 40, 89, 175, 176, 196

National Wildlife Federation, 18, 51, 83, 86, 131, 137, 138, 141, 142, 145, 194, 199
Natural gas, 98, 124, 127, 128, 135, 140, 144, 145
Natural Resources Defense Council (NRDC), 4, 18, 83, 86, 127, 137, 194
   Natural Resources Defense Council v. Morton, 77(table), 80–81, 194
Natural Resource User Charges (Bureau of Budget), 77(table)
Navajo Power Plant, 143, 195
Nebraska, 25
Neocolonialism, 106
NEPA. *See* National Environmental Policy Act
Nevada, 11, 19, 28(nn 5, 6), 29(n13), 32, 95, 103, 104, 112, 116, 140, 181
New Jersey, 102
New Mexico, 17, 25, 26, 28(n5), 29(n14), 104, 181, 184
New Mexico Wilderness Act of 1980, 184
NFMA. *See* National Forest Management Act of 1976
NIMBY syndrome, 122–123, 140, 147
Nixon administration, 123, 124–126, 130, 147, 157–158, 187(n1)
   New Economic Policy, 125, 126
North Cascades complex, 178, 187(n5)
North Dakota, 129, 132
Northern goshawk, 62
NPCA. *See* National Parks and Conservation Association
NPS. *See* National Park Service
NRDC. *See* Natural Resources Defense Council
Nuclear power, 142, 143
Nuclear waste, 123, 135, 139–140, 143–144, 146, 148(n)
Nuclear Waste Policy Act, 139–140
Nuclear weapons sites, 144

Office of Management and Budget (OMB), 2, 89
Office of Science and Technology, 160
Office of Surface Mining and Reclamation (OSM), 99, 100, 131–132, 133, 137, 138, 143, 144
Office of Technology Assessment, 100
Ohio, 143
Oil, 12, 22, 23, 26, 98, 102, 128, 140, 144, 145, 198
   offshore drilling, 144
   oil shale, 127, 129, 140
   prices, 124, 125, 126, 128, 135, 147–148
   spills, 141
   U.S. imports, 126
   See also Energy, crises
Oklahoma, 138
O'Leary, Hazel, 146
Olympic National Park, 139

OMB. *See* Office of Management and Budget
One-Third of the Nation's Land (PLLRC), 40, 77(table)
OPEC. *See* Organization of Petroleum Exporting Countries
Ordinances, 29(n11)
Oregon, 28(n5), 56, 63, 181
Organic Act of 1897, 1, 49, 51, 114
Organization of Petroleum Exporting Countries (OPEC), 123, 126
OSM. *See* Office of Surface Mining and Reclamation

Pacific Legal Foundation, 29(n10)
Pacific Northwest, 52, 53, 55–60, 62, 139
Pacific Railway Act, 173
Payment in Lieu of Taxes (PILT) Act of 1976, 13–14, 26
Pennsylvania, 132, 143
People for the West!, 107
Persian Gulf War, 142
Pesticides, 51, 122
Phoenix, 145, 146
Pilon, Roger, 23
PILT. *See* Payment in Lieu of Taxes Act of 1976
Pinchot, Gifford, 15, 18, 22, 49, 75, 178, 196
Pitstick, Randall, 194
Planned market, 130
Planning, 123, 127, 128, 129–130, 136, 150, 160–161, 166
    opening of process, 155, 158–159
    See also under U.S. Forest Service
PLLRC. *See* Public Land Law Review Commission
Pluralism, 34, 35, 55, 128
    pluralist legalism, 51
Plutonium, 122, 144, 148(n)
Policy subsystems, 1–2, 55, 118, 199
Political appointments, 5–6, 56, 88–89, 133, 137, 138, 140, 141, 143, 144, 165
Political partisanship, 122, 123
Pollution, 51, 106, 111–115, 122, 127, 135, 143, 155, 167
    acid drainage, 112, 113, 117
    See also National parks, and automobiles
Populations, 103, 104, 117
Preservation. *See* Conservation
Presidency. *See* Executive branch
PRIA. *See* Public Rangelands Improvement Act of 1978
Prices, 198. *See also under* Oil
Primitive areas, 176, 187(n3), 200. *See also* Wilderness areas
Private landholders, 14, 15, 16, 26, 104, 118(n5), 122
    of commercial forests, 48
    See also Property rights
Privatization, 21, 26, 82, 98, 107, 117

Progressive Era, 16, 41, 49
Property rights, 23, 24, 25, 29(nn 9, 11), 66, 107, 117
    extralegal systems of, 96, 97–98
    See also Private landholders
Public Land Law Review Commission (PLLRC), 37–38, 40, 77(table), 79, 89
    study by, 115
Public land policy
    changes in, 2–3, 4, 13, 16, 17–21, 32, 47, 48, 50–51, 54, 60, 63, 65–68, 76, 79–80, 82, 85–90, 91–92, 107–108, 117, 150–151, 152, 153, 155–161, 165, 166, 168, 194–201. *See also* Energy, changes in policy; Reforms
    economic arguments concerning, 197–198
    future of, 201
    major laws, 3(table)
Public Lands Commission, 115
Public Lands Council, 19, 85, 195
Public opinion, 52, 57, 68, 106–107, 114, 141, 155, 158, 162, 168, 185, 201
Public Rangelands Improvement Act of 1978 (PRIA), 17, 78(table), 81–82, 89, 90–91
Public range policy, 74–92
    chronology concerning, 77–78(table)
    See also Grazing
Pulp mills, 60, 63

Radon, 134
Rahall, Nick, 108
Railroads, 174
Rangeland Reform '94, 78(table), 84, 90
RARE. *See* Roadless Area Review and Evaluation
Ray, Dixy Lee, 33
Reagan administration, 5, 17, 18, 20, 21–22, 24, 25, 32—33, 55, 78(table), 82–83, 107, 110, 111, 115, 122, 123, 135–140, 162, 165
    appointees, 56, 89
    strategic minerals policy in, 100
Receipt sharing programs, 13–14, 16, 27, 49, 128
Recissions Act of 1995, 67
Recreation, 2, 3, 4, 5, 34, 48, 50, 78, 83, 104, 106, 153, 159–160, 161, 167, 178, 179, 187
Redwoods National Park, 156
Reforms, 16, 22, 47, 51, 65, 117–118, 196
    of Mining Law of 1872, 95, 99, 102, 107, 115–116, 117
    of rangeland policy, 79, 80–85, 91, 92
    See also Public land policy, changes in
Regulatory issues, 6, 12, 14, 20, 22, 23, 25, 26, 51, 52, 114, 132, 137, 182, 199
    concerns regulated by Congress, 184
    price controls, 125, 126, 135
    regulatory takings, 24, 27, 28(n7), 29(n10), 66, 194, 194

Reid, Harry, 84, 116
Reilly, William, 143
Republican Party, 25–26, 66, 67, 78(table), 87,
    88(table), 91, 100–101, 101(table), 102,
    117, 136, 144, 147, 156, 168, 185
Research, 99, 166, 167
Resource Conservation and Recovery Act, 112
Rey, Mark, 66
Roadless Area Review and Evaluation (RARE),
    181, 182
Roads, 160, 174, 178
Robertson, Dale, 54
Rockefeller, Nelson, 127
Rocky Flats, 144, 146
Rocky Mountain Legal Foundation, 137
Rocky Mountain states, 103, 104, 107, 200
Rogers, Paul, 134
Romer, Roy, 29(n12), 84
Roosevelt, Theodore, 15
Royalties, 118(n1), 128, 130, 140–141, 195
Rural areas. *See* Urban/rural areas

Sabatier, Paul, 85
Sagebrush Rebellion, Inc., 19, 20, 27
Sagebrush rebellions, 14–15, 16, 18, 19, 22, 24,
    32, 33, 66, 82, 101, 107, 158, 162, 193, 194
    and environmentalists, 19–20, 21
    organizations, 19–21
Salmon, 64, 139. *See also* Fish
Santini, Jim, 110, 111
San Juan Mountains, 112
Schechter Poultry v. United States, 39
Scientists, 15, 19, 62. *See also* Biology
SCLDF. *See* Sierra Club, Legal Defense Fund
Second homes, 103, 117
Section 318. *See under* Litigation
Seiberling, John, 86
Selway-Bitterroot Wilderness, 180
Sequoia National Park, 173, 178
Shenandoah National Park, 167
Sierra Club, 18, 86, 125, 156, 157(table), 182
    Legal Defense Fund (SCLDF), 4, 55–56, 64,
    70(n22)
    Sierra Club v. Hardin, 51
Sights and sounds doctrine, 183, 184
Silver, 96
Silviculture, 49, 178
Simpson, Alan, 117, 166
SMCRA. *See* Surface Mining Control and
    Reclamation Act
Smith, Loren, 24
Smog, 134
Smoky Mountains, 152
Snowmobiles, 162, 167, 182
South Africa, 111
Southeast Alaska Conservation Coalition, 61
Southern Utah Wilderness Alliance, 107
Soviet Union, 111

Spotted owls, 5, 25, 52, 56, 57–58, 59, 63, 194
State of the Parks, 1980, 160, 162, 167
States, 11–14, 17, 26, 28, 48, 82, 100, 114, 132,
    133–134, 137, 138
    land transfers to, 28(n5)
    legislatures, 19, 21, 25
    states' rights, 12–13, 15, 16, 19–20, 21, 27
    See also Rocky Mountain states; Western
    states
Steamtown, 166
Stearns v. Minnesota, 28(n6)
Stegner, Wallace, 2, 42
Stevens, Ted, 62, 66
Stone, Deborah, 36
Strategic minerals. *See under* Mining
Subgovernments, 74, 76, 107, 122, 198
Subsidies, 60, 61, 64, 65, 74, 76, 83, 90, 129, 196,
    197–198
Subsystems. *See* Policy subsystems
Sulfur oxide, 127
Superfund, 112, 113, 194
Supreme Court, 12, 13, 24, 28(nn 4, 6), 29(nn 8,
    9, 10), 57, 102, 185, 195
Surface Mining Control and Reclamation Act
    (SMCRA), 13, 123, 131, 132, 133, 137,
    138, 142
Surface Resources Act of 1955, 98–99
Synar, Mike, 83, 86, 90
Synthetic fuels, 127, 136
Synthetic Fuels Act of 1980, 128, 129
Synthetic Fuels Corporation, 136

Takings, 195. *See also* Regulatory issues,
    regulatory takings
Taxes, 130, 144
Taylor Grazing Act of 1934, 1, 15, 37, 75, 80, 81
Tennessee, 138
Texas, 13, 26, 138, 140
Thomas, Jack Ward, 54
    Thomas report, 58
Timber harvesting/sales, 48, 49, 53, 54–55, 57,
    70(n30), 177, 178, 179, 195, 196, 197, 198,
    201
    below-cost sales, 60, 64–65, 116
    decline of, 104
    harvest levels, 59, 61, 63, 64, 65, 68
    injunctions on sales, 56, 58
    and old-growth forests, 51, 52, 55–60, 67
    proportionality requirement, 61, 62
    See also Logging
Time magazine, 57
Tongass Land Management Plan, 61, 62
Tongass National Forest. *See under* Alaska
Tongass Timber Reform Act of 1990 (TTRA),
    61
Tongue River, 138
Tourism, 103, 104, 106, 117, 150, 153, 179. *See
    also* National parks, use of

Toxic waste. *See* Hazardous waste
Trade associations, 2
Truman, Harry S., 76
TTRA. *See* Tongass Timber Reform Act of 1990
Turner, John, 141

Udall, Stewart. 76, 79, 86, 101, 115, 123, 131, 153
Unemployment, 59, 106
United States v. New Mexico, 185
Uram, Robert, 144
Uranium, 134, 135, 143
Uranium Mill Tailings Reclamation Act, 134–135
Urban/rural areas, 4, 17, 48, 49, 101, 160, 198
 urbanization, 103(table), 103, 104, 117
U.S. Court of Federal Claims, 24, 28(n7)
USDA/DI. *See* Agriculture, Department of;
 Interior, Department of
US Energy Outlook (report), 125
U.S. Forest Service (USFS), 1, 2, 3, 5–6, 18, 25, 26, 35, 36–37, 42(n), 47–68, 70(n30, 74, 75, 82, 109, 114, 129, 140, 142, 173–174, 177, 178, 179–180, 180–181
 vs. Park Service, 174
 personnel, 53–54, 55, 65, 68, 69(n10), 86
 planning by, 52–53, 183
 pro-timber orientation of, 49, 68
USFS. *See* U.S. Forest Service
U.S. Geological Survey (USGS), 97, 99, 100
USGS. *See* U.S. Geological Survey
Utah, 25, 28(n5), 29(n12), 103, 104, 107, 113, 140, 181, 185
 Bryce Canyon National Park, 132–133, 134, 162
Utah Public Lands Management Act, 185

Venezuela, 126
Vento, Bruce, 66, 86
Virginia, 132, 143
Vision for the Greater Yellowstone Area (Mintzmayer), 165
Vistas, 186. *See also* Integral vistas

Walker, Ron, 161
Wallop, Malcolm, 166
Wall Street Journal, 153
Washakie Wilderness, 135
Washington state, 28(n5), 56, 63, 181
 Glacier Peak Wilderness, 109
 Hanford, 140, 144, 146
 Olympic National Park, 139
Watercraft, 160, 167, 177, 182
Water projects, 17, 20, 178
Water rights, 184–185, 186, 188(n9), 199
Water supply, 112

Watkins, James, 143
Watt, James, 20, 32, 78(table), 82, 83, 89, 110–111, 135, 136, 137, 162, 165
Wayne National Forest, 143
Western Lands Act, 20
Western Livestock Grazing Survey (USDA/DI), 77(table), 79
Western states, 100–101, 103(table), 103, 106, 117, 118(n3), 131, 132
West Virginia, 51, 129, 132, 143
Wetlands, 141
Wild and Scenic Rivers Act, 3
Wilderness Act of 1964, 3, 18, 42(n), 50, 110, 153, 156, 172, 175–181, 183, 184, 185, 196
 and mining exemptions, 108–109
Wilderness areas, 34, 42(n), 48, 50, 55, 61, 78, 107, 108–109, 110, 117, 135, 145, 199, 200
 distributive policy, 175–181, 183, 187(n4), 198
 future policy, 185–187
 management issues, 182–185, 186, 188(n8)
 policy, 172–187, 198
 wilderness reviews, 109, 111, 119(n8), 199
 See also Primitive areas; Wilderness Act of 1964; Wildlife preservation
Wilderness Impact Research Foundation, 182
Wilderness Society, 18, 51, 86, 90, 125, 156, 157(table), 162, 182
Wilderness Watch, 183
Wildlife preservation, 2, 12, 52, 58, 159, 167, 177, 178, 184
Wilkinson, Charles, 50
Winters Doctrine, 184, 188(n9)
Wirth, Conrad, 152
Wirth, Tim, 61, 142
Wise Use Movement, 22–25, 27, 66, 85, 101, 107, 118, 162, 182, 195
Wolves, 187
Wyoming, 25, 26, 28(n5), 104, 124, 132, 135, 181, 200
 Medicine Bow and Red Rim areas, 138

Yates, Sidney, 135
Yellowstone National Park, 36, 42, 151, 160, 166, 167, 173, 178, 186
Yom Kippur War, 124, 125
Yosemite National Park, 139, 150, 153, 159, 160, 166, 167, 173, 178
Young, Don, 66, 101, 102
Yucca Mountain nuclear waste repository, 148(n)

Zahniser, Howard, 175, 176
Zero-sum games, 35–36, 37, 40